Rebel Life

Rebel Life

The Life and Times of Robert Gosden,
Revolutionary, Mystic, Labour Spy

Mark Leier

New Star Books
Vancouver
1999

New Star Books Ltd.
107 · 3477 Commercial Street
Vancouver, BC V5N 4E8
www.NewStarBooks.com

PHOTO SOURCES
p 10 · British Columbia Archives and Records Service (BCARS) E-00230
p 4 · in author's possession, photographer, date unknown
p 14: BCARS G-04702; p 23 · BCARS D-06368; p 30 · BCARS E-01194
p 32 · City of Vancouver Archives CVA 259-1; p 52 · BCARS A-2467
p 65 · BCARS B-2950; p 74 · Cumberland Museum and Archives CMA-110-2
p 80 · Provincial Archives of Manitoba N 2762, Foote Collection 1696
p 115 Vancouver Public Library, Special Collections VPL 1312
p 125 · Saskatchewan Archives Board R-B 171-1
p 127 · postcard in author's possession, photographer, date unknown
p 138 · in author's possession, photographer, date unknown.

Designed & typeset at The Cardigan Press
Cover image: BC Archives and Records Service E-00230
Printed and bound in Canada by Transcontinental Printing and Graphics

1 2 3 4 5 03 02 01 00 99

Publication of this work is made possible by grants
from the Canada Council, the British Columbia Arts Council, and the
Department of Canadian Heritage Book Publishing Industry Development Program.

CANADIAN CATALOGUING IN PUBLICATION DATA

Leier, James Mark.
Rebel life

Includes bibliographical references and index

ISBN 0-921586-69-8

1. Gosden, Robert, 1882–1961.
2. Labor unions–British Columbia–Biography
3. Labor unions–British Columbia–History
4. Working class–British Columbia–History. I. Title.
HD6525.G67L44 1999   331.88'092   C99-910872-7

To Adam and Jim,
and the road trip of '98

Rebel Life

INTRODUCTION

Few people will have heard of Robert Raglan Gosden. He won no elections, headed no corporation, led no troops into battle. He wrote no books, painted no art, invented no useful gadget, performed no act of great heroism, inspired no myths. He had little education and lived in poverty most of his life. Why then write a book about him?

The story of his life provides us with several useful lessons. It reminds us that all lives are important and interesting, not just those of the rich and famous or notorious. It reminds us too that the history of British Columbia was not made solely by politicians and business heads. Not one of their programs or enterprises could have been accomplished without the labour of thousands of men and women who rarely make it into the history books. Yet they, not the premiers or coal barons, paid the price for prosperity and progress. Their stories also deserve to be told if we are to understand the history of the province.

Gosden's life reminds us of something else. If the individual lives of workers are important, they become a determining force of history when workers act collectively. Through striking, voting, demonstrating, even sabotaging, workers constantly force government and business to listen to them, accommodate them, and suppress them. Politicians change and enforce laws, and employers pressure governments, create new technology, and move capital about in the attempt to respond to the actions of workers. We cannot understand historical change without understanding this constant tension between workers, capital, and the state, and examining the life of one worker gives us some insight into this process.

But a life cannot be understood in isolation. The people, events, ideas, and culture that surrounded Gosden influenced him just as he influenced them. To understand his life, we need to understand its historical context. British Columbia's traditional political, economic, and cultural history, with its focus on elites, is easily available, but its labour history is not. That is the context this book focuses on, and it is Gosden's context. Because

I

this story is centred on Gosden's life, there are gaps in the book's coverage of labour history. Gosden lived much of his life in the male world of the migrant worker. He made little mention of women in the labour movement, and that has skewed this account. The contribution of the skilled worker is similarly given less treatment than it deserves, and there is little mention of working-class culture and other important aspects of labour history. They await another book.

There are many stories in BC's labour history that need to be told. My hope is this book will interest more people in writing these stories, and therefore I've included a chapter on how to write labour history, including tips on research, oral history, and understanding historiography. An extensive bibliography, put together by a number of graduate students in the Simon Fraser University (SFU) History Department, will give those who are interested some places to begin their research.

As the footnotes and the section on doing research make clear, this book could not have been written without the help of a great many institutions and people. I note with gratitude the funding provided by Simon Fraser University in the form of a President's Research Grant and by the Social Sciences and Humanities Research Council, and the financial assistance of the Boag Foundation, the Canadian Labour Congress, the BC Federation of Labour, and the New Westminster and District Labour Council for the BC labour history bibliography. The staff at SFU's Inter-Library Loans, University of British Columbia Special Collections, the Vancouver City Archives, and the BC Archives and Records Services were always helpful, patient, and informative.

Thanks are due to Allen Seager, who first suggested several years ago that I look for Robert Gosden. Greg Kealey has provided support, both moral and financial. Keith Ralston gave invaluable insight and advice, often at a moment's notice. A number of my former students undertook research on different parts of the book. The work of John-Henry Harter, Denine Marasco, Andy Neufeld, Juanita Nolan, Dennis Pilon, David Sandquist, and Jennifer Whiteside is greatly appreciated. Audrey McClellan's firm but gentle editing has made this a much better book.

In particular, I would like to thank Todd McCallum, Andy Parnaby, and Dennis Pilon. As researchers, they were quick to ferret out important information; as friends, they listened endlessly to the Gosden saga; as historians, they offered sage advice. Todd is responsible for the index, and Andy for the final work on the bibliography.

Sean Cadigan first suggested I turn the story of Gosden into a book, so I have much to thank and blame him for. I admire his work and black humour and greaty appreciate his friendship. Thanks are also due to Laurin Armstrong and Tina Loo, colleagues and friends. My parents, Jim and Margaret, and my brother, Ben, have, as always, been supportive. So too have Heather Way and Drew, Sheena, Connor, and Zöe DeFaveri. My biggest debt is to Annette, who put up with Robert Gosden for a long time, and continues to put up with me.

Robert Raglan Gosden, circa 1950s

CHAPTER 1

"The Workers Can Do No Wrong"

April 18, 1961, was much like any other spring day in Vancouver. It was overcast and damp; the temperature, measured on the Fahrenheit scale in those years before Canada adopted the metric system, was about 50 degrees, or 10 degrees Celsius. The Stanley Cup was going into its fourth game, and the smart money was on the Chicago Black Hawks to take the Detroit Red Wings. There was no Vancouver team to break the hearts of local fans, but a special commission was investigating sites for a downtown sports arena.

Movie fans were talking about the Academy Awards show televised the previous evening. Elizabeth Taylor had won the Best Actress award for her role as a prostitute in *Butterfield 8*, and Burt Lancaster took the Best Actor award for *Elmer Gantry*. Shirley Jones, later to become famous to TV audiences as the pure and perfect musical mom in *The Partridge Family*, won the Best Supporting Actress title for her performance in *Elmer Gantry*, while Peter Ustinov was named Best Supporting Actor for his role in *Spartacus*.

There were weightier concerns, of course. Debate over health care raged, as some argued for a national public plan or an extension of private plans. Unemployment was high, with over 700,000 Canadians looking for work, but it was, as one newspaper reported, "still possible to make a killing in real estate." Business, then as now, complained that wages were too high and made it difficult for Canada to compete on world markets. The provincial government sided squarely with business: W.A.C. Bennett's notoriously anti-labour Social Credit government had just made it illegal for unions to contribute to political parties. The law was intended to prevent the labour movement from supporting Bennett's left-wing rivals, the Co-operative Commonwealth Federation, soon to become the New Democratic Party.

Overshadowing provincial affairs was the tension of the Cold War. Allies only sixteen years earlier in the Second World War, the Soviet Union and the United States now faced each other warily. Even outer space was an arena for their political manoeuvring. Less than a week before, the Soviet Union had launched the first human into space, and Yuri Gagarin's flight shook the confidence of the United States in its technological superiority.

Worse, the Cold War threatened to turn hot as the two sides sponsored a series of local, bitter conflicts. American troops were fighting in Viet Nam, and the undeclared war there was escalating. Civil war split the Congo, and Berlin, already split in two, would soon be physically divided by the Wall. In Cuba, the US-sponsored invasion at the Bay of Pigs was easily beaten back by Cuban troops who rallied behind Fidel Castro in the face of Yanqui aggression. In the meantime, schools drilled students to "duck and cover" in the event of nuclear war.

In such a world, it was perhaps not surprising that the funeral of an elderly man in Vancouver went unnoticed by all but a small group of mourners gathered at the T. Edwards Chapel on Granville Street on that grey, damp, spring afternoon. The death of Robert Raglan Gosden did not warrant a story in the metropolitan dailies, only a few short lines in an obituary in the back pages of the paper. No reporter was sent out to bear witness, no crowd gathered to pay respects. To those few at the memorial service, Bob Gosden was a husband, a friend, a relative, remembered warmly for his loyalty, his ideas, even his eccentricities, nothing less, nothing more.

But forty-five years earlier he had shocked the province with his speeches and actions. He provoked headlines in the daily newspapers and even pushed the First World War from their front pages for a time. His name was synonymous with radicalism, revolution, political scandal, and violence, and he inspired and outraged thousands. Robert Gosden had taken part in labour strikes from Prince Rupert to San Diego and advocated violence and sabotage in newspapers, at public meetings, and on picket lines. He had helped drive a BC attorney-general from office and may have fought alongside the Mexican revolutionary Pancho Villa. He was the president of the Miners Liberation League, formed to aid imprisoned miners during the bitter Vancouver Island coal strike of 1912–14, and he had denounced the Socialist Party of Canada as cowardly and conservative. He boldly declared that capitalism was "a system based on theft" that should be "sabotaged at every conceivable opportunity," and he even hinted darkly that the BC premier, Richard McBride, should be assassinated.

Some at his funeral knew parts of his history, though the details were sparse and conflicting. They knew he had been a fiery radical, a revolutionary, an anarchist, even a saboteur. But none knew Gosden's final secret. The real secret of his past was that he had been a labour spy for the Royal Canadian Mounted Police. His reports on labour leaders and political figures, advocating measures ranging from political reforms to the "disappearing" of trade unionists and socialists, were read in the prime minister's office. However ordinary his death, there was nothing ordinary about Bob Gosden's life.

Who was this contradictory, shadowy man? In many ways he was typical of the migrant workers who did much of the work on the industrial frontiers of North America. His story reveals the world of the blanket stiff, the hobo, the rough worker. The violence of this world and its inhumane treatment of working men and women, proved a fertile ground for anger and despair, hope and passion, radicalism and treachery. In examining the life of Robert Gosden, we learn something about the labour history of North America as well as the life of one man.

Many of the details of his early life are unknown; others have been stretched, even fabricated, by Gosden himself. He was born in Surrey, England, in 1882 and left England around 1896. He claimed to have fought in the Boer War of 1899–1902 and told people years later that he had been in Lord Kitchener's army and had met the British hero. He went back to England but soon left again, never to return. He made his way to North America by 1904 and travelled throughout Canada and the United States. Somehow he always ended up back in British Columbia. Later he told friends that he had met the writers Jack London and Robert Service in his travels. Like many of Gosden's claims, this cannot be proved, but it is possible, perhaps even likely, for both authors had spent time in the Canadian north. Gosden worked at a variety of jobs: he was a miner, logger, painter, seaman, janitor, garbage man, and labourer. This diversity was typical of the transient male worker with few specialized skills. By 1910 he was in Glace Bay, Nova Scotia, and had observed first-hand the labour strife in the district, though Gosden apparently played no part in the coal mining strikes there.[1]

Leaving the Nova Scotia coal mines, Gosden travelled back across Canada to the coast, probably walking and hopping rides on freight trains. In Prince Rupert he found work as a labourer, building roads and right of ways. His experience was common to hundreds of thousands of men who tramped across North America, following jobs and seasons. The industrial economy depended on this transient army of workers. Often disparaged as hoboes, tramps, bindlestiffs, or bums, their labour was essential. They built the infrastructure of roads, railways, and dams, and cut the trees, harvested the crops, and mined the minerals of the resource economy.

Their lives were hard and brutal. Even travelling to the job was dangerous. It is estimated that 50,000 men were killed or injured riding freight trains in North America between 1901 and 1905. Jumping on board a moving train was dangerous: one mis-step and the hobo would be crushed by the wheels. If the tramp were lucky, he could ride on top of or inside a freight car. Often, however, that was not possible, and he had to ride on the rods underneath the boxcar, perching there precariously, the rails and wheels inches from his face.

"Riding the rods," which came to mean any travel by freight train, was illegal, and getting caught could mean a jail term or a beating at the hands of railway police. It could even mean death. Jack London, who rode the rods himself, described in The Road one tactic used by brakemen, or "shacks," to get hoboes off the trains. The brakeman would tie a piece of rope to a large bolt or coupling pin and drop the pin between two cars as the train sped along. There it would bounce and rebound between the ties and the bottom of the car. A hobo under the car would be subjected to what London called "a veritable tattoo of death."

Getting a job was no guarantee of security or comfort. One migrant worker, Albert Roe, described his experience in Alberta in 1910. He got his job through a "shark," or employment agent, who charged him half a day's pay. Roe was put on a train at Edmonton and shipped with a hundred other men to Wolf Creek.

We arrived in Wolf Creek about 3 a.m. and it was raining hard. We were all lined up after leaving the train and marched through the woods about three miles, wading through the mud and soaked by the rain ...When we arrived in camp we were wet to the skin and hungry as bears, but there was no sign of anything to eat. We were all so tired that we flopped down any place we could in our wet clothes and slept until breakfast time. The grub in this camp was something fierce. It was so rotten and so poorly cooked that it made nearly everyone sick including myself. I hiked to Camp 38 [38 miles from Wolf Creek] and hit the boss for a job, getting a team of mules to drive on a dump wagon. I started to work about 9 a.m. and worked till quitting time. After supper I went to the boss and asked him where I was going to sleep. He told me that they didn't charge anything for flopping in the bunkhouse, but that I would have to furnish my own blankets, and towels and soap. Upon enquiring I found that before going to work I was in debt to the extent of fare advanced from Edmonton to Wolf Creek, $1.25; meals eaten from Wolf Creek to camp, 50¢ each, $6.00; hospital fee $1; and mail 25¢ making a total of $8.50. If I had stayed on the job I would have bought a pair of blankets at cost of $4.50 and soap and towels would have cost some more. I sat down and figured it out and I saw that if I held the job down the first twenty or thirty days I would have to work for nothing ...The contractors have got it figured out so that it is impossible for anyone to make anything on the job because it will take you at least a couple of weeks to get square with the company and when you get ready to make a few dollars for yourself they fire you.[2]

Gosden's job on the Prince Rupert road construction was marginally better, but the work was still hard and the conditions poor. The labourers were paid $3 for an eight-hour day. It was better pay than working in railway construction, where they might get $2.50 for a ten-hour day, but railway navvies were put up in company camps. In the city, construction workers had to pay for their own room and board, and these were expensive in the isolated towns and cities of northern BC.

The workers, Gosden among them, resolved to win better conditions. By December 1910 they had formed the Prince Rupert Industrial Association (PRIA), a local organization of construction labourers that soon affiliated with the Industrial Workers of the World (IWW or "Wobblies"). This alarmed the employers and local politicians, for the IWW was the most radical and revolutionary organization of the period and, by some measures, to the present day.

Created in 1905, the IWW was both a union, prepared to fight for better conditions and wages, and a revolutionary organization determined to end capitalism and create a democratic, socialist society.

The Wobblies believed that there should be no bosses, for employers were parasites who stole the wealth created by workers. As famous Wobbly

Workers at the Grand Trunk Pacific Railway's First Cut, Prince Rupert, 10 May 1908

leader Big Bill Haywood put it at the founding convention, "The aims and objects of this organization should be to put the working class in possession of the economic power, the means of life, in control of the machinery of production and distribution, without regard to capitalist masters."

The IWW also believed that there should be no government. Government, it believed, was little more than the "slugging committee" of the bosses. At best government and politics, even those of socialists, were as harmful, as undemocratic, as the boss. Voting, Wobblies argued, could do little to change the system. What was needed was direct action, workers taking affairs into their own hands, without politicians as middlemen. The IWW's program could best be described as a variant of anarchism, often called syndicalism or anarcho-syndicalism. One unidentified BC Wobbly summed it up clearly when he wrote, "It is the purpose of all authority, whether economic or political, to enslave the wage worker. Give any person enough property or enough political authority and he will be a despot to the full extent of his power."[3]

This democratic ethos was also applied to the labour movement. Wobblies were quick to denounce "pie cards," "porkchoppers, " and "labour fakirs" (often mis-spelled "fakers"; a fakir is a magician or con artist), that is, union officials who were more interested in looking after themselves than the members. The IWW insisted that union officers should serve limited terms, be subject to recall, and be paid little more than the members made at their jobs. They also opposed

THE INDUSTRIAL WORKERS OF THE WORLD

In BC the Wobblies organized railway and road construction workers, miners, loggers, city workers, and the unemployed. In 1912 the IWW led a strike of 8,000 railway workers on the Grand Trunk Pacific and Canadian Northern railways to protest camp conditions. The famous Wobbly songwriter Joe Hill wrote the song "Where the Fraser River Flows" when he came to Yale to support the strike. Folklore has it that the nickname "Wobbly" came from this strike, from a Chinese restaurant owner who supported the strike and pronounced IWW "I Wobble Wobble." From the nickname "Wobbly" came the verb "to wobble," that is, to pull a wildcat, or illegal, strike.

But a union that took on employers, government, and conservative trade unionists had to fight on three fronts. During World War One the union was declared illegal, and many of its members were arrested in Canada and the United States. After 1917, with the success of the Russian Revolution, many radicals left the IWW for the fledgling Communist Party. The IWW is still around today; its newspaper, the *Industrial Worker*, is published regularly, and it has a web page (http://iww.org/). The preamble to its constitution, written originally in 1905, is still a powerful, clear, radical document: (see over)

PREAMBLE TO THE
CONSTITUTION OF THE
INDUSTRIAL WORKERS
OF THE WORLD

The working class and the employing class have nothing in common. There can be no peace so long as hunger and want are found among millions of working people and the few, who make up the employing class, have all the good things in life.

Between these two classes a struggle must go on until the workers of the world organize as a class, take possession of the earth and the machinery of production, and abolish the wage system.

We find that the centering of the management of industries into fewer and fewer hands makes the trade unions unable to cope with the ever growing power of the employing class. The trade unions foster a state of affairs which allows one set of workers to be pitted against another set of workers in the same industry, thereby helping defeat one another in wage wars. Moreover, the trade unions aid the employing class to mislead the workers into the belief that the working class have interests in common with their employers.

These conditions can be changed and the interest of the working class upheld only by an organization formed in such a way that all its members in any one industry, or in

the dues check-off – the automatic deduction of union dues from the paycheques – as it made the leadership less accountable to the rank and file and gave officials easy access to large sums of money that could be diverted from organizing and education. The union provided for initiatives, that is, motions put forward by the rank and file and referenda, so all members could vote on important issues.

The IWW differed from the labour movement of the trade unions in two other respects. First, it believed in organizing all workers into one big union, regardless of trade, skill, sex, or ethnicity. In this way the IWW was a continuation of the dream of industrial unions taken up earlier by the Knights of Labor. Only in one union could workers be united to fight the boss and the government effectively. Once workers were organized into a single union, they could bring about a new society, not through violent revolution or through voting, but with a general strike of all the workers. Once the factories and railways and mines and offices were shut down, they would be expropriated from the employers and the workers would run them, producing for human need, not profit.

Second, Wobblies believed that it was wrong to sign a contract with the boss. Contracts, then and now, forbade strikes during the term of the agreement. The Wobblies believed they should be free to strike when conditions favoured them, not when the law said they could.

If the IWW's tactics terrified employers, they attracted the Prince Rupert workers. The PRIA soon signed up 1,100 members and confronted candidates during the municipal election. At open candidates' meetings and rallies, union members asked each candidate whether he would support the union demand for 45-cents-an-hour pay and the eight-hour day. One of those running for city council was Dufferin Pattullo, who would become the Liberal MLA for Prince Rupert in 1916 and premier of the province in 1933. As chairman of the city's finance committee, in 1910 Pattullo had raised wages by five-and-a-half cents an hour and supported the eight-hour day. This had angered Prince Rupert businessmen, and in 1911 Pattullo played a cagier game. When asked where he stood, Pattullo answered that

all industries if necessary, cease work whenever a strike or lockout is on in any department thereof, thus making an injury to one an injury to all.

Instead of the conservative motto, "A fair day's wage for a fair day's work," we must inscribe on our banner the revolutionary watchword, "Abolition of the wage system."

It is the historic mission of the working class to do away with capitalism. The army of production must be organized, not only for the everyday struggle with capitalists, but also to carry on production when capitalism shall have been overthrown. By organizing industrially we are forming the structure of the new society within the shell of the old.

> he never posed as the particular champion of the working man. He was absolutely friendly to him, but always consistent to the conception of his duty to the public in general. He was not the extreme champion of the working man yet he believed that the working man trusted him just the same.[4]

This of course was no answer at all, for it left workers wondering whether Pattullo supported their request or not. Undoubtedly that was the budding politician's intention. In another speech he was more clearly on the side of business when he warned workers that "in demanding increased wages they must be careful not to kill the goose that lays the golden eggs – that is, not to make their demands so exorbitant as to scare off investment from Prince Rupert."[5] In this way, Pattullo neatly dodged the issue without unduly alienating either voters who supported the reforms or those who opposed them. Indeed, this rhetorical position of appearing to favour reform while actually doing little for working people would become the hallmark of Pattullo's politics and premiership.

At one meeting, another candidate, W.H. Montgomery, rose to speak in favour of Frank Mobley, whom Pattullo also supported for council. Montgomery, who had not come out in favour of the wage increase despite being a labour candidate, received what the newspaper called "a rather mixed reception." One of those who denounced Montgomery, according to the Prince Rupert newspaper, was Robert Gosden. Montgomery responded in kind, accusing Gosden of being of "disreputable character." He then charged that Gosden was no longer a real worker, for he was now a caterer in the tenderloin, or skid road, district of Prince Rupert.

As he would time and again throughout his life, Gosden met the accusation by going on the attack. He took the stage and frankly admitted that he made his living catering in the tenderloin. It was "as much a part of the social fabric as any other part," he thundered, and "surely it was no sin to serve meals to the people who came in need of them." His rejoinder silenced Montgomery, and the newspaper noted that "the speech made a splendid effect."[6]

Industrial Workers of the World on strike against Canadian
Northern Railway, Yale District, 1912

The union continued to press candidates for a wage increase for construction workers hired by the city. Despite the political pressure, workers still had to hold a short strike after the election to secure a raise of sixty cents a day, or about 16 percent. In March 1911 the PRIA demanded that private contractors engaged in municipal works pay their employees the same rate that the city workers were paid for the same work. The private contractors refused, claiming that a pay raise would eliminate their profit. The workers were unsympathetic. At a union meeting that opened with the singing of the labour anthem "The Red Flag," a worker pointed out that often the cost of materials rose after a contract had been signed. When that happened, the contractors did not stop work; they simply made some adjustments. Why could they not do so when the cost of labour was altered? Again it was clear that a strike was necessary for workers to improve their lot.[7]

Whether they could afford a raise or not, the contractors preferred to fight. They hired scabs to break the strike, going as far as Vancouver to round up strikebreakers. The IWW, however, warned workers in Vancouver, Victoria, and Seattle of the strike and the bad conditions, and it proved difficult to import scabs. The strike escalated: the PRIA widened the action to include those workers who were hired directly by the city. Meanwhile, employers and the city council held a secret meeting in the office of railway contractors Foley, Welch, and Stewart, better known to workers as "Frig 'em, Work 'em, and Starve 'em" for the harsh conditions of their camps and work sites. There they decided to ask the provincial government to send the militia or the RCN *Rainbow*, a light cruiser from the naval base in Esquimalt, to Prince Rupert to quell the strike. The request was significant, for there had been no violence or threats from the workers; clearly business leaders and civic authorities hoped to use military force to break the strike. The *Rainbow* was sent up, but played only a minor role in the events.[8]

In a letter to the Wobbly newspaper, the *Industrial Worker*, Gosden let other workers know about the strike. In scathing words, he outlined conditions in the city:

The cost of living is so high here that a man cannot live on three dollars a day and it rains every day. There was 155 inches here last year, and the rest of the time it was bitter cold, so you can guess that it is something fierce. This jerk-water city is composed of tar-paper shacks filled with wage slaves, and the owners of this rock and muskeg are waiting to realize a little hard cash on the patch if they can boom it up and get suckers to come here and buy it up. At the present time it is just a dumping place on this desolate coast for freight and wage slaves being sent up to build railroads for the masters, and let me assure you the conditions in the camps up the line are hell...Yours for the IWW and the whole world.[9]

On 6 April the angry strikers held a march through the city streets. Several hundred strong, the marchers urged others to down tools and join the strike. When they reached a section of roadway known as Kelly's Cut, a fight broke out between the strikers, scabs, and police. Several on each side were injured. The violence gave employers the excuse to have several unionists arrested, including the union secretary. Gosden was appointed to take his place, then was arrested with several others on charges ranging from attempted murder to rioting to assault. Charged with counselling assault, Gosden spent three months in prison.[10]

The harsh reaction to the attempt to secure decent work and wages strengthened Gosden's belief that capitalism was a cruel and exploitative system. Many of the arrested were kept in a hastily built bullpen until their trials, and the trials themselves were denounced as an attempt to "railroad some of the agitators." According to Gosden, one man, Steven Rudo, was convicted of rioting even though the police could not agree when and where he was arrested. One officer testified that Rudo had been arrested at Kelly's Cut during the battle, while another testified he arrested him the next day in his cabin. Several witnesses testified Rudo had been sick in bed the day of the riot and played no part in the events. Despite this testimony, Rudo was sentenced to one year in jail. The prisoners were fed a watery soup they mocked as "shadow soup" until local union supporters brought them food. The prison itself would "make a dog blush with shame," according to one of the men. The boards in the flooring were so far apart, he wrote, he "nearly fell through to be buried alive in the muskeg beneath." In a letter to the *Industrial Worker*, this Wobbly pointed out the desperate irony of a country that had a law "whereby you must not abuse animals but the capitalists and hired thugs can massacre men and women by the thousands and there is nothing done to them." So frightful was the jail, Gosden wrote, Rudo soon went insane.[11]

His experience in Prince Rupert also soured Gosden on the conservative unionism of the American Federation of Labor. During the PRIA strike, local craft union carpenters had no qualms about building the bullpens that held the arrested strikers. One PRIA member remarked bitterly, "We cannot expect anything else from the old craft form of disorganization. If it was a gallows to hang those innocent men, it would be all the same."[12]

Gosden himself reported with scorn on the efforts of an AFL organizer to bring local unions into the American federation. Gosden deplored the organizer's closed meetings, his "secret craft dope," and his refusal to make public the proceedings of the meetings with local unionists. Gosden sarcastically suggested that such tactics could work, if only the AFL man "was the omnipotent ruler he thinks he is." Ridiculing the closed meetings as the "secret confines of the holy of the holies," Gosden ended his report with the optimistic observation that despite the AFL's fulminations, "the knowledge and sentiment of the ONE BIG UNION is growing apace."[13]

Gosden was not alone in his attack on the craft unions. As the name indicates, craft unions (also known as trade unions) organized workers by craft or trade. Carpenters, for example, would join the United Brotherhood of Carpenters and Joiners, while painters would sign up with the International Brotherhood of Painters. Craft unions affiliated to the American Federation of Labor (AFL) in the United States and to the Canadian or Dominion Trades and Labour Congress (CTLC or DTLC; often just TLC) in Canada. These were central organizations that did not control the unions but put forward policies and lobbied for political reform.

Early unions tended to be formed by skilled workers who did the same job and thus were members of the same craft or trade. In Canada, shoemakers, printers, machinists, and carpenters were some of the first skilled

KNIGHTS OF LABOR

One of the first attempts to organize industrial unions was the Knights of Labor. Formed in the United States in 1869, the Knights spread quickly to Canada. By the 1880s there were locals of the Knights throughout the country, especially in Ontario. While the Knights welcomed skilled workers, it actively organized the unskilled, women, and immigrants. In British Columbia the Knights organized coal miners on Vancouver Island and stevedores, longshoremen, and loggers in Vancouver. The union helped form the Vancouver Trades and Labour Council in 1889 and played a vital role in the defeat of a pro-business candidate for mayor in 1887. The Knights, like the Wobblies a generation later, argued that it was crucial for the labour movement to organize all workers, regardless of skill, race, or gender. If labour did not include everyone, the employer would use the unorganized to break strikes, and skilled workers would often ignore the efforts of the unskilled, even crossing their picket lines and breaking their strikes.

But the vision of the Knights of Labor was not successful. Internal factions; the open hostility of the craft unions, which purged the Knights from many labour councils, including the VTLC;

workers to form craft unions in the 1840s and 1850s. It was relatively easy for them to organize, because they shared the common bond of the craft or trade. They had a great deal of power when they organized because without them and their skills, the job could not be done. Scabs could not be used effectively as they could not do the work. Thus the fight for organized labour was often led by skilled workers in craft unions.

But craft unions had many weaknesses. They tended to be exclusive. The law of supply and demand suggested that if there were too many skilled workers, employers could lower wages. To reduce the number of competing workers, the craft unions controlled apprenticeship programs and made entry into the craft difficult and expensive.

Because they were organized around the craft and skill, these unions looked after the skilled but ignored the unskilled. In practice, this often meant that women, immigrants, and members of racial minorities were excluded and unprotected by unions. Because craft unionists had a monopoly on skills and could not easily be replaced in a strike, they were often relatively successful in bargaining with the employer and won better wages. As a result, craft unionists sometimes believed they had little in common with other workers and put their own narrow interests before those of the working class as a whole. These unions were usually politically conservative and were rarely interested in fighting for the rights of others. They were sometimes called "pure and simple" unions because they were concerned only with wages and conditions of work rather than issues of social justice. They were also called "business unions," for they tended to regard the union as a kind of business that should not take risks or lose money on strikes or organizing drives.

In contrast, industrial unions did not sign up workers by craft or trade but by industry. The United Mine Workers of America, for example, organized everyone in the mining industry, regardless of their specific job. They represented those workers ignored by the craft unions. Industrial unions were also crucial to avoid what the IWW called union scabbing. In the construction industry, for example, there might be ten or more crafts on a single job site: carpenters, plumbers, ironworkers, pipefitters, electricians, painters, glaziers, operating engineers, labourers, drywallers, bricklayers, teamsters, plasterers – each organized into a separate union. Each union would have a separate contract that compelled its members to keep working if one of the unions went on strike. If the carpenters' contract expired and they went on strike to win better conditions, all the other unions on the job would have to keep working or risk fines and imprisonment. That, the IWW said, was union scabbing. With work on the building continuing, the employer could defeat the carpenters, then turn on the next union. Organizing by industry would solve this problem. If all construction workers were in one union, regardless of their trades, they would take action as a single union and prevent the employer from dividing and conquering.

and changes in industry made it difficult for the organization to fight the employer effectively. In 1902 at the Berlin (Kitchener, Ontario) Conference of the Dominion Trades and Labour Congress, the DTLC voted to expel the Knights. In truth, it had ceased to be significant a decade earlier, but the dream of industrial unions would be taken up again by the IWW in the early 1900s, and by a new generation of unionists in the 1920s and 1930s.

UNION SCABBING AND THE UBRE STRIKE

The most vivid example of union scabbing in BC was the United Brotherhood of Railroad Employees' (UBRE) strike of 1903. The running trades on the railways – the engineers, firemen, brakemen, and conductors – were considered skilled workers. They worked for big corporations, were paid well, and were trained to think of themselves as an elite. Their unions were craft unions, and they did not organize the so-called unskilled railway workers. These workers created their own union, the UBRE, in the United States in 1901 and elected George Estes to head it. The union affiliated with the American Labor Union, a radical federation that included the Western Federation of Miners and would in 1905 merge with the IWW.

By 1902 the union had spread to Canada and organized clerks, freight handlers, and labourers in Toronto, Calgary, Revelstoke, Nelson, and Vancouver. The Canadian Pacific Railway (CPR), however, refused to recognize the union and began a campaign of espionage, intimidation, and provocation. When the company suspended a union worker in February 1903, the union demanded he be reinstated. The company refused, and Vancouver UBRE members went on strike.

The strike soon spread as

His experience in Prince Rupert convinced Gosden of the need for industrial unionism and revolution. After his release from prison he made his way down to San Diego by the end of October 1911. From there he may have gone into Baja, California, to take part in the Mexican Revolution. Certainly in later years he claimed to have ridden with Pancho Villa and to have "expropriated" horses from William Hearst's San Simeon ranch to aid the revolutionaries. In a short autobiographical sketch he wrote in the 1950s, Gosden described how he met IWW martyr Frank Little in Taft, California, "after completing a mission in Mexico for the 'insurrecto' fleeing before the new 'presidente,' Huerta." His story is possible, for several IWW members were active participants in different events in the Mexican Revolution.[14]

In California, perhaps not surprisingly, he encountered a group of spiritualists. He denounced the mystics in harsh language in a letter to the *Industrial Worker*:

Whether it is the climatic conditions or not I cannot say, but their metaphysical dope especially appeals to some emasculated persons who have been so degenerated by this system that they are preaching the doctrine of absolute non-resistance and the curious phase of it is that they are deluding themselves that they are evolutionists and that they have got such an enormous individual WILL POWER that whatever they will they can do and that the individual creates his own environment, etc., instead of the usual course of procedure. I am deeply interested in this curious human phenomenon and I purpose to study it a little deeper so that when the species are sent to the museum we can describe their habits and customs before they become extinct.[15]

Although he would later become fascinated with mysticism, at this time in his life Gosden preferred what he defined as a more materialist direct action in the here and now rather than investigating metaphysics. In 1912 he took part in the IWW's San Diego free speech fight. In several cities throughout North America, including Vancouver and Victoria, city officials banned the union from holding meetings and speaking in the streets. Since these meetings were a crucial tactic for organizing, the IWW fought back, usually by calling upon its members to flock to the city and get arrested for defying the ban. The resulting publicity, unruly demonstrations, and strain on the city's jails and coffers were designed to force the municipal authorities to relax their assault on the right to free speech and to allow the union to continue its organizing drives. This was the theory. In San Diego, however, it was proved tragically wrong.[16]

In December 1911 the city council voted to ban street meetings from the entire downtown core, ostensibly to avoid the blocking of traffic. The IWW joined with socialists, civil libertarians, religious groups, and trade unions to maintain the right to free speech. When the ordinance went into effect in February 1912, police arrested

CPR workers joined in. Other Vancouver workers supported the strike: longshoremen refused to unload CPR ships, and teamsters declared CPR freight "hot" and would not haul it. Even some CPR machinists, notably those in Revelstoke, went out in sympathy with the strikers, while Nanaimo miners put an embargo on shipping coal to the CPR.

The running trades unions, however, did little to help the UBRE. Many of them crossed the pickets and scabbed. Other trade unions aided the company as well. Perhaps the worst example was that of Joseph Watson. Watson was head of the boilermakers local in Vancouver and had for a time been president of the Vancouver Trades and Labour Council. A staunch craft unionist, he was a member of the Liberal party and an organizer for the Dominion Trades and Labour Council. He even applied to AFL president Samuel Gompers for a job as an organizer, but Gompers turned him down. During the UBRE strike, Watson ordered members of his boilermakers union not to join in sympathy strikes, and at public meetings and in the press he agitated against the UBRE, the ALU, and socialists.

The provincial government sided with the CPR too. When UBRE president George Estes went to Victoria to help the strikers, he was arrested on trumped-up charges; after three weeks, the charges against him were dropped. With the company, conservative trade unions, and even the government against them, the strikers had little chance for success. That did not stop the CPR from continuing its terrorist activities against the UBRE.

On 13 April, union organizer and socialist Frank Rogers went down to the picket line at the foot of Abbott Street around midnight. Rogers and others confronted CPR thugs and were fired upon. Rogers fell, mortally wounded, and died two days later.

A CPR special policeman and a strikebreaker were arrested, but the policeman was not charged. The strikebreaker was defended by a CPR lawyer and was found not guilty. Rogers had been active in the longshoreman's union and had helped organize Fraser River fishermen during their strike of 1900–01. His funeral procession drew a large turnout of union members and supporters; the running trades, however, did not send official delegates or support. Socialist MLA James Hawthornthwaite spoke at a Labour Day celebration later, and accurately noted that if Rogers "had been a magnate of a corporation the papers would not have ceased to this day to call for the avenging of his murder, rewards would have been offered and the

forty-one people who had gathered in the city centre. The following weeks saw more arrests, and the IWW called upon its members to come to the city to fight back. The authorities continued to arrest speakers, and in short time nearly three hundred were imprisoned in the city jail. Fire hoses were turned on crowds, and vigilante groups were organized to purge the city of the activists. Often with the connivance of police and officials, the vigilantes kidnapped and beat free speech fighters. At least two IWW members were killed by mobs during the several months of the free speech struggle.[17]

One of the Wobblies picked up by police in the February dragnets was Bob Gosden. Arrested and charged with violating the city ordinance forbidding gatherings, Gosden was held in county jail without trial for nine months. Again, his imprisonment served largely to make him more determined to overthrow capitalism.

From his cell, Gosden continued to write to the Wobbly newspapers. His letters reveal an intelligent man, keen to draw lessons from his experience and observations. His second stint in jail reaffirmed his views on capitalism, revolution, and the role of craft unions. In his first dispatch to the IndustrialWorker he insisted that a proletarian revolution was necessary. The most effective tools for revolutionaries, he argued, were direct action and sabotage. Gosden urged the IWW to "act in more direct and aggressive ways...." While the IWW talked a revolutionary line, in practice its tactics were little different from parliamentary socialists or traditional labour unions. So far, Wobblies were "only advocating revolution, we are not living it." Worse, the strikes and free speeches of the IWW usually resulted in its members being jailed, and the resources that could be used to organize went instead into legal fees. In Gosden's view this was both unproductive and hypocritical, for "from every street corner we are telling the workers what a farce the courts are (and we prove it too) and still we play their game." Without revolutionary action, he wrote, "we are just a set of philosophers. Philosophy may do for recreation, but it is a damn poor thing to fight the capitalist with."

Gosden pointed out that though the IWW had been around for eight years, it had only about 100,000 members, and these were diffused across North America. With so few numbers, a general strike was obviously impossible; indeed, "in no industry have we enough men to call for and enforce a stoppage of work merely by

criminal however clever would have been run to earth. That murder will be a stain on the justice of this province until it is avenged."

If Rogers's story was the most tragic, the failure of the running trades to support other workers was widespread.

Arrests at the Free Speech Demonstration in Vancouver, 18 January 1912

23

striking." The only way to be a revolutionary union, the only possible hope for success for a "militant minority," was "for every member of the IWW to sabotage at every conceivable opportunity." Through sabotage, he wrote, "we are forcing the slaves to go the way we want them to, instead of persuading and pleading and getting clubbed trying to get them to act." By destroying capitalist machinery and factories, the IWW would remove itself from its untenable position of sitting "on the fence and advocating radical action and excusing cowardice by saying that the workers won't organize. We have," Gosden concluded, "enough members in America to tie up every industry at any time if we use sabotage, and by such action alone will we have the liberty to organize in the industries so that we can feed and clothe the world's workers when the class war has ceased."[18]

The advocacy of sabotage grated on the ears of many moderate unionists and could in itself raise the suspicion that the speaker was an agent-provocateur. But in the 1910s, IWW members and other left-wingers and unionists were fiercely debating the merits of sabotage and direct action as tactics in the class war. In 1913 the Industrial Worker, under the editorship of Walker C. Smith, came out unreservedly in favour of sabotage. In a series of editorials Smith called upon Wobblies to counter the violence of the capitalists with violence "not against their person but against their profits." The editor asked rhetorically, "Is the machine more than its producer? Sabotage says 'No!' Is the product greater than its producer? Sabotage says 'No!' Sabotage places human life – and especially the life of the only useful class – as higher than all else in the universe." The paper even went so far as to print tips on how to destroy machinery. In advocating sabotage, Gosden was not advancing a new strategy or suggesting ideas that were beyond the pale for the IWW. He was simply presenting one, admittedly provocative, side in an ongoing and serious debate. Sabotage had a great deal of appeal to men and women who stood outside the existing order and had little ability as individuals to shape their world in their day-to-day affairs. It suggested that a new society was possible and gave adherents at least the illusion of autonomy and effective power. In his calls for sabotage Gosden was expressing a sentiment and tactic that was widely accepted by the IWW.[19]

In a second letter, Gosden commented acerbically on the habits and conditioning of union workers he observed from his prison cell. The letter uses puns and irony effectively and reveals a sense of humour as well as a contempt for capitalism and conservative unionism:

> As I gaze from our bedroom window I can see the Free Born Citizens mustering upon the foundations of a new hotel ... which they are erecting for their masters ... It has been an interesting and instructive study to watch the Dig-in-ity of Labor perform its function for the boss. It is now about quarter to eight and already the slaves are unpacking their tools and climbing into position to have a good start in their eight hour race against each other.

Gosden singled out a bricklayer who was keen to out-work the others:

> He is already stripped off, waiting for his master's voice. He is a splendid "bricklaying machine," and like all machines is unable to think for himself. If he did think, he would realize that the faster he builds the sooner he will be out of a job, and that means out of his rented house. In fact, the faster he builds houses, the sooner he will be "homeless." Gee, it's a great system.

Next he observed a carpenter the prisoners nicknamed the "Bell Horse because he is always in the lead. One morning he started work five minutes before the whistle blew, but we shouted at him so that he was forced to wait, much against

SABOTAGE

Modern readers tend to associate sabotage with wilful destruction of property, with images of the French Resistance movement during World War II – blowing up bridges and tunnels, for example, or igniting oil tanks. And this is one meaning of the word. But there is another, older meaning that is more accurate and useful when discussing labour history and labour relations.

The English word *sabotage* is from the French verb *saboter*, which means to botch, or to do in a clumsy way. In turn, the French verb comes from *sabot*, a wooden shoe or clog. How do we get from a shoe to the word's present meaning? Some authorities claim that French workers, forced into a speed-up of work, threw wooden shoes into machinery to cause it to stall and thus slow down production. Others claim that the wooden shoe was worn by peasants and unskilled workers who were brought into factories to scab against skilled workers who were on strike. The scabs were clumsy and unskilled and performed their work poorly, and thus the sabot became a symbol of sloppy work, intentional or not.

In either case, in labour history the word *sabotage* more accurately refers to working slowly or poorly to force the boss to meet workers' demands or to register dissatisfaction, rather than to outright destruction of machinery. It is closely related to the Scottish term "ca' canny," meaning "to go slow."

Used in this sense, sabotage is a regular feature of industrial relations and one that most working people have engaged in at one time or another. Booking off sick when one is healthy could be considered a form of sabotage, as could taking a breather between tasks. Obeying all the safety rules set out by employers and the Workers' Compensation Board would likely result in a slow-down. Giving customers a little more coffee than company regulations dictate, or telling customers the truth about unhealthy conditions in a restaurant, would also be forms of sabotage. Each of these is a way of reducing profit and, from the boss's point of view, interferes with production. That these tactics are often necessary to preserve workers' health, sanity, and dignity is obvious to anyone who is not a boss.

The IWW discussed sabotage as a tactic at great length. It published articles, poems, and stickers on the subject, often using pictures of a wooden shoe or a black cat — the "sabo-tabby" — as symbols for sabotage. Elizabeth Gurley Flynn wrote a long pamphlet for the union in 1915, where she defined the word this way:

his will ...We are sorry if we have offended him, but it was necessary for us to prevent him from scabbing on himself as well as us." The jeers and catcalls continued when the prisoners noticed a nine-year-old boy working on the site, in open contravention of the child labour laws. The noise they made affected the job so much the foreman spoke with the guards to see if they could quiet the men down. The effort failed, however, for as Gosden put it, "we are advocates of Free Speech and we would criticize Jesus Christ if he attempted to work a boy of that age."

He ended his spirited, sardonic letter by noting that

the waiters arriving with the breakfast, we adjourned with the unanimous opinion that things were pretty rotten, but perhaps, after the State Convention of the Federation of Labor has been wined and dined and welcomed by our masters, it may be all right — for the boss, I mean. Say, I wonder whether those AF of L guys will ever get wise and kick the fakirs out. Yours for the whole cheese, and to hell with the Bosses.

A third letter, entitled "Jail Bird Philosophy," started, "There used to be a saying that 'All Roads Lead to Rome,' now it is 'All Roads Lead to the Overthrow of Capitalism.' I am in one of the cages where rebels are made, having time to rest and think, I can see the process of evolution going on, slowly but surely."

"Democracy," he continued, "is the order in jail. The aristocrat of labor bums his cigarette from his Oriental brother, and the white man argues with black. All race prejudices are swept aside." This anti-racism was crucial to the IWW view of industrial unionism. Craft unionists had often sought to restrict immigration; in British Columbia, the Vancouver Trades and Labour Council had helped found the Asiatic Exclusion League in 1907. Their racism reflected the skilled workers' beliefs that an over-supply of labour would lower wages and that Asian workers, by virtue of their different languages and customs, could not be organized. In contrast, Gosden reported that several of his fellow prisoners were Japanese and Chinese men who had long ago learned that industrial unionism was crucial if their lives were to improve.

Even the "Free Americans," he noted with satisfaction, were learning political lessons behind bars. One was still "pretty strong on 'political action,' but by the time he gets out he will be safe and sane." "Blackie," a veteran of the US military invasion of the Philippines, "confessed" that "he really deserved punishment, for, says he, 'I went to the Philippines to fight for "my" country – why, I have no country, I am a Jew! Of course the other suckers had none either, but I ought to have known better, they had been trained that way.'"

Pete, a "down and out wage slave," still viewed "capitalism through a business man's spectacles." Pete expected to "get the 'millennium' through the Initiative, Referendum, etc. At present Pete's mind is in a whirl, but when it settles down a bit (which it will do in the eleven months' sentence he has) he will be a real live little rebel."

Finally Gosden came to "the piece de resistance. Enter 'Shorty' O'Donnell, once the Cowboy

Sabotage means primarily: the withdrawal of efficiency. Sabotage means either to slacken up and interfere with the quantity, or to botch in your skill and interfere with the quality, of capitalist production or to give poor service. Sabotage is not physical violence, sabotage is an internal, industrial process. It is something that is fought out within the four walls of the shop. And these three forms of sabotage – to affect the quality, the quantity, and the service – are aimed at affecting the profit of the employer. Sabotage is a means of striking at the employer's profit for the purpose of forcing him into granting certain conditions.

Other Wobblies pointed out that employers engaged in sabotage all the time when they watered the liquor they served, built with cheaper materials than contracts called for, or told workers to ignore rules and standards to produce more profitably. If it was fair for employers to squeeze out extra profit this way, the Wobblies maintained, it was fair for employees to use similar tactics in self-defence.

Sabotage was practised by the Luddites in Britain in the late eighteenth and early nineteenth centuries. These were textile workers who smashed machines. We are often told that the Luddites feared

27

progress and thought they could stop it by breaking the new technology. This is wrong. The Luddites understood technology very well, for they were highly skilled workers who used the most modern equipment of the time in their daily work. They smashed the machines because they knew that employers introduced them to reduce their labour costs by firing workers and making the remaining ones work harder.

Sabotage is an ancient tactic: it is alleged that Hebrew slaves in Egypt tampered with the bricks they were forced to make for the Pharoah's buildings. It is a modern tactic: many computer viruses are created by disgruntled employees. In 1997, Canadian postal workers who were ordered back to work threatened to withdraw efficiency to protest unfair treatment. Sometimes it is a conscious, group tactic; often it is an individual protest that ranges from slacking off to damaging a machine. But it is unlikely to disappear as long as we have a society divided into bosses and workers.

King at thirty a month; then penitentiary range rider...and last but not least, a member of the Intelligence department of the San Diego police department during the free speech fight – a la stool pigeon." Little had Shorty thought that "he would ever enjoy the comforts which are to be found only in jail, to which place he helped send so many of the IWW for two dollars a day." But when the job as police spy ended, Shorty needed work. Desperate, he turned to crime. He proved a failure and was arrested, Gosden noted wryly, for "stealing a piece of string." Unfortunately, "there were five horses on the end of the piece of string."

"Alas, how are 'the mighty' fallen!" Gosden continued:

Shorty now occupies a bunk in our ward and lice spring from our shirts and bite him (in a playful way, of course) just as impartially as they do the humans of coarser clay ...Oh, the irony of fate! To think that this notorious gun man should be forced to wallow with the agitators. ... Stripped of his glory, deserted by those whose dirty work he so willingly did, his cheeks sunken by starvation, despised by the rest of his class, he is a pitiful picture of abject slavery and degradation.

Shorty learned a hard lesson, Gosden concluded, when he discovered for himself "how well the boss treats his 'gunmen' when they have done his dirty work." But redemption was possible even for Shorty. "A little sense is springing up even in this barren soil," and Shorty would have "long months ahead" to "develop his thinking powers, and if he can manage it, he may yet emerge from this depravity, stand on his legs AND BE A MAN."[20]

The comment on being a man was more significant than it might first appear. As an unskilled, transient worker, Gosden had little status in society, little way to reaffirm his existence and worth. In a world that defined adult males by the ability to secure a wife, a family, steady work at a decent wage, and a home, he had nothing. Nothing, that is, except his revolutionary politics, which helped define his life and acted as a yardstick by which to judge others. Real men did not kow-tow to the boss or suffer exploitation cheerfully; they fought back with whatever tools they found to hand. By defining manhood this way, Gosden could find some satisfaction even from his jail sentence.

In November 1912, Gosden and sixteen other defendants finally went to trial on charges of violating the street speaking ordinance and assault with a deadly weapon. He was found guilty but was released on probation and deported to Vancouver.[21] The *Industrial Worker* noted his deportation, complaining that the immigration officials were "working in harmony with the vigilante-loving town of San Diego." The paper went on to comment on the futility of removing Gosden from the United States, for "as the IWW is not particularly patriotic and there is a class struggle in Canada, we fail to see how a system based on theft has gained by making the change."[22]

Certainly his stay in jail had not dampened Gosden's enthusiasm for class war. On his return to British Columbia he continued to agitate for the IWW. At Steveston, a fishing village outside of Vancouver, Gosden addressed audiences of Native and Chinese cannery workers. Dressed in the black shirt often affected by Wobbly organizers, symbolic of the black flag of anarchism, he outlined the principles of the IWW. Careful not to openly advocate violence or sabotage, he rhetorically asked the workers "what it mattered to them if the machinery was to fall to pieces or the roofs of the cannery were to fall in."[23]

He took a stronger line among the striking miners of Vancouver Island's coal fields. In September 1912 the miners at Canadian Collieries, formerly Dunsmuir and Sons, took a one-day "holiday" to protest the company's discrimination against two of the members of the workers' gas committee, responsible for ensuring mine safety. The work stoppage began a strike and lockout that lasted two years. Led by the United Mine Workers of America (UMWA), the strike centred on the demand for collective bargaining and union recognition. It was a fierce strike that saw miners thrown out of company housing and the province's Conservative government, headed by Richard McBride, side with the company as the bayonets and machine guns of the militia were brought to help break the strike. Beatings, sabotage, and charivaris or shivarees – loud protests accompanied with banging on pots, taunting, and noisemakers – were common. Miners demonstrated and rioted to protest the use of troops to escort scabs, and miners and police exchanged gunfire in pitched battles at the mineheads. Over two hundred miners were arrested and charged with unlawful assembly and given sentences of one to two years in prison.

Though the IWW was involved only peripherally in the UMWA strike, Robert Gosden strode boldly into the fray.[24] He headed to the island and travelled up and down the strike region, giving speeches and counselling radical action. Asked later if he approved of the looting and burning that had taken place, Gosden side-stepped the issue, saying that he had not done any of it and if in charge would have urged the strikers to take "pos-

Canadian Collieries miners being marched off to jail in Ladysmith, 1913

session of the mines." Did he approve of violence? "Under circumstances as they existed there ...when all peaceful protests fail, I am a man and if I am satisfied my cause is just I will fight," he replied.[25]

But Gosden's chief contribution to the strike and to class antagonism came some months later. By November 1913, BC unionists and socialists formed the Miners' Liberation League (MLL) to work for the release of the miners arrested for taking part in demonstrations and riots during the strike. Gosden, representing the IWW, spoke at a mass meeting of the MLL on 10 November, along with prominent socialist leaders E.T. Kingsley and Jack Kavanagh, and Vancouver Trades and Labour Council president J.W. Wilkinson. There he made what the labour newspaper, the BC Federationist, called "a fighting speech." Gosden warned the crowd that the bosses "were putting you to the test ...You must have the might. The workers can do no wrong. The capitalists have called your bluff; make good or lie down." His speech was greeted with applause, and Gosden was made executive chairman of the MLL.[26]

His success evidently emboldened him. At the next open meeting of the MLL, held at the horse-show building at Vancouver's fairgrounds, site of the Pacific National Exhibition, Gosden went further. The last speaker at the meeting, his words were calculated to leave the crowd in a charged mood:

By the end of this month every last peaceful appeal which is necessary or possible for us to make as citizens of this Dominion for the release of our brothers in prison will have been made. By the end of this year all peaceful measures will have been exhausted. If they are not released by the time the New Year is ushered in, if Sir Richard McBride, Attorney-General Bowser, or any of the minions and politicians go hunting, they will be very foolish, for they will be shot dead. These men will also be well advised to employ some sucker to taste their coffee in the morning before drinking it if they value their lives. In addition, it will cost them one million dollars a week for every week that our brothers remain in jail after the New Year.[27]

His speech, given to a crowd of at least one thousand, was greeted with "tremendous cheering," and the *BC Federationist* later printed a letter supporting both Gosden and his call for industrial sabotage. More significantly, Gosden was elected president of the Miners' Liberation League shortly after his rousing speech.

His remarks gained him considerable notoriety. The mainstream press railed against the threats of violence, and moderate labour leaders of the province distanced themselves from Gosden's fiery call to arms. Robert Foster, president of UMWA's District 28, the Vancouver Island local, denounced the speech as "extremely foolish utterances" that "in no way expresses any of the views or aims of the United Mine Workers Union." Most of the executive of the Miners' Liberation League repudiated Gosden in the hope that the miners would be freed if the MLL disassociated itself from the radical faction. Gosden himself jumped before he was pushed and tendered his resignation from the presidency on 23 January, citing the MLL's refusal to move beyond protest and its rejection of direct action as his reason. "If they do not consider their own comrades' liberty of enough importance to take some more decisive action," he wrote, "I consider that the league will be wasting its energies." Nonetheless,

MLL Tag Day, in front of the Vancouver Labour Temple.
The figure second from left in the front row is believed to be Gosden.

despite, or perhaps because of, his militancy, Gosden was elected to the vice-presidency and to the press committee of the MLL.[28]

After his coffee speech, Gosden went to Vancouver Island and addressed strikers and their supporters in Ladysmith and Nanaimo, encouraging them to take direct action and seize the mines. He may also have advocated violence.[29] He appears to have done little more with the MLL, however, and his coffee speech marked the high point of his involvement with the miners' strike and with radical labour politics. In fact, his forced resignation from the MLL presidency indicated that Gosden was outside the mainstream of the labour movement. His politics and his actions would become increasingly more complex and entangled. Soon it would be almost impossible to tell which side Robert Gosden was on.

CHAPTER 2

"I Have No Moral Conception of Party Politics"

If the rallies of the Miners' Liberation League were the most significant moments in Gosden's career as a labour agitator, they signalled the decline of the Vancouver Island coal strike. The militia patrolled the streets and mines and helped employers use scabs to resume production. Many of the miners were in jail. Some had left the district to search for work while still others were urging an end to the strike. At a few mines, miners called off the strike, signed agreements with their employers, and returned to work; at other mines, miners were crossing picket lines and scabbing. Calls for a general strike were rejected by union leaders, and labour was unable to apply more pressure on government and employers. In the summer of 1914 the UMWA was forced to cut off strike pay, and the strike was effectively over by the end of July.

The slow collapse of the coal strike reflected the decline of the labour movement generally. The province started to slide into a depression in 1912. It would not recover until 1916, when war production invigorated the regional economy. By the winter of 1912, prices for raw materials and land were dropping as foreign investors, worried about the possibility of war in Europe, moved their money into safer investments. The great railway schemes of the Laurier years, the Grand Trunk Pacific and the Canadian Northern, had made fortunes for their creators, who built the railways with public money. But the railways failed to generate long-term prosperity for the province, and by 1914 they were nearly bankrupt. Millions of dollars were owed to sub-contractors and workers. Soon the owners would ask the federal government to bail them out, and the railways would be taken over

SOCIALIST PARTY
OF CANADA

While many trade unionists were prepared to accept the capitalist system as long as they could continue to increase their wages, other workers believed that more fundamental changes were necessary. For them, capitalism was an unjust system built on exploitation. No real gains for workers could be made unless the system was abolished. Capitalism would be replaced with socialism. Then goods would be produced to satisfy human needs, not make a profit, and workers themselves would control the means of production. These workers, together with some members of the middle class, formed left-wing parties to educate and organize.

The first of these socialist parties in BC was the Socialist Labor Party (SLP), formed in Vancouver in 1898. It was a branch of the American SLP, which was headed by Daniel De Leon, and it took up De Leon's fiery, intellectual brand of socialism. But some members objected to the party's politics, especially its belief that working with trade unions was pointless. These members soon split off to form the United Socialist Labour Party. Under that banner, William MacClain became the first socialist to contest a BC election. Endorsed by the Canadian Socialist League and supported by the Vancouver

by the federal government and merged to form the Canadian National Railway.

With the collapse of the resource industries and railway construction, unemployment rose. Many workers left the province hoping to find work elsewhere. Those who stayed found it difficult to organize unions or to press for better wages, for employers benefited from the high unemployment rate. With a pool of desperate workers to choose from, they could easily fire and replace those who talked union or complained about conditions. Union membership dropped precipitously. In 1911, BC unions reported a membership of about 22,600. By 1915 the number of union members had been slashed by more than half to about 10,800. Unions represented more than 12 percent of the work force in 1911; by 1915 it was less than 6 percent. Strike activity, another measure of labour's strength, slumped. In 1911 more than 12,000 workers were involved in twelve strikes; in 1915 fewer than 1,000 workers took part in only five strikes. Not until 1918, with the war economy in full production, would the BC labour movement recover the strength it had in 1911.

The left-wing movement suffered as well. The socialists were divided and squabbling and unable to mount a consistent challenge during provincial elections. The Socialist Party of Canada (SPC) received about 11.5 percent of the popular vote and elected two MLAs in 1909. In 1912, socialists received about the same percentage of votes and elected two members, but now the votes and seats were split between the SPC and the Social Democratic Party. More telling, the SPC could only field candidates in seventeen of the forty-two provincial ridings. The 1916 election would be even worse. Between them, the SPC and SDP could run only seven candidates, all of whom were defeated. Only Parker Williams, running as an Independent Socialist, was able to hang on to represent the left, and he soon joined the Liberal party.

Even the IWW collapsed as Wobblies were increasingly persecuted and work ran out. The most famous Wobbly, Joe Hill, was framed on a murder charge in Utah and executed by firing squad on 19 November 1915. On the day of his execution, Hill sent a telegram to Big Bill Haywood that read, "Goodbye, Bill. I die like a true blue rebel. Don't waste any time in mourning. Organize." To commemorate his death, the IWW printed postcards with Hill's picture and a version of his telegram that read, "Don't Mourn But Organize."

Events in BC paralleled those across North America. The Victoria IWW local folded in May 1914 as most of its members left town to seek work elsewhere. In Vancouver and Kamloops, Wobblies spent as much time fighting each other as they did the boss. Not surprising in a union that stressed rank-and-file activity and democracy, the IWW was often wracked by disputes over whether the union should be One Big Union, with decisions made by the General Executive Board, or a federation of autonomous industrial unions that would decide policy independently. Vancouver Wobblies split on the issue. It is not clear which side Gosden was on, but his close friend Matt

Trades and Labour Council, MacClain received 683 votes, a respectable showing for a new candidate and a new party in a riding where the winning candidates received only about 1,660 votes. Very little is known about MacClain, who left the city soon after the election. He was British, had likely jumped ship in Seattle before making his way to BC, and was a member of the machinists' union. Together with Frank Rogers, he helped organize fishermen along the Fraser River and helped lead their strike in 1900–01.

More significant was the Socialist Party of Canada (SPC). It was created in 1904 when the Socialist Party of BC merged with the Canadian Socialist League and other socialists. The SPBC's newspaper, the *Western Clarion*, became the official paper of the new party, and its editor, E.T. Kingsley, set the tone. Kingsley was an "impossibilist." That is, he argued that trade unions were of little use to workers, for they could rarely win meaningful reforms. Worse, reforms would only delay the socialist revolution, for if workers got some relief, they would be less inclined to overthrow the capitalist system. In some elections, the official SPC platform consisted solely of the call to abolish capitalism.

But there was always a tension in the party between

the radical impossibilists and more moderate socialists. Certainly those SPC members who were elected to the legislature were quick to call for reforms and even to work with the Conservative government. While writers like Kingsley might attack trade unions, most of the rank and file of the SPC were trade unionists, and political candidates actively sought the votes of union workers by promising reform measures.

Both the reformist and the revolutionary wings of the party believed in using the electoral system to press their demands. Reformists believed much could be accomplished within the system, while the revolutionaries believed that voting for the revolution would make it so. Neither side advocated violence or armed revolution, but both sides believed in the necessity of parliamentary procedure.

The SPC has been interpreted in different ways by historians. In large part this is because the party contained many different people with many different points of view. Kingsley was an impossibilist, and for a time impossibilism was the official party stance. Yet 60 to 90 percent of the SPC's rank-and-file members were trade unionists, while its MLAS, James Hawthornthwaite and Parker Williams, were moderate reformers, judging by their work in the legislature. At times the party lead-

Fraser was active on the side of the decentralizers, and it is likely that Gosden, with his distrust of authority, also sided with them. The conflict was never fully resolved, but it undoubtedly contributed to the decline of the IWW in BC.[1]

Faced with the collapse of his union and the end of his role in the MLL, Gosden dropped out of public view. He became disillusioned with radical politics; as he put it later, some of his views "have been shattered," though he continued to endorse the IWW "principles which are contained in its preamble." He took up a number of casual labouring jobs, most of them short-lived and ill-paid. He worked as a longshoreman for a time, and in the winter of 1915–16 he cleared snow, removed garbage, and excavated sewers in Vancouver and Victoria. Unemployed in February 1915, he took a six-week job washing windows at the provincial legislature, but left when he was cut to half-time.[2]

During this period Gosden was a regular boarder in houses owned by a widow named Ethel Cuthbertson, moving residences as he found different jobs. Cuthbertson owned houses in Victoria, Vancouver, and Cloverdale. In 1916 Gosden resided in the house at 432 Almas Road, now Aberdeen Street, in the working-class area of Collingwood in East Vancouver, paying Cuthbertson five dollars a week when he could. He shared the house with Cuthbertson, his friends Matt Fraser and David Grey, and other boarders. For a time, these included the wife and children of Isaac Portrey or Portray, one of the miners whose ill-treatment by Canadian Collieries had led to the Vancouver Island coal strike.

Portrey, Fraser, and Gosden worked together for a short time, inspecting a well for a farmer at Gordon Head near Victoria in the winter of 1915–16.

In addition to keeping boarders, Mrs. Cuthbertson wrote and published poetry and small tracts on sociology, temperance, and prohibition. Her writing and her boarders allowed her to live in relative comfort with her six-year-old daughter and another woman, sometimes referred to as her nurse.

It is difficult to know exactly what Gosden's relationship with Cuthbertson was. Later, when Gosden was under scrutiny for his role in an election scandal, the press hinted, in the guarded, coded language of the day, that Cuthbertson, Gosden, and the other tenants were more than landlady and boarders. One paper referred to the arrangement as a "menage," and when questioned, the tenants refused to discuss the details of their relationship with Mrs. Cuthbertson. It seems safe to suggest that Gosden and Cuthbertson were a couple. They first started living together, at least as owner and boarder, in 1912 or 1913, and they stayed in the Vancouver house until 1917. By 1918 they were living together in Alberta, and Gosden was said to have treated Cuthbertson's daughter as his own. This was the beginning of a pattern of living with women who had some independent income, which Gosden would follow for the rest of his life.

In addition to their unconventional relationship, the two shared an interest in spiritualism. Although he had denounced mysticism during his trip to California, by 1916 Gosden was keen to

ership was elitist, insisting that prospective members pass an exam on left-wing theory and more interested in discussing Marxist philosophy than in taking part in labour struggles. George Hardy, a staunch Communist activist and functionary, denounced the "leading lights" of the party as "spittoon philosophers" who "Nero-like…fiddled while the armed forces of the State suppressed the miners and locked up resisters" during the Vancouver Island coal strike. But Hardy's harsh assessment is unfair. More often the SPC membership played an active role in the battles of the day and supported workers on strike. Many SPC officials worked with the trade union movement, and several became officers of the Vancouver Trades and Labour Council and the BC Federation of Labour. The range and complexity of the party should not be surprising; even today, in the homogenous, "lowest common denominator" parties such as the Liberals and Reform, there is a wide spectrum of politics and ideas.

Much of the work of the party went into elections. The SPBC had some success at the polls, converting Nanaimo City MLA James Hawthornthwaite from the Independent Labour Party and electing Parker Williams in 1903 to represent the riding of North Nanaimo.

The party captured about 8 percent of the popular vote, but this figure understates its efforts. The party contested only ten of the forty-two provincial ridings and, where it ran losing candidates, polled between 20 and 40 percent of the popular vote. Even in the multi-member riding of Vancouver, the SPBC polled between 3 and 5 percent in an election that gave the winners about 10 percent of the popular vote.

The SPC did substantially better in the popular vote, but could not elect many more members. In 1907 the SPC received 9 percent of the popular vote and elected three MLAS; in 1909, 11.5 percent and two MLAS; in 1912, 11 percent and one MLA. By comparison, the Liberals won only two seats in 1909 and none in 1912.

Despite the electoral successes, the tension between the two wings of the party did not go away. By 1910 the more conservative socialists had left the SPC to form a new party, the Social Democratic Party (SDP). They elected John Place in Nanaimo City and during the 1912 election Parker Williams left the SPC for the SPD.

Both parties effectively collapsed during the First World War, at least as parliamentary parties. The SPC could only contest four ridings in the 1916 election; the SDP, only three. Neither party won a seat. By

investigate the occult, and Ethel Cuthbertson was rumoured to hold seances and to be clairvoyant. Perhaps because of the collapse of radical politics, the eclipsing of his own role in the movement, and his grinding round of casual jobs, unemployment, and hard physical labour, Gosden began to explore eastern religions and metaphysics.[3]

The material world, however, kept intruding. By February 1916 Gosden was unemployed again. This time, however, he was determined to avoid the labouring jobs that had been his lot for years. 1916 was an election year in BC, and Gosden went to the Liberal party headquarters and offered his services. He was directed to John T. Scott, an ambitious Alberta newspaperman who had been hired by the Liberals as a campaign manager. His first task was getting the up-and-coming lawyer M.A. Macdonald elected in the by-election for the riding of Vancouver City. The Liberals were courting the labour vote, but Scott, a newcomer to the city, had few connections among Vancouver workers, especially those on and around the waterfront. Gosden, with his longstanding ties to the radical and labour movements and his work as a longshoreman, was ideally placed to help the Liberals. Scott hired Gosden, at the respectable salary of twenty dollars a week plus expenses, to supply him with "correct data about the waterfront men."[4] Scott particularly wanted help in drawing up a roll of men who could be put on the voters' list. In 1916, voters' lists were not drawn up by an impartial government office; they were created by the political parties themselves.

Gosden could put together an accurate list of

waterfront men, and the job was a welcome break from the manual labour he had been doing. It paid relatively well – about what a union carpenter or machinist would make. It held the promise of long-term employment, for Scott promised to keep Gosden on the payroll to build up an organization for the upcoming general election. That it was political work aimed at dislodging the Tories was another bonus, for as Gosden remarked, "There was some satisfaction in seeing the Liberals get in to beat the Conservatives for once. Do you think I don't remember the troubles up on the Island?"[5]

The upcoming election was widely viewed as a crucial one that could realign the politics of the province. The Conservative party was tired after thirteen years in power. The prosperity of Premier McBride's early years was over, and the province had been in a recession since 1912 as cautious financiers pulled their money out of risky investments like mining and railway building on the BC frontier. Then, as now, provincial governments could do little in the face of decisions made in the financial centres of the world, but the Tories were blamed for the slowing of the economy. The party was plagued with scandals ranging from patronage to conflict of interest to Richard McBride's quixotic purchase of two submarines to defend the BC coast when the First World War broke out. McBride himself suffered from diabetes and kidney disease and retired from politics in December 1915. The choice of his attorney-general, William Bowser, to replace him angered many and further divided a party already splitting at the seams.

1920 the SDP was unable to run a single candidate, while most of the labour and socialist leaders had left the SPC for a new party, the Federated Labour Party. The SPC was split even further as some members moved into the One Big Union and some into the fledgling Communist Party of Canada. Others continued to give a socialist, but anti-Communist, analysis of politics. In 1933 many SPCers, led by Ernie Winch, joined the Co-operative Commonwealth Federation (CCF), now the NDP. A few diehards resurrected the SPC in the 1930s, and the party still exists today but plays no real role in politics.

The SPC is significant for the role women played in it. Activists such as Bertha Burns contributed to the socialist press and organized for the party. Especially in areas outside BC, women played a critical role in the party. The views of the male leadership on "the women question" were not always consistent: some writers argued that women's suffrage was an important cause, while others insisted it was only a diversion from the "real" class struggle. Nonetheless, the SPC was an important forum for women and their struggles.

Historians continue to debate the politics and significance of the SPC. Certainly its impact cannot be judged by its performance in elections or the legislature, for these were not great. More important perhaps was its ability to inspire and train working-class activists and unionists. This is admittedly hard to measure, but even a short list of SPC members includes people such as Ernest Winch, leader of the Lumber Workers Industrial Union and CCF MLA from 1933 until 1957; William Pritchard, participant in the Winnipeg General Strike and reeve of Burnaby in the 1930s; and Helena Gutteridge, union activist, CCFer, and in 1937, the first woman elected to Vancouver City Council.

It was hard to imagine anyone voting for the Conservatives. The middle class viewed the party as corrupt and out of touch. For a number of British Columbians, the proof of this was the government's refusal to give women the vote and to prohibit the sale of liquor. Both women's suffrage and prohibition were widely supported, but the Tories had stalled and dithered on both issues for years. Working people remembered Bowser's suppression of the Vancouver Island miners and the party's opposition to labour legislation such as workers' compensation reform and the eight-hour work day for hardrock miners.

On the other side, the Liberal party was united, confident, and dynamic. Unable to win a single seat or even field a full slate of candidates in the 1912 election, the Liberals had spent the next four years canvassing the province and reinventing themselves as the party of political purity and change. Headed by a new, capable leader, Harlan Brewster, the party attracted reformers of all stripes. It presented itself as the working man's friend and worked to undercut the socialist and labour parties that had been the opposition during McBride's reign. The Liberals successfully courted Vancouver Island socialist MLA Parker Williams and could rely on an old Liberal-Labour politician, Ralph Smith.

The test of the Liberals' rejuvenating formula came in the three 1916 by-elections that preceded the September general election. The Liberals easily won the by-elections in Vancouver and Victoria, and their candidates, party leader Harlan Brewster and rising star M.A. Macdonald, received over 60 percent of the popular vote in each election. This was particularly significant, as both ridings had long been Tory strongholds. The Liberals lost the by-election in Rossland City, but the Conservative's margin — a mere nine votes — was so slim that the Liberals could be pleased with the result. They consoled themselves with the knowledge that their victory had been spoiled by the SPC. If the socialist candidate, Wallis Lefeaux, had not run, his forty-nine votes would probably have gone to the Liberals to give them the riding.

The victories of Brewster and Macdonald gave hope to reformers and progressives around the province. Even former Wobbly Robert Gosden was cautiously optimistic that the Liberals would usher in a new era of change and justice. In a letter to Harlan Brewster the day after the Liberal victory in Vancouver, he outlined a program for reform. His letter reveals him as an astute political observer with a practical program that would help the unskilled and migrant worker, and as a schemer hoping to impress the Liberals with tales of electoral support he could throw their way. "Having done my little bit in the campaign," he began, "I am now taking the liberty of making some suggestions for your consideration which may or may not meet with your approval." He then hinted that he belonged to a number of organizations representing "a large body of men and women" whose support he could deliver to the Liberals if they proved to be genuine reformers. He suggested to Brewster that the Liberals could introduce bills in the legislature, even though they would have no chance of being

PARKER WILLIAMS

Although the two men would be bitter political enemies, the lives of Robert Gosden and Parker Williams had some similarities. Unlike Gosden, however, Williams managed to parlay his native intelligence into a successful and lucrative career as a politician, while Gosden was forced by circumstance to remain a labourer all his life. As a result, the two had very different political trajectories: one became a revolutionary and then a labour spy; the other a socialist reformer and then a Liberal patronage appointee.

Parker Williams was born in Glamorganshire, South Wales, in 1873. The son of a farmer, he received a limited education and worked in the Welsh coal mines. At nineteen he emigrated to Canada, and with his wife Eleanor he raised two children in Ontario. But the family was unhappy there, and Williams left to find a better life. In a journey that took thirty months, he worked in logging and railway camps in Ontario, made his way across the Prairies, worked in coal mines in Alberta, and headed to Oregon and Washington state. He worked in the logging and railway construction camps of BC and finally made his way to Nanaimo in January 1898. Perhaps because the hills and coast reminded him of Wales, he decided the family would move to

Nanaimo and he sent for his wife and children.

He started work in the coal mines, making $100 a month, but soon abandoned the dark shafts of the mine for the halls of political power. In 1902 he ran as a member of the Socialist Party of BC against W.W.B. McInnes in a by-election in the riding of North Nanaimo. Williams lost, but in the general election of 1903 he won a three-way race with 40 percent of the popular vote in the riding of Newcastle. He held the riding in the elections of 1907, 1909, 1912, and 1916, winning a majority of the popular vote in the last three elections.

Although he was a member of the SPBC and later the SPC, Williams was no radical or impossibilist. A member of the Freemasons, his politics were pragmatic and reformist, and after the 1903 election he propped up the Conservatives in a number of close votes in the legislature. Along with fellow socialists James Hawthornthwaite, John Place, and John McInnis, he managed to extract minor reforms from the Tories in return for their support. As one Conservative put it, the government could well afford to support a few reform bills "which are not necessary but can do no harm."

By 1916 Williams was a member of the SPC and the more moderate Social Demo-

passed by the Conservative government. But introducing the bills would place the Liberals "in a commanding position, against all those Socialist candidates, so called, independents, labor party men, etc. and other of that ilk who will be financed for the purpose of splitting your vote."

Chief among the reforms he advocated was women's suffrage, "which rightly handled will make your party the real power in BC after the general election." He attached a lengthy list of other reforms, including a bill to provide for direct legislation, that is, the initiative, the referendum, and recall. Gosden called for an eight-hour day with time-and-a-half for overtime, a minimum wage, the replacing of employment sharks with a government employment bureau, government-funded hospitals and first-aid supplies for work camps, land and homes for returning soldiers, and compulsory citizenship for eligible immigrants. Those who were not eligible for citizenship, he argued, should not be allowed to immigrate; ineligible immigrants already in BC should be forced to leave and their property sold and the proceeds sent to them.

Gosden noted that "Many of these measures if submitted will undoubtedly be killed or scientifically sidetracked, at this time," but he was convinced that merely putting them forward would convince many people that the Liberals were truly committed to reform and were worth supporting. He concluded:

A short time ago these measures would have been considered too revolutionary, today, such measures as these are the only ones which can be used to allow the "awakening conscience" of the people to have intelligent and progressive legal expression. Statesmen will see this. MACHINE POLITICIANS will not.

Have we those statesmen in the Legislature now? We shall see, and seeing, act accordingly.[6]

Gosden was sent a formal, brief reply from Brewster that thanked him for his letter and noted that "many of the suggestions enclosed therein will no doubt be acted upon during this Session by members of the Opposition." Brewster closed by assuring Gosden that "it is our intention to live up as strictly as possible to the demands of the democracy of the province."[7]

How should Gosden's letter be interpreted? It outlines Gosden's belief that some reform in the short term was as important as long-term revolution. Nonetheless, while he was now prepared to work within the system, Gosden remained keenly interested in reforms that would meet the needs of men such as himself, those transient workers forced to turn their hands to many jobs, all ill-paid and arduous. A minimum wage, shorter work hours, publicly funded hospitals, the closing of the employment sharks, the use of public lands and seized property to reward soldiers and those deemed worthy of citizenship – each of these measures would remove some of the most keenly felt abuses. In addition, Gosden was aware of the growing pressure for women's suffrage. His relationship with the political Mrs. Cuthbertson and his involvement with the Wobblies and their advanced views on the equality of

cratic Party of BC, but abandoned both parties to run as an independent socialist. He was viewed by many as a closet Liberal in 1916, and he campaigned for Liberal candidates in Vancouver. He probably cut a deal with the Liberals, who did not run a candidate against him in Newcastle, the only seat the party did not contest. Williams won comfortably, but resigned in 1917 when the Liberals appointed him commissioner on the newly reformed Workmen's Compensation Board.

Lauded by the press for his years of service, Williams sat on the Board until 1943, when he retired to his 200 acres at Oyster Bay, near Nanaimo. He lived another fifteen years and was survived by four sons, four daughters, and several grandchildren and great-grandchildren. He died in 1958, aged 85.

women no doubt made Gosden himself a supporter of women's suffrage.

His disillusionment with the "so-called Socialists" is clear. This disillusionment reflected two political trends within the left. First, the socialists had given up any revolutionary aims. Second, they were no longer able to provide an effective voice in the legislature. If they had no radical vision and were unable to push for reform, there was clearly no point in supporting the parties of democratic socialism and social democracy. Any political change would have to come from the Liberals, who were poised to form the next government. Gosden was in touch with the reform sentiment that was sweeping the province and was thinking strategically.

His skepticism about politics still remained, however. The Liberals could take either of two paths: that of statesmen or that of machine politicians. Hoping they would take the former, he was obviously aware that the latter was equally possible.

The letter may also be seen as an attempt to cash in on the political debts Gosden believed the Liberals owed him for his work during the by-election. No doubt he hoped the Liberals would make good on Scott's promise of employment during the general election. To this end, Gosden reminded Brewster that he had done his "little bit" during Macdonald's by-election and hinted that he could bring more support to the Liberals in the general election through the organizations he was connected to. Bright, articulate, able to work with politicians and the "common working man," tired of brutal physical work, Gosden, now thirty-five years old, probably looked forward to a more comfortable life that would make better use of his brain and less use of his brawn.

It was not to be. His letter and his "little bit" would soon come back to haunt the Liberals and Gosden, damaging Macdonald's political career and pushing Gosden into the seamy world of machine politics and ultimately his career as a labour spy.

At first the by-elections were cause for celebration. Confident and ambitious, the two new Liberal MLAs used their toe-hold in the legislature to step up the campaign against the Tories. Smelling victory, the Liberals were aggressive and ambitious, keen to outmanoeuvre the Tories in the build-up to the general election. Their campaign, however, started to founder. Out of the triumph of the by-elections came dark hints of election fraud, of illegal voters and mysterious pay-offs. In the middle of the rumours and charges, in what would become known as the "plugging scandal," stood Robert Gosden.

Shortly after Macdonald's victory, the daily press, especially those newspapers friendly to the Conservative party such as the Victoria *Daily Colonist* and the Vancouver *Province*, started printing stories of voters paid to vote for the Liberal candidate and of men shipped in from Seattle to cast illegal ballots. The Tories seized the issue, for it was the perfect counter to the Liberals' promise of clean government. The rumours refused to die down, and in April, Conservative leader Bowser gleefully appointed a commission to investigate the allegations. Three Conservatives, Liberal leader Harlan Brewster, and socialist/Liberal Parker Williams made up the commission and began a series of hearings and interviews.

The commission heard testimony from a number of people, and it was soon obvious that a complicated scheme of voter impersonation and fraud had taken place. The evidence clearly implicated high-ranking Liberals, including Macdonald's campaign manager, John T. Scott. Did Macdonald know of the plugging scheme? Was he implicated directly? Had he authorized it or had he turned a blind eye to his overzealous campaign workers? Had Scott operated on his own initiative or on orders from others higher up in the Liberal party? Was Macdonald himself guilty of election fraud? This was the key to the investigation and Scott held the answers.

WORKMEN'S COMPENSATION

Was Parker Williams's success with workers' compensation proof that the system could be used to benefit working people? Did it indicate a victory for working people over the interests of business? Not really.

As John Keelor has demonstrated in his MA thesis, Workmen's Compensation in BC and elsewhere was promoted by corporations. Before Workmen's Compensation (as it was known until the 1970s, when it became Workers' Compensation to reflect the number of women in the work force), workers had to sue their employers to receive any payment for injuries received on the job. Companies were liable only if they were found to be negligent in a court of law. This was often a drawn-out process that could cost the companies more money in lawyers' bills than they paid out in compensation. Even if the company won the suit and paid nothing to the injured worker or to the family of a dead worker, it still had to pay the lawyer. As a representative of the BC Electric Streetcar Company put it in his testimony to the BC Royal Commission on Labour in 1913, the company was keen to find a "way of saving money so it can be given to the unfortunate victim of accident...There is a lot of money wasted in law costs."

If the worker won the suit, the company would be found negligent, and that could be bad publicity for companies that dealt with the public. If the BC Electric Streetcar Company, for example, was held to be negligent in the death of a worker, this would make the public wary of taking the streetcar.

Lawsuits also carried the potential of a large settlement in favour of the workers. Although this rarely happened in BC, corporations disliked the unpredictability of juries and preferred a low-cost insurance scheme, with costs that could be rationally and accurately calculated.

Workmen's Compensation cut employers' costs. It eliminated liability, as workers were forbidden to sue employers under the act, even if the employer was clearly negligent or violated the law. The insurance scheme reduced individual costs by spreading them among all companies, eliminated legal fees, and made taxpayers ultimately responsible for paying for the injuries caused by private companies.

Workmen's Compensation did three other things that benefited business. First, it shifted blame. Employers were no longer accountable for the injuries and deaths of their workers. "No-fault" insurance treated injuries and deaths as accidents, acts of God, rather than the result of the failure of employers to

But Scott could not be brought before the commission. He had left town in a panic, fleeing to the United States. While he promised to testify in return for immunity, the Liberals did not want him back in BC and helped fund his refuge in Seattle. They needed a scapegoat, and Scott was perfect. If he testified, he might connect Macdonald to the illegal activity, but if he did not appear, the Liberals could place all the blame on him. Another witness who was in a position to implicate Macdonald was whisked away to Seattle by Scott and kept locked in a hotel room while the BC Provincial Police searched for him. For a time, the Liberals' damage control worked. The scandal still made headlines, but Macdonald seemed in the clear.

Robert Gosden upset the Liberals' plan. Subpoenaed and brought before the commission against his will, his testimony electrified the province. His revelations cast light on the shadowy corners of Liberal and Conservative politics, and provide some insight into his own politics and life. His story drew in two future BC premiers — Brewster and John Oliver — as well as a Nanaimo mayor and a future Conservative MLA — Albert E. Planta and his son Clive — and ultimately shaped at least two political careers, those of Macdonald and his successor.

Cocky, self-assured, and combative, Gosden revealed the details of the plugging scandal, his role, and the connection to Macdonald. He told the commission that he had been hired originally by Scott to prepare lists of electors. But it quickly became clear that Scott wanted much more than a detailed list of eligible voters and a reading of the political sympathies of the working man. Scott wanted to win the by-election, and he did not want anything left to chance. He asked Gosden to give him "complete information about the waterfront workers, dead or alive, here or there, good, bad or indifferent." The object was to create a list of absentee voters so "pluggers" could assume their identities and cast ballots in their place. On the day before the election, Scott gave Gosden $400 to cajole real voters to support the Liberals and to help others cast illegal ballots. He also hired Phil "Brocky" Robertson to help them round up voters. Brocky was a colourful figure with some experience in rigging elections, for he spent eighteen months in prison for "plugging" for the Liberal North Vancouver candidate in 1903. Brocky, a one-eyed, weatherbeaten, congenial, alcoholic longshoreman with a "voice like a young foghorn," cheerfully "ginned up" several voters during the 1916 by-election and helped them vote for the candidate of his choice.[8]

His work was no secret to other Liberals, including Macdonald, Gosden testified. But Scott's plans were discovered shortly before the by-election, not by the opposition or the press but by some prominent Liberals who were appalled at Scott's machinations. The Liberals were not as unified as they appeared. Two factions, the "machine" Liberals based in the Vancouver City riding, and the "Purity Squad," a collection of Vancouver and hinterland Liberals, vied for control of the party. The machine Liberals saw politics as a pragmatic,

maintain a safe workplace. The only responsibility employers had was to follow the letter of the often meagre regulations. Employers could still encourage workers to avoid following regulations to improve production, perhaps by speeding up the work process or by hinting that "real men" didn't worry about silly safety rules, or by encouraging people to take dangerous, timesaving shortcuts. If workers were injured, companies were safe as long as they had officially obeyed the rules, even if they had effectively subverted them unofficially.

Second, the WCB soon behaved much like any insurance company. It looked for ways to avoid paying claims. It hired its own doctors, whose mandate was to find ways to refuse claims as much as it was to help workers. WCB doctors might, for example, suggest that injuries were the result of a pre-existing condition, or that workers were malingering. Many workers came to view the WCB as their enemy, not their ally, when they were injured.

This led to a third effect. Angry injured workers now blamed the WCB, not their employer, for their fate. This helped employers evade responsibility, and made workers distrust the state more than employers. In this way, the WCB helped create a climate in which government, not business, was seen as the real problem in the work place. This was useful for business, for it helped sow distrust of any government intervention in industrial relations and of reform, let alone socialism.

So the creation of Workmen's Compensation in BC cannot be seen as a progressive measure that primarily benefited workers. Nor does it suggest that the government of the day was taking on capital on behalf of workers. Many businesses supported Workmen's Compensation, for they understood it would benefit them. Certainly some businesses complained about their premiums, just as we all complain about insurance premiums. The alternative for business, though, would be much worse, just as having no insurance when your house burns down is worse than paying the premiums.

This does not mean that Workers' Compensation was of no use to workers. But it does show how measures that workers fight for can be watered down and ultimately used to help business more than workers.

hardball game in which winning was the only goal. If winning meant adopting the corrupt but effective methods of their enemies, the goal – Liberal victory – was worth it.

The Purity Squad, however, was dedicated to reform and cleaning up politics. Its members believed the Liberals had to be different, better, than the Conservatives, otherwise there was no point in replacing the Tories. The discovery of Scott's dirty tricks dismayed them. At the same time, the fight over means and tactics was also a fight over who would divide the political spoils. The machine Liberals were more successful, leaving the Purity Squad out of the real corridors of power. The plugging scandal gave the Purity Squad, led by Ashworth Anderson and Prince Rupert businessman and newspaper editor J.S. Cowper, some ammunition to fight back against the Liberal machine. The Purity Squad cut off Scott's funding and grilled him for details of the plugging scheme. The machine Liberals went along with the housecleaning in the hope the potential for scandal could be contained. The party made it clear to Gosden that he was no longer welcome; as he put it, "the moment there was a squeal I could not get near them with a Gatling gun."

With Scott unable to pay Gosden the money owed him, Gosden was in a precarious financial position. He too owed people for their election work, such as copying out the lists and campaigning to get the Liberal vote out. He paid his colleagues out of his own pocket, for "There's still some principle left among us people, and I had to pay my fellows even though Scott did not pay me." Gosden pressured Scott for the money he was owed. Scott put him off with promises and small sums of money, but Gosden suspected he was stalling. He also suspected that the Liberals were planning a frame-up. Their plan was to pay men to sign affidavits claiming they had plugged for the Conservatives and thus take the heat off the Liberals. Gosden refused to discuss the plot with its instigators, worried that the Liberals would try to "make a goat" out of him.

Desperate for money, Gosden warned Scott that if he wasn't paid soon he would go over Scott's head and hit up Macdonald for the money. But Scott still did not pay, claiming he too had been abandoned by his employers. When Brocky Robertson suggested they go see Macdonald himself, Gosden agreed.

Gosden then testified that he and another friend approached the candidate at his Vancouver home. Macdonald said he had no money on him but would meet Gosden in Victoria the next day and settle up with him then. They met near the Victoria post office, Gosden said, around six o'clock, but Macdonald still had no money. Later that night, however, they met again at the post office, and Macdonald gave Gosden fifty dollars.

This was the link the Tories and the press had hoped for. There was already some circumstantial evidence that linked Macdonald to the election irregularities: he was president of the provincial Liberal association that hired and paid Scott; Scott had left the country rather than testify, presumably to protect himself and others; and Scott had undoubtedly brought in men to vote illegally. He had even printed up cards with the name and occupation the substitutes were to adopt. None of this, however, touched Macdonald. Gosden's testimony tied the MLA directly to the plugging scandal.

The Liberals had to discredit Gosden to protect themselves, and they swung into action. Macdonald, upon hearing Gosden's allegations, swore out a charge of perjury and had him arrested pending his trial. Gosden continued to testify before the commission, but now did so with a police guard and was returned to his cell at the end of the day. The Victoria Times, a pro-Liberal newspaper, characterized him as "a man who would do anything for a price," whose testimony to the commission was suspect. He might

LIB-LABISM AND RALPH SMITH

One wing of the Liberal party had always sought the vote of working people through a platform of mild reform. The career of Ralph Smith illustrates the party's strategy nicely.

A member of the provincial legislature and the federal House of Commons, and the first British Columbian to head the Trades and Labour Congress of Canada (TLC, now the Canadian Labour Congress), Smith was a Liberal-Labour, or Lib-Lab, politician: a member of the Liberal party who was friendly to labour.

Smith was born in Newcastle-on-Tyne, England, in 1858 and started to work in the coal mines when he was eleven years old. He left the pits to become an office worker for a mining company and was soon involved in politics. In 1891 Smith and his wife, Mary Ellen, emigrated to Canada and settled in Nanaimo in 1892, where Smith again worked his way from the mines to the office.

But his real vocation was politics. Smith was elected general secretary of the Miners and Mine Laborers Protective Association, a small,

even be a Tory agent, the paper suggested, planted in the Liberal organization to aid the plugging scheme to discredit the party later. The paper made much of Gosden's exhortations to Vancouver Island miners and of his 1913 speech when he suggested the premier and the attorney-general would be wise to hire someone to taste their coffee. That indicated that Gosden was entirely unscrupulous. His job as a janitor at the legislature was also suspicious, the paper added. Despite his threats, Gosden may well "have cleaned the windows of the attorney-general's office with no more danger to the safety of that gentleman than if a dyed-in-the-wool Conservative had the task. It may be, though, that that description would fit him." The combination of the radical speeches and the janitor's job were, the paper concluded, "grounds for sinister surmise."

Brewster and Williams tried to shake Gosden's testimony by challenging his politics, his honesty, and his lifestyle. Parker Williams in particular went after Gosden, implying alternately that he was a notorious radical and a Tory spy. Williams, now cozying up to the Liberals, pushed this line when he grilled Gosden at the commission hearing. Gosden, however, refused to be browbeaten. Instead, he used the commission to defend himself and to outline his own political views. In response to Williams's questioning, Gosden stated that he was not a Liberal or a Conservative, that he belonged to no political or industrial organizations. When Williams asked if he was a socialist, Gosden, with a dig at the socialist cum Liberal, answered, "Certainly not, Parker!" The former Wobbly made it clear that he did not identify with the established parties and politicians but rather with "every man who is on the bum, who has been blacklisted by this rotten order of things." When Williams suggested that these men had been driven out of the province, Gosden coolly replied, "Have they? Well, they can come back. The S.O.S. signal would bring them back a thousand strong." In the meantime, Gosden's work with the Liberal party might not bring about many political gains for these men, but the election day handouts were at least "a financial benefit to them."

Williams then tried to brand Gosden as a Wobbly, hoping to awaken all the fear and anger that label stirred in middle-class voters. He asked Gosden if the IWW had been involved in the election scandal. When Gosden answered, "There is no such organization," Williams asked, "Then you helped kill it?" "Yes," Gosden replied, adding sardonically that he was preparing a new organization, "which would arise Phoenix-like from the ashes." He led Williams into a lengthy discussion of socialist politics, principles, and organizations that revealed Gosden as "an anarchist, or in some way opposed to the existing order of things," according to the unsympathetic Victoria *Times*.

Williams tried to paint Gosden as an irresponsible rebel whose brash statements during the coal strike had injured the cause of the miners. Gosden took him head on, scoring several telling points against the MLA, even embarrassing him on occasion. Their heated exchanges revealed the gulf between the comfortable social democrat and the angry revolutionary. Williams sought to establish

local union that represented Vancouver Island coal miners. With the failure of their strike in 1890–91, the miners decided they needed a voice in the provincial legislature. They elected Thomas Keith in 1890, and in 1894 Smith ran as a Reform candidate along with Keith and Tully Boyce. The three were defeated, but in 1898 Smith was elected with a sizeable majority.

His platform was one of moderate reform that included the eight-hour day, women's suffrage, and safety inspections of mines and factories. He also called for a law that would ban Chinese men from working underground. This racist measure was demanded by the miners, who were angry that Dunsmuir had used Chinese workers as scabs to break strikes and to lower wages. Smith was elected vice-president of the TLC in 1896 and was president from 1898 to 1902.

By 1900, however, Smith's political base was being challenged. While he was moving to the right, Nanaimo miners were moving to the left. He retained his seat in the 1900 election, but his local support was weakening. Smith resigned his provincial seat and was replaced by the socialist James Hawthornthwaite. Elected as a federal MP in November 1900, Smith declined the post of deputy minister of labour (the position went instead to William

Lyon Mackenzie King).

As president of the TLC in 1901, Smith launched an attack on American international unions in the Congress. These unions had always been an important part of the Canadian labour movement, and by 1900 approximately 80 percent of Canadian unionists were members of international unions such as the International Typographical Union, the International Brotherhood of Carpenters and Joiners, and the International Association of Machinists.

Smith argued that Canadian unions should replace the international unions. In part this reflected his belief that Canadian problems should have Canadian solutions, and that it made no sense for Canadian workers to send dues to American union headquarters. It also reflected his desire to swing the labour movement's votes to the Liberal party and to rid labour of the influence of socialists.

Smith's plan, however, united conservative AFL supporters and radical unionists against him. At the 1902 TLC convention in Berlin, Ontario, Smith was replaced as president by John Flett, a Hamilton carpenter and the Canadian organizer for the AFL.

Smith concentrated on his federal political career and was elected in 1904 in the riding of Nanaimo. He did lit-

himself as a legitimate, respectable politician, one fit to take his place in the mainstream of BC's politics. Gosden remained intransigent and defended his revolutionary speeches and direct action.

When Williams brought up the infamous coffee speech to discredit him, Gosden readily admitted making the remark and added, "You can call it a threat or a statement, and I have no apology to make, understand that, Parker."

Pressing on, Williams said, "I had to straighten that out at the Globe theatre the next Sunday, you remember that?"

Scornfully, Gosden replied, "Had you the same courage I had there would be a different story to it."

Williams then suggested that Gosden's inflammatory speech "did not help us any," again implying that Gosden was irresponsible and reckless.

But Gosden refused to be cowed and objected to Williams's attempt to identify with the miners and their cause. "Help us any!" he scoffed. "You were not on trial."

Williams quickly changed the subject to Gosden's speeches on Vancouver Island. "Did you suggest in Extension that it would be a good night to make trouble?" he asked.

Gosden snapped back, "I exposed your cowardliness, Parker, and your own son was there, and I think he had the manliness to be ashamed of you." He then got a laugh from the audience at Williams's expense when he reminded him that they had spoken on the same platform on one occasion during the strike, suggesting that their politics had been rather more similar than Williams now cared to remember.

Williams pushed on, hinting broadly that Gosden must have been working for the Tories during the strike. After all, Gosden had advocated the use of violence and had even offered to lead Ladysmith miners in action. Yet he was not arrested, and had had little trouble travelling throughout the disturbed region. Surely that was suspicious, Williams suggested.

Finally, he probed Gosden's janitorial job. "Were you working a twelvemonth ago last March?" he intoned.

"I was," Gosden answered.

Williams prepared to drop the final argument that he believed would impugn the witness, the revelation that Gosden had been hired by the Tories to work at the legislative buildings. Gosden, however, turned the tables on him and again revealed the difference between the respectable and the rough. When Williams asked where Gosden was working, he replied, "Right here in this building, and so were you. I was cleaning windows," implying that he at least was doing honest work in the legislature.

Williams abandoned his interrogation, and Harlan Brewster took over. He preferred not to engage Gosden on the ground of politics as Williams had done. Instead, he tried to expose Gosden as a man without principles. "Have you no qualms about plugging?" he asked. "Do you think it is right?"

"No, I do not think it is all right," Gosden answered. "I think it is a rotten, damned business, absolutely." That did not mean that he thought it was wrong because he believed in the

tle in office but he held his seat until 1911. He returned to provincial politics, losing in the Tory sweep of 1912. President of the Vancouver Liberal Association and vice-president of the provincial association, he helped rebuild the party and fashion it as a reform party for the 1916 election. He won a seat in Vancouver that year and was named minister of finance in Brewster's cabinet. His success was fleeting; he died a few months after the election, on 12 February 1917. Ironically, the career of his wife, Mary Ellen, is better known today. After Smith's death, she was elected to replace him and was appointed to the cabinet, becoming the first woman in the British empire to hold a cabinet seat. Ralph Smith's career is notable, for he helped create an image of the Liberals as a reform party that lingered until the 1980s.

sanctity of parliamentary politics, however. True to his earlier Wobbly beliefs, Gosden made it plain: "I have no moral conception on the question of party politics," for "politics is based on a rotten structure." This did not mean he was unprincipled, but rather that Brewster could not "measure my morality by yours whatever that is." "Necessity," he continued, "dollars and cents," had forced him into working with Scott.

The election commission continued its work for two more weeks and finally concluded that "a conspiracy to carry on personation on an extensive scale was entered into with the object of securing the election of the Liberal candidate." The report pinned the illegal activity squarely on John Scott, but left open the question of Macdonald's involvement, preferring "to leave to the country final judgement in this matter." Gosden had defended himself ably against the charges of Williams and Brewster, even turning the tables on them occasionally. He now had to face a more serious challenge, the perjury charge laid by Macdonald.

CHAPTER 3

"Opposed to Me is A Strong and Powerful Organization"

Macdonald's perjury charge appeared to be an odd way to silence Gosden. If Macdonald believed his reputation was injured by Gosden's testimony, a libel charge would have been more appropriate. But charging Gosden with perjury would bring the whole power of the state to bear on Macdonald's side. Formally, this meant Bowser's Conservative government, not the Liberal Macdonald, was prosecuting Gosden. This gave Macdonald two advantages. It forced the Tories to take action against the most important witness they had against the Liberals, and it spared Macdonald the expense of launching his own civil suit. At the time some speculated that Macdonald hoped the criminal proceedings against Gosden would silence him, for the court might rule that Gosden's testimony to the plugging committee should be stopped until the criminal proceedings were over.[1] This did not happen, and the trial began in late May, just as the committee report was released.

Macdonald's perjury case was simple and unadorned. He maintained that Gosden lied when he claimed to have met Macdonald in Victoria and received money from him. Later he added a second charge: that Gosden had lied when he testified that Scott had accused another Liberal of the theft of party funds. Macdonald admitted to meeting with Gosden at his Vancouver home but denied he met Gosden in Victoria or gave him money. His proof was the testimony of his wife of four months, Ida. She

JAMES HAWTHORNTHWAITE

James Hurst Hawthornth-
waite's career as a socialist
politician was intertwined
with that of Ralph Smith. Born
in Ireland in 1869, Hawthornthwaite emigrated to BC in
1885, where he worked as the
secretary to the US consul in
Victoria and as a white-collar
worker in the Vancouver Coal
Company. A member of
Smith's reform movement in
Nanaimo, Hawthornthwaite
moved to the left as Smith
moved to the right. In 1901,
when Smith resigned his
Nanaimo provincial seat to
run in the federal election,
Hawthornthwaite was
acclaimed to the seat as a
member of the Nanaimo
Independent Labour Party, a
local party with close ties to
Smith and the Liberals. But he
soon joined the Socialist Party
of BC and in 1903 defeated
both a Conservative candidate and a candidate from the
Independent Labour Party.

Hawthornthwaite moved
farther to the left and joined
the Socialist Party of Canada.
Together with Parker
Williams, he brought forward
legislation for the eight-hour
day for miners, workmen's
compensation, and women's
suffrage. A fiery speaker,
much respected by the
Nanaimo miners, he beat out
the Tories and the Lib-Labs
again in 1907, then resigned
to take on Ralph Smith in the
federal election of 1908. The
race was close, and

swore that she and her husband had met at the legislative buildings before six o'clock on 25 April and had walked through Beacon Hill Park. They then had dinner and retired to their room at the Empress Hotel for the night. At no time, she said, had Macdonald left her and at no time had they met Robert Gosden. Macdonald's fellow Liberal politician John Oliver, who would become premier in 1918, backed up part of their story, stating that the couple had left the legislature together around 5:30 p.m.[2]

Gosden's defence was equally straightforward. He said he had come over on the midnight boat to Victoria, walked around the city that morning, and visited James Hawthornthwaite for an argument. A friend bought him dinner, and Gosden met Macdonald around six o'clock in the evening. He telephoned Macdonald at the Empress Hotel later that night and met him again at the post office around nine o'clock, when Macdonald paid him fifty dollars. Corroborating his account was more difficult, but several witnesses confirmed parts of his story. An acquaintance, Anthony Silvene, an engineer on the Esquimalt and Nanaimo Railway, testified that Gosden had come up to his room in the St. James Hotel on the night of 25 April and had underlined the Empress Hotel telephone number in his phone book. Silvene was charged for a telephone call from his room on 25 April and had made no calls himself. He had not, however, seen Gosden make the call, for Silvene testified that he had spent a great deal of time in the bathroom. The prosecution's implication that someone else might have sneaked into the room and made a mysterious call was ludicrous, but Silvene's testimony could not prove Gosden did use the telephone to call Macdonald, and the judge emphasized this in his summing up. The hotel clerk remembered that Silvene had had a male visitor that night and that a man other than Silvene had placed a call from the room. He thought the call had been to the Empress Hotel but could not be positive, and no records of the number were kept. A number of witnesses, including Gosden's plugging partner Brocky Robertson, Ethel Cuthbertson, and one of his fellow boarders, established that Gosden had been broke before he went to Victoria. He had to borrow money for the ferry fare and was looking "rather seedy," even though he had borrowed better clothes to wear. But when he returned a day or two later he paid Cuthbertson the back rent he owed, was sharply attired in new clothes, and squared some of his debts from a thick roll of bills. The money, he told those who asked, had come from Macdonald.[3]

Gosden's friend and fellow Wobbly Matt Fraser told the court that he had been with Gosden when he met Macdonald and received the money. Fraser, like many Wobblies, refused to swear on the Bible, which he believed to be little more than a superstitious relic and a prop of capitalism. He made a non-religious oath to tell the truth instead. Fraser said he had arrived in Victoria around eight o'clock that night and had visited Silvene, who told him Gosden was out eating. He found Gosden, who told him he was going to meet Macdonald, and the two of them walked down to the post office. According to Fraser, "A man came up and

Hawthornthwaite outpolled Smith in the mining regions of the riding. But the riding also included the town of Esquimalt, site of a federal naval base. Voters there were keen to keep the base well-funded and thus supported Smith for his ties to Wilfrid Laurier and the Liberals. Their votes were enough to keep Smith in power.

Hawthornthwaite returned to provincial politics and easily won re-election in Nanaimo City in 1909, defeating Conservative candidate Albert Edward Planta. But Hawthornthwaite soon came under attack from the Socialist Party. While he was to the left of Lib-Labs like Ralph Smith, Hawthornthwaite was in the centre of the socialist movement. Never a member of a union, Hawthornthwaite was a white-collar worker with no trade apart from politics and deal-making. His deal-making finally got him in trouble in 1911. Heavily involved in real-estate speculation, Hawthornthwaite neglected his constituency and could not justify his political inaction to fellow SPC members. Forced out of the party, he went to London where he floated a number of financial and commercial ventures.

He returned to BC, and when Parker Williams took up his patronage appointment on the Workmen's Compensation Board, Hawthornthwaite ran in the by-election to replace

him. He won a crushing victory over his Liberal opponent in 1918 and sat as an
independent socialist/labour
MLA for Newcastle.

His stay in office would be
short. In 1918 he helped create the Federated Labour
Party (FLP), a hodge-podge of
former SPC and SPD members,
labourists, and radicals,
formed to fill the vacuum left
when the SPC collapsed during the First World War. Officially supported as labour's
party by the BC Federation of
Labour, the FLP brought
together people such as
Hawthornthwaite, VTLC and
SPC stalwarts James McVety
and Parm Pettipiece, the
moderate trade unionist
Helena Gutteridge, and
William Pritchard, soon to be
a leader of the One Big
Union. Its program was a contradictory amalgam of left
socialism and reformism, its
members united largely by
anti-Communism and anti-
Bolshevism. Hawthornthwaite
was especially opposed to the
Bolsheviks and to those
Canadian leftists who were
inspired by the Russian revolution.

For reasons that are not
clear, however, Hawthorn-
thwaite did not run under the
FLP banner in the 1920 election. Likely many miners still
did not trust the would-be
financier. Hawthornthwaite
ran as an independent
labour/socialist candidate but
was soundly defeated by the

Gosden said to me, 'Beat it, here comes Mac.' So I beat it and stood behind the big pillars at the post office." The man was in shadow, with his back to the streetlights, but Fraser heard him say, "Here's fifty. I'll fix up with you when I come over again." The man left, and Gosden treated Fraser to two beers and gave him five dollars – nearly two days' pay for unskilled workers – before getting on the ferry for Vancouver. Fraser then went to the White Lunch restaurant, where he saw Parker Williams and Social Democratic MLA Jack Place. When a juror asked Gosden why, if he was so broke, he would give Fraser five dollars, Gosden immedi- ately replied, "Fraser can have half I've got at any time. Fraser has shared his last crust with me, and I would share mine with him. If I could, I would have given him one-half of what I got."[4] In a wel- come moment of humour in the proceedings, Fraser answered one questioner, who asked if he had "a grudge against the world so far as capital is concerned," with the quip, "I would like more of it myself."

A number of witnesses testified that they had seen Macdonald alone on the night of 25 April. Albert Edward Planta, former mayor of Nanaimo, three-time unsuccessful Tory candidate for the provincial riding, and friend and former business partner of James Hawthornthwaite, swore he had seen Macdonald pacing up and down Govern- ment Street that evening. Planta's son Clive, who would himself serve as an MLA in the 1930s, was with him, and he too testified to seeing Macdon- ald. James Rooke, a fruitgrower from Grand Forks, took the stand and stated that he had seen

Macdonald leave the Empress Hotel alone shortly before nine o'clock.[5]

Gosden's lawyer, H.W.R. Moore, also introduced some circumstantial evidence that bolstered the defence. A law clerk at the legislative buildings testified that on 25 April, Macdonald had requested an advance on his MLA's sessional allowance. When the clerk could not advance him the money, Macdonald then borrowed fifty dollars – the exact sum Gosden said he had been paid – on account at the Empress Hotel. He repaid the money when he paid his hotel bill. Macdonald claimed he needed the money to send the secretary of the Liberal party to Seattle to continue the plugging investigation, but the man had never shown up.[6]

On the face of it, Gosden had a strong defence. Four people had sworn under oath that Macdonald, contrary to his evidence, had been near the post office on 25 April around nine o'clock. One witness had sworn that Macdonald had met Gosden, and several witnesses provided uncontested proof that Gosden had been broke the day he left for Victoria and was flush upon his return, while others testified that Macdonald had borrowed fifty dollars the day he allegedly met Gosden. All Macdonald could offer in his defence was his testimony and that of his wife.

But class and status mattered in BC as much then as they do now, and some witnesses were more equal than others. Furthermore, the highly charged political atmosphere tainted the proceedings. The politics of the case were obvious to all, and the issue of Gosden's own political alle-

FLP candidate, Samuel Guthrie, a miner who had been imprisoned during the 1912–14 coal mine strike on Vancouver Island.

Hawthornthwaite then retired from active politics and turned again to deal-making, this time in northern BC mining properties. He died in Victoria, BC, in 1926.

giance was an important one. Clearly, his testimony before the plugging commission aided the Conservatives, and as a witness for the commission he had been paid five dollars a day.

Most of Gosden's witnesses had ties to the Conservative party, and the jury wanted to know whether Gosden was being supported and aided by the Tories. A juror asked him who had paid his bail after his arrest on the perjury charge. Gosden answered that he didn't know. Did he have any political bias? the juror pressed. "No," came the answer, "I am an absolute free lance."

When asked who was paying his lawyer and providing for his subsistence, his attorney replied that he was acting without fees. No doubt his generosity was due to his desire to hurt the Liberals, for Moore was a staunch Tory. At the same time, Moore told the court, "the subsistence of Mr. Gosden is being provided for by friends among the Socialist party." This seems likely despite Gosden's attack on Parker Williams, for socialist and trade unionist John Sidaway observed years later that, "while Gosden's actions were morally wrong, there was considerable sympathy and excuse for his part, being a victim of capitalist cruelty at its worst."[7]

For his part, Moore argued that Gosden had been a tool of both political parties, first used and deserted by the Liberals to commit election fraud and elect Macdonald, then used by the Tories to blacken the Liberals. The attorney-general's office put its resources and those of the BC Provincial Police to work finding and transporting Gosden's witnesses to the trials. While this was necessary if Gosden were to receive a fair trial, undoubtedly the chance to tarnish the Liberals gave the authorities especial zeal.[8]

The prosecuting attorney argued that Gosden was simply out to get Macdonald, to engineer a "frame-up," either for the money or as part of a Conservative plot, or both. His only tactic, in the face of the witnesses who directly contradicted Macdonald and his wife, was to attack Gosden's character and that of his witnesses to convince jurors they could not be trusted under oath. During the cross-examination of Gosden, the prosecutor brought up his labour activities, his arrests in San Diego and Prince Rupert, and his speeches during the Vancouver Island coal strike. He accused Gosden of threatening to poison the premier in his famous coffee speech, but Gosden denied this, stating that his speech had not advocated poisoning but had only indicated that such an action was possible.

Nonetheless, the speech was used against him by the prosecutor. Gosden's character was the real issue on trial, and the prosecutor worked hard to turn the jury against him and his most important witness, Fraser. "I do not quarrel with my learned friend Mr. Moore," he intoned, "…when he says that the evidence of a poor man is as likely to be truthful as that of any other man. But when you get a poor man of the type and character of Gosden, when you get a poor man of the type and character of Fraser – you can only judge a man by his associates and Fraser associates with Gosden – then that kind of evidence is evidence I do quarrel with and it is not evidence that can be believed."

John Oliver was called back to the witness stand to refute Fraser's testimony. The future premier gamely testified that he had conducted several experiments with the lighting near the post office where Gosden and Macdonald allegedly met, checking the shadows, the brightness, and the visibility at night. He concluded that the alcove behind the buttress, where Fraser claimed to have hidden, would have been lit well enough for Macdonald to have seen him. The jury was taken to visit the spot, but Oliver's experiments had a desperate, almost bathetic ring, and of course proved at best that Macdonald could have seen Fraser, not that Fraser wasn't there.[9]

The prosecutor then attacked Gosden's other witnesses, including his fellow boarders and Mrs. Cuthbertson, inviting the jury to "infer what you like as to the circumstances under which they live, whether it is a nice little select party or not." Gosden, the prosecutor continued, had admitted that "he would not stop at murder.…Can you wonder then that he would make up his mind to follow up some scheme of obtaining money…? Did you see his demeanor in the box, and the way he pounded it? Did you see his eyes blaze?" The best Gosden received was a backhanded compliment when the prosecutor was forced to "give him this credit, that he is one of the most skillful witnesses I ever saw. He was the greatest fencer in the witness box I have come in contact with."

His attack on Gosden reached a fever pitch when he recounted Gosden's political career. Playing on the jurors' prejudices, he asked them rhetorically, "Who is Gosden? Almost as soon as he lands in Canada he takes part in labor troubles that attracted notoriety at Glace Bay. He then gets to San Diego and is found in trouble and in jail for attempting free speech. You can infer what else you like as to his activities there. Men are not kept in jail for nine months in a civilized country unless they have done something wrong. You have a right to draw that inference." The prosecutor went on to remind the jurors of Gosden's time in jail in Prince Rupert, his actions during the Vancouver Island coal strike, and his coffee speech, "and then," he concluded, "he got into this," meaning the plugging scandal.

Finally he argued that Gosden, Portrey, and Fraser had already taken part in a similar blackmail scheme at Gordon Head while they were inspecting and repairing the well of a farmer named Fullerton. The prosecutor alleged that the men had seen Fullerton shoot a pheasant hen out of season and had extorted money from him to keep the crime a secret. He produced a receipt signed by Gosden and the others for a cheque that had been subsequently cancelled by the farmer. Each of the men denied the charge under oath and told the court that the cheque was for their work on the well. The prosecutor pointed out that the receipt was for "all claims against Fullerton, reasonable and unreasonable," and suggested the "unreasonable claim" was payment for their silence. Again, all the men denied the charge, and Fraser added that it was not surprising that what a working man thought was reasonable pay was not what an employer might think reasonable. In other words, this was a dispute over wages owing, not an attempt at blackmail. Oddly enough, even though Fullerton was in the courtroom, the prosecutor did not call him to the stand to clarify whether he had indeed been blackmailed by the men.[10]

The judge also participated in this attack on Gosden's politics and character. He played down the corroborative evidence of Gosden's witnesses and told the jurors that in assessing Gosden's testimony "it was fair that a man's character should be taken into consideration, and his peculiar conceptions of right and wrong, if he had any, had to be judged by present standards...if people followed along certain lines they could not quarrel when the country took them at their own valuation." In contrast, the judge told the jury, "Macdonald may be lying and trying to railroad this man to jail. But you have got to consider whether these people, Mr.

and Mrs. Macdonald, starting out in married life, both young, could spoil all their future by such an action."[11]

That, then, was the issue for the jury to decide – who was telling the truth? Should they side with the happy, respectable newlyweds or the revolutionary who scorned conventional politics and morality? Shaped that way, the result seemed preordained, and many people expected a quick verdict of guilty.

The jury retired to make its decision around seven o'clock on 7 June. By midnight, however, it still could not reach a verdict, and the jurors were kept overnight. When the jury came back on 8 June with no decision, it was declared a hung jury and dismissed. The vote was variously reported as 8 to 4 and 9 to 3 for conviction.

Gosden had won a victory, for he had not been found guilty of perjury, but his legal troubles were not over. The second perjury charge, regarding his testimony that Scott had accused another Liberal of the theft of party funds, was still outstanding, and the judge directed that there would be a new trial on the first charge in the fall. For the time, however, he was free.

His foes were not content to let justice take its course. There was, after

The Vancouver Labor Temple, 411 Dunsmuir Street, where Gosden addressed the open meeting. The VTLC later sold the Labor Temple to prevent it from being taken over by labour radicals. In the 1930s it was the provincial relief office; today it is a senior's centre.

all, an upcoming general election to be won. In a series of well-publicized speeches around the province, Harlan Brewster and M.A. Macdonald denounced Gosden as a perjurer and a criminal in an obvious attempt to clear Macdonald.

They underestimated the former Wobbly. On 11 September, two days before the provincial election, Robert Gosden struck back. At a public meeting at the Vancouver Labour Temple he attacked the Liberals, accusing them of plugging the by-election and of framing him. Spectators filled the hall, and many could not find seats. The crowd spilled into the aisles, onto window ledges, and jammed the entrance to strain to hear Gosden speak. Veteran Socialist Party member E.T. Kingsley chaired the meeting and kept order by pounding the table with a massive walking stick. At precisely eight o'clock, Kingsley called the meeting to order and turned the floor over to Gosden. He spoke for an hour and twenty minutes, and his revelations electrified the audience.

In a strong, steady voice that carried to all parts of the hall, Gosden laid bare the entire plugging scheme. Gesturing expansively, using his voice and talent for rhetoric effectively, Gosden soon had the crowd hanging on his every word. His supporters cheered and applauded throughout the performance. He confessed his own role freely and admitted that what he had done was "crooked work." It was "nothing to be proud of," he declared, but he needed to tell his "side of the story" in self-defence. Brewster and Macdonald were telling lies about him in order to prejudice prospective jurors for the upcoming perjury trial. Gosden insisted that he had taken the floor, not for political motives, but only to defend himself against their falsehoods and accusations. He was "one who has not a social standing in the accepted sense of the word," and arrayed against him was "a strong and powerful organization." His fight for justice was also a fight for the people of the province, for "whether I am guilty or not, if such a precedent as that can be carried out in this province, your liberty as citizens is in jeopardy the moment that precedent is established."

He told the audience how he had met with Scott, how the plan had been devised, and how they had implemented it. He filled in details that had not been brought out by the investigating commission, such as the "disinformation" campaign to have Brocky Robertson gin up legitimate voters. Anyone who was suspicious would investigate the crowd around Robertson and miss the real pluggers. Gosden's own work was much more extensive than he had told the commission. In addition to helping prepare the lists, he told the eager crowd, he himself had arranged to send people to Seattle, Tacoma, and Revelstoke to recruit pluggers. Through conversations and notes placed in freight cars, he said, it was made known to "men who were travelling, not those who travel on cushions," that "Vancouver was a place where a piece of change could be pocketed." Many of the men used simple disguises to change their appearance and vote repeatedly, some as many as ten times. The scheme started to unravel, he continued, when the Purity Squad became suspicious. Macdonald feared that the Squad was out to get Scott but would unwittingly implicate him. Gosden and others then compiled a special list of voters that contained legitimate names of real voters known to Gosden. This list was to be called the "not to be challenged" list, in the hope that it would in fact make investigators suspicious. If they did investigate that list, each of the voters could be produced. That would allay suspicion and divert attention from the fraudulent lists.

Of course the crucial question was, what was Macdonald's role in the plugging scheme? Gosden made it clear. "Macdonald," he said, "was the man through whose brains these ideas came...Scott referred to every new move, and had it sanctioned by Macdonald before he would move." Furthermore, once elected, Macdonald planned to use his MLA sessional allowance to build a more effective machine for the provincial election. Other candidates would be invited to contribute to a war chest, and the machine would be extended throughout the province. Gosden also explained why the Liberals fought amongst each other as the plugging scheme came to light. The Purity Squad candidates "were never taken into the plan as they had no money. They were to be ditched." Liberal hopeful John Wallace de Beque Farris "was going to be approached, and if he did not come through he was 'to get his.'"

Gosden soon had, according to the press, "the sympathies of the crowd." They laughed at his witticisms, applauded his arguments, and threatened the few hecklers into silence. When he was interrupted by a questioner from the floor in the middle of his speech, the crowd drowned out the question and urged Gosden to continue. He assured them the question "can not break the thread of my remarks, for this reason, that my liberty is at stake, and my liberty is my life against Macdonald's $50." The crowd cheered him wildly and shouted to have the questioner thrown out. Gosden calmed the crowd and continued.

He had one final thrill for them, one last secret to be revealed. Three days before his trial for perjury, he said, Harlan Brewster had approached him in the halls of the legislative building. There the leader of the opposition offered Gosden $1,000 to skip bail and flee the province. Angered by the offer, Gosden said he had told Brewster "to go – you know where," to the great amusement of the audience. He promised to swear an affidavit affirming the truth of his statements and dared the Liberals to take legal action against him, for "I am not running out of British Columbia, and I shall not run out of it. I have never run from anything."

The audience remained lively and peppered Gosden with more questions. How did he know of Macdonald's involvement in the plugging scandal? He knew of it from Scott's statements, he replied. Had anyone else heard Brewster make the offer of $1,000? That was not the sort of offer one made in front of witnesses, Gosden answered. What about his job as a janitor at the legislative buildings the year before? Wasn't that suspicious? Visibly moved, Gosden said he had taken the job because his "mother and father, both over 80 years of age, were threatened with the foreclosure of a mortgage and that they needed $100 to wipe that out...." He hounded Richard McBride and Thomas Taylor, minister of public works, for a job, he said, and secured six weeks' employment.

Not everyone was convinced by Gosden's moving tale of filial loyalty. One skeptic asked from the back of the hall if Gosden had bothered to send that money to his parents. "Shame!" and "Don't answer!" came the cries from the audience. Gosden waved the protests aside and replied that indeed his parents had received the money, as well as some of the money he had made from the plugging adventure.

Soon the meeting threatened to get out of hand. One man climbed the platform to speak but was shouted down by the crowd; when another questioner was hissed down, Kingsley finally declared the meeting over. A collection was taken, and about forty dollars was raised to cover expenses.[12]

The meeting was a personal triumph for Gosden. Whatever his guilt, whatever his role in the plugging scandal, he had vindicated himself in the eyes of his public and won its support. But the Liberals came to power, Macdonald was elected, and Gosden was about to be re-tried for perjury. His attorney applied to change the venue from Victoria to Kamloops, alleging that the earlier speeches of Brewster and Macdonald made it impossible for Gosden to secure a fair trial in the capital, "where political leanings run very strong." The judge refused the motion, however, and on 3 November 1916, Gosden was tried again for perjury.[13]

This trial was nearly identical to the first. Gosden stood by his original testimony, as did his witnesses, while a new prosecutor attacked Gosden's character. When the coffee speech was raised yet again, Gosden replied as he had before, adding that "tyrants should be handled in a tyrannical way, the same as they attempt to handle others…If the Kaiser had been dealt with that way," he elaborated, "thousands of men would have been saved from slaughter – slaughter caused by his insatiable thirst for power and desire for tyranny." This judge too made Gosden himself the issue. Gosden was, the judge commented, a "picturesque character," "a man of strong convictions and with lots of courage." While these could be the "attributes of an honest man," he warned the jury that they could also be "the attributes of a man who might set himself against organized society."

The defence did add one new piece of evidence: another witness who testified he had seen Macdonald leave the Empress Hotel on the night Macdonald swore he had stayed in with his wife. One defence witness, the legislative clerk who had been unable to advance Macdonald fifty dollars on 25 April, avoided his subpoena and left town for the duration of the trial. The judge admonished him in absentia and promised to bring the matter to the bar association, but it is not clear that the witness could have added much to the proceedings.[14]

After a week of evidence and testimony, the jury went off to render its verdict. After three and a quarter hours of sitting, it announced that it too was divided. The jury was declared hung, and the prosecution indicated that it would not pursue Gosden a third time. As the newspapers noted, the hung juries meant that there was no real answer to the question of the guilt of Macdonald and Gosden. One man had to be lying, but who? Whose corroborative witnesses were more likely to lie – Macdonald's wife or the several people, some with personal ties to Gosden, others with ties to the Conservative party, who testified that they had seen Macdonald that night? Why was the one man who could clear either man, John Scott, never called as a witness, even though he and Macdonald were in contact? Could the Tories have asked loyal members to deliberately commit perjury to discredit the Liberals? Was it probable that they had? If the juries could not decide, perhaps it remains impossible for us to decide as well.[15]

The issue heated up again in late December 1916 when Macdonald was made attorney-general. Until 1929, MLAs appointed to cabinet had to run in a by-election to have the voters confirm the appointment. The Purity Squad was out to get Macdonald, while his supporters insisted nothing wrong had been done. Again Gosden's name was vilified in the press as a perjurer, an outcast, and a criminal. One Macdonald supporter, the journalist J. Francis Bursill, also known as Felix Penne, inspired Gosden to counter-attack with a poem entitled "Gosden's Ode to Bursill," printed in the BC Federationist:

> Bursill, you've made an immoral name
> By defending politicians of "plugging" fame.
> You prescribe for me a hempen rope
> In reply I ask you be given soap.
> Soap with water, used with vim,
> Will kill the "vermin" you specialize in.
> Razor and scissors, well applied
> Destroy "noxious weeds" in which they hide.
> Mr. Bursill
> otherwise Felix Penne
> You're at your filthy game again.
> Dirty you are, dirty you'll be
> Until bathing is made compulsory.[16]

If each man had suffered as a result of the plugging scandal, the consequences were very different for the two men. Macdonald was re-elected and confirmed in his cabinet post. In Gosden's case, the damage to his reputation nagged at him, and he could not let the matter die down.

He wrote to the federal minister of justice, hoping the minister could offer him help or advice. He outlined the plugging investigation and the subsequent perjury trials, concentrating on incidents that he believed had been distorted during the trial. His witnesses had all been forced to testify during the plugging investigation – that is, before the perjury trials – which gave Macdonald ample opportunity to create an alibi. During the second trial, he maintained, Mrs. Macdonald had been "helped by signs from Macdonald" and John Oliver. Only when she had concluded her testimony did the judge recall that witnesses should have been kept out of the courtroom until they had testified. Crucial errors of timing had been made in the transcripts, he said, errors that hurt his case. For example, the prosecution claimed that Fraser and Gosden had had opportunity to cook up their story, when in fact Fraser gave his testimony before they could have spoken. If the events were "transcribed correctly," he insisted with heavy underscoring, they would prove how futile it was to expect "a fair deal for my witnesses or myself." Nor was he allowed to seek redress from the courts for the insults he had endured from Macdonald, Brewster, and the press. The hung juries had left open the question of his innocence; his reputation, and that of his friends, had been damaged. More than his reputation was at risk. Twice, he claimed, he had been physically attacked and had required medical attention for forty-eight hours in one case. He had been blacklisted and as a result, "it is impossible for me to go to work anywhere." Even Mrs. Cuthbertson had suffered; she had been "subjected to the vilest of tricks," and someone had thrown rocks through her glass door at 2:30 in the morning, narrowly missing her daughter. Threatening notes, "containing vile and scurvilous [sic] matter," were thrown over her fence and caused her to have "a serious nervous breakdown which may cost her life." The letter concluded in a way now typical of Gosden. "Sir, I have tried to put my case before your notice," he wrote. "It is my duty as a citizen to do so, as a last forlorn hope of legal redress. If this fails, then my duty to myself as a man is plain, and I shall follow it let it lead where it may."[17]

The letter was not Gosden at his finest, and it is not surprising that it appears to have gone unanswered. Four typed, single-spaced pages long, it alternately rambled and ranted. The writing was loose and the thread of his argument was lost, barely regained, then lost again as he seemed unable to distinguish insignificant facts from more important ones. It is not clear why he thought a federal minister would be willing or able to help him, and he did not present the minister with a clear description of events or ask him for specific help. The overall impression is of a man too angry and desperate to be rational, and this may well describe his state of mind after the months of legal harassment, threats to his liberty, and, if he is to be believed, threats to his life.

Compared to his earlier letters to the Industrial Worker, this letter shows a very different Robert Gosden. There is no hint of the confidence, the cockiness, of his letters from Prince Rupert, his letter on sabotage, and his letters from the San Diego jail. There is none of the humour and feistiness Gosden displayed in his earlier writings and on the political platforms where he spoke; even his testimony on the witness stand showed a strength of personality and a charm that are utterly lacking in the letter to the minister. Undoubtedly the legal proceedings wore him down and left him with few resources. Perhaps more important, he was now isolated from the vibrant political culture that helped sustain him earlier. Even in prison, perhaps especially in prison, Gosden was with men who held similar ideas and shared similar experiences. They had worked hard to keep their spirits up by singing, writing to inform the world of their struggle, and debating politics. They could also take some pride that they were a militant minority, a brave band persecuted by government and capital. Remaining true to their beliefs and facing their persecutors with resolve and defiance allowed them to claw out small but important victories every day. In a word, solidarity gave them support and strength.

By 1916, however, the left in BC had declined and Gosden had isolated himself from the movement that remained. If the venerable socialist Parker Williams had gone over to the Liberals, what place was there for a revolutionary who called for direct action, sabotage, and violence? Gosden was now thirty-six years old. His life had been a hard one. He had travelled across North America several times, riding the rods, with hard labour his only employment along the way. He had shared platforms with politicians and jail cells with criminals. He had been in physical and political battles, fought for his liberty in court and won a Pyrrhic victory, and was used by political parties. His private life had been exposed to the harsh light of publicity, and his name was practically a synonym for corrupt politics and violence. From the zenith of his work with the Miners' Liberation League, Gosden had now become something of a political pariah. Conservatives, Liberals, Socialists, all had attacked him during the plugging scandal. His calls for direct action had made him popular with some workers but had also led the more "respectable" among the left to distance themselves from him. There were those rumours that he had worked for the Conservatives. Worse, he was now portrayed as an opportunist who loved grandstanding and would do anything for money. Though he had often given as good as he got, his counter-attacks undoubtedly isolated him further and made it more difficult for him to find a suitable place to use his considerable gifts of rhetoric and courage.

It is of course impossible to glean the psychology of a man from a few letters and notes. We do know, however, that for whatever reason, Robert Gosden was about to begin the strangest chapter of his life.

Ginger Goodwin

CHAPTER 4

"The Unseen Hand Would Intimidate the Weaker"

Robert Gosden disappears from the public record for a time at the end of 1916. The political turmoil of 1917 to 1920, however, would soon bring him back into view.

While nationalist historians claim Canada was forged as a nation during the First World War, that conflict led to tensions that divided the country as it never had been before. The war had first been greeted with some enthusiasm in English Canada. Many Canadians, especially those of British ancestry and those affected by the pre-war economic slump, volunteered to fight, believing it would be over quickly. But the battle on the western front soon became a static contest of trenches and futile, bloody charges against barbed wire and machine guns. The terrible slaughter convinced many that military service was little more than a death warrant, and the rate of volunteering dropped quickly. In Quebec, many French-Canadians had opposed the country's entry into the war from the beginning, believing that an independent Canada had no obligation to save British imperialism. The war was also strongly opposed by many in the labour movement and on the left, including future Co-operative Commonwealth Federation (CCF) leader J.S. Woodsworth. While the war sacrificed working people on the altar of patriotism, capital remained untouched. Indeed, some companies stood to make huge profits from supplying the government with materials and goods for the war effort.

GINGER GOODWIN

The most famous of the men who objected to the war was Albert "Ginger" Goodwin. His story is well known. Goodwin was born in Yorkshire, England, on 10 May 1887. The son of a coal miner, Goodwin started in the pits in 1902. Four years later he emigrated to Glace Bay, Nova Scotia, where he worked as a miner for the Dominion Coal Company. He took part in the United Mineworkers of America (UMWA) coal strike of 1909–10 and moved to Cumberland on Vancouver Island in BC by early 1911. There he went to work for Canadian Collieries, the company that had bought out Dunsmuir's company in 1910. Goodwin was active in the UMWA and the 1912–14 strike against Canadian Collieries, served as delegate to the BC Federation of Labour, and was an organizer for the Socialist Party of Canada (SPC). Blacklisted after the strike, he went to Trail, BC, and worked in the Consolidated Mining and Smelting Company (Cominco) smelter there. He organized for the International Union of Mine, Mill, and Smelter Workers (Mine-Mill) and was elected secretary of the local as well as regional vice-president of the BC Federation of Labour. A provincial candidate for the SPC in 1916, Goodwin was an outspoken opponent of Canada's involvement in the First World War. Initially

Read one way, that meant that war – the organized murder of millions – was good for business. Not surprisingly, many rebelled against such a system. Some wondered what it meant to fight a war for democracy when they suffered daily tyranny on the shop floor.

With the war becoming more unpopular, the Conservative Prime Minister Robert Borden found it difficult to maintain the troop levels he had promised to supply for Britain. To keep his pledge to the empire, he brought in conscription – the enforced enlistment of men into the military. Many Canadians believed conscription to be morally wrong. The labour movement bitterly pointed out that while working men would now be forced to fight and die, none of the war profiteers risked even their money. Furthermore, conscription meant that workers who fought for better conditions could be punished by being drafted and sent overseas. This was especially likely as businessmen were often appointed to the conscription boards. Instead of signing up, many Canadians took to the bush rather than fight in an unjust and imperialist war.

Robert Gosden appears to have taken part in the anti-conscription movement and to have helped resisters in their camps in Alberta, perhaps by bringing them food and supplies. For a time Gosden, his friend Owen H. Paulson, Ethel Cuthbertson, and her daughter lived in Pincher Creek, Alberta, where they may have aided draft resisters. According to a letter to the BC Provincial Police from the RCMP, 36-year-old Gosden was arrested for evading the draft.[1]

By April 1918 he was in Calgary. There he and Owen Paulson organized labourers into the Federated Workers' Union, a quasi-industrial union chartered directly by the Trades and Labour Congress. Both he and Paulson, however, were ordered out of town by the police, for "their presence was not exactly desirable here."[2]

The police were increasingly alarmed by attempts to organize unions in this period, part of a growth of unionization and radicalism that had begun well before the war. This trend was brought to a halt with the depression of 1912–15, but now World War One presented workers with new challenges and opportunities. The economy boomed to meet the needs of the war for material and goods; the siphoning of men into the armed forces helped create a labour shortage; women entered the work force in increasing numbers. One consequence of the expanding economy was inflation. As the cost of living rose, workers pressed for higher wages. Because employers did not have a surplus work force to draw from, and because government wanted production to continue without strikes or lockouts, it was easier for workers to win their demands. As a result, wages rose, though usually more slowly than the cost of living. The number of people in unions rose to levels that would not be seen again until the 1940s, and workers experimented with different tactics, such as industrial unions, joint bargaining committees, and general and sympathy strikes. And of course, in 1917, the success of the Russian Revolution inspired workers around the world to believe they had a world to gain.

exempt from conscription because of ill health, he was later reclassified as fit for service and ordered to report for duty. Like many others, he refused to fight in a war he believed was unjust and took to the bush around Cumberland to avoid the draft and arrest.

The federal government sent police after Goodwin and other resisters. On 27 July 1918, Dominion Police Special Constable Dan Campbell encountered Goodwin near Cumberland. According to Campbell's testimony, he and Goodwin surprised each other in the bush. Both were carrying rifles. Campbell ordered Goodwin to surrender. Goodwin raised his rifle and Campbell shot him in self-defence. The coroner's inquest ruled Goodwin's death accidental, and the grand jury at Campbell's later trial for manslaughter held there was no evidence to proceed with the charge. Subsequently the case against Campbell was dropped.

Goodwin's death enraged the province's labour movement. In Vancouver, a one-day general strike was held on 2 August 1918 and thousands attended his funeral in Cumberland. Controversy immediately surrounded Campbell's version of the shooting and continues to this day. It is often suggested that Campbell was under special military orders to kill Goodwin, and that such orders came from the federal government at the instigation of Cominco, whose workers Goodwin had tried to organize at its Trail smelter in 1917–18.

While some claim the mishandling of evidence, conflicting testimony, and unasked questions at the inquest and manslaughter trial indicate a possible conspiracy, none of these proves anything save perhaps incompetence and confusion. The conspiracy argument stands or falls on the forensic evidence, hinging on three claims that dispute the official verdict of self-defence and justifiable homicide.

The first claim is that Goodwin was shot in the back. This would strongly suggest that Campbell had ambushed him and had not shot him in self-defence. The second is that Goodwin was shot with a soft-nosed, or dumdum, bullet rather than a steel-jacketed military bullet. The contention is that this type of bullet is more deadly than the military bullet and was selected by Campbell to ensure his victim would be killed. The third claim is that Goodwin was not shot from a distance of four or five yards, as Campbell maintained, but from a distance of a few feet. If true, this would again suggest that Campbell had waited in ambush, got the drop on Goodwin, and killed him from this vantage point. Each of

The most significant of the workers' tactics was undoubtedly the One Big Union. A number of unionists and socialists believed that it was necessary to organize workers in industries such as logging, mining, and the metal trades, and to organize them in industrial, not craft, unions. Many also believed that the craft unions and the TLC were too conservative. At the TLC convention of 1918 in Quebec City, for example, radicals were angry that motions calling for opposition to conscription were defeated and that the official TLC response was one of inaction and compromise with the government and employers. Many started to suggest that a new labour organization was needed.

In 1919 that organization was created when the One Big Union was launched. The core of the union was the miners and loggers of western Canada, who together made up the bulk of the membership. Many other unions, locals, and even labour councils such as the Vancouver Trades and Labour Council (VTLC), voted to join the OBU. It soon had nearly 50,000 members, of whom about 30,000 were in BC. It also organized workers in the US.

Radicalism was not restricted to the OBU. Across Canada, workers were mobilizing, sometimes for traditional ends such as wages and conditions of work, but often in support of each other and for more radical ends. A wave of strikes, starting in 1916 and lasting until 1920, swept the country. The most famous of these was the Winnipeg General Strike, in which 30,000 workers in virtually every industry – many of them not even in unions – left their jobs in support of construction and metal trades workers. The strike, which lasted from 15 May to 25 June 1919, was finally broken when leaders were arrested and police and military attacked demonstrators and seized the streets.[3]

Gosden's radical and labour credentials were well-established by 1918. He appears, together with his friend Paulson and "Mrs. Cuthbutson," in the RCMP Personal Files Register for 1919–29, and clearly the two men were regarded by Calgary police as labour organizers to be watched.[4]

By early 1919, Gosden was in Hillcrest, Alberta, working with the miners there. In March he attended the Western Labor Conference in Calgary, the conference that would launch the One Big Union. The conference, however, would prove his undoing.

Originally called as a strategy session for western unions to prepare for the upcoming Trades and Labour Congress convention, the Western Labour Conference quickly went far beyond the initial intent of its planners. Over 230 delegates attended the conference, their politics ranging from the syndicalism of the Wobblies to the socialism of the SPC to the labourism of AFL officials. If their politics differed, most were keenly aware that labour was about to make a resurgence, and they were determined to shape the new movement. Regardless of their politics, they wanted action, not talk. This was made clear when the Resolution Committee, chaired by BC radical Jack Kavanagh, reported in the afternoon session of the first day. The first resolution said:

these claims strongly indicates premeditated murder rather than self-defence. If Campbell did set out to murder Goodwin, presumably he did so under orders and not on his own initiative, and these orders from higher-up would constitute conspiracy.

How well do these three forensic claims stand up to investigation? The first, and most easily dismissed, is the suspicion that Goodwin was shot in the back. The autopsy records are imprecise in the description of the entry wound; it was either in the side of the neck or more forward, in the side of the throat. In either case, the location of the wound does not suggest Goodwin was shot from behind.

The second charge is that Goodwin was shot with a dumdum bullet, that is, a soft-nosed bullet designed to expand or mushroom on impact and create wounds more deadly than those of a military bullet. According to the theory, use of this type of bullet indicates Campbell's murderous intent. But Campbell was a special constable of the Dominion police. That means he was sworn in for a short period of time, probably for a single specific task (to pick up draft resisters). He would have used his own rifle, which was a hunting rifle designed to fire soft-nosed hunting ammunition. This was not a dumdum bullet specially issued by the police, but simply the type of bullet Campbell would have had on hand. Furthermore, the bullet hit something, probably Goodwin's arm, before entering his body; that would cause the bullet to tumble and create a much larger entry wound.

The final allegation made by conspiracy theorists is that Campbell shot Goodwin at virtually point-blank range. It is not clear how this implicates Campbell, for the two men could have stumbled across each other at any distance. The doctor who performed the autopsy suggested that the two were at least two feet apart and no more than ten feet apart; Campbell estimated the distance at no more than fifteen feet.

The issue of the distance at which Goodwin was shot depends on the interpretation

Realizing that the aims and objects of the labor movement should be the improving of the social and economic condition of society in general, and the working class in particular;

And whereas the present system of production of profit and the institutions resulting therefrom, prevent this being achieved,

Be it resolved that the aims of labor as represented by this convention are the abolition of the present system of production for profit, and the substituting therefore, production for use, and that a system of propaganda to this end be carried on.

The resolution was unanimously passed by the delegates. So too was the second resolution, which read:

Whereas great and far-reaching changes have taken place during the last year in the realms of industry;

Strikers in Winnipeg (1919) topple a streetcar sent into the crowd by the Citizen's Committee of 1000.

And whereas we have discovered through painful experiences the utter futility of separate action on the part of the workers, organized merely along craft lines, such action tending to strengthen the relative position of the master class;

Therefore be it resolved that this Western Labor Conference place itself on record as favoring the immediate reorganization of the workers along industrial lines, so that by virtue of their industrial strength, the workers may be better prepared to enforce any demand they consider essential to their maintenance and wellbeing;

And be it further resolved that in view of the foregoing, we place ourselves also on record as being opposed to the innocuity of labor leaders lobbying for palliatives which do not palliate.[5]

Despite the stuffy language of the formal resolutions, the implications were obvious. The delegates realized that if workers were to have real improvements in their lives, they had to replace capitalism with something else. They also realized that the old-style craft unions with their conservative leaders could not deliver. The resolutions were firm: industrial unionism, radical politics, and an end to business unionism.

Could they work for these ends within the traditional labour movement? Many thought it was impossible, that the international craft unions were unable and unwilling to take the necessary action. The BC Federation of Labour

of powder marks. However, powder marks are not a reliable indicator of distance. One author has claimed that it is impossible to calculate from the wound or powder marks whether a shot was fired from six feet or sixty feet. Each weapon, barrel length, type of ammunition, and type of powder, and the condition of each of these, gives different results. Only repeated firings with identical bullets at known distances can allow investigators to give accurate estimates of distance from the gun barrel to the victim. That is to say, no examination of the wound itself can reveal the distance of a gun from the victim.

Furthermore, it is very difficult even for modern forensic experts to identify powder burns or marks. Lead particles, soot, dirt, and lubricant from the bullet may resemble powder marks. The edges of the dried wound itself may have a powder-like appearance, and insect bites obtained after death may, to the untrained examiner, look like powder marks. Only microscopic and other analysis can determine whether these different marks are caused by powder from the weapon. Thus it is highly likely that the doctor and other witnesses were mistaken to insist that powder burns were found on Goodwin's body.

Taken together, all of these qualifications and reservations make it impossible to know whether Goodwin was shot from a distance of six inches or sixty feet. For this reason, it impossible to base a conspiracy theory on the powder marks.

At the end of this analysis, we are left not with certainties but with unknowns. What was the position of the two men when the shot was fired? It is impossible to know. Was Goodwin shot with a soft-nosed bullet? Yes, but that is irrelevant. Was he shot at a closer range than Campbell asserted? Maybe, maybe not. It should be clear that there is no forensic evidence that disproves Campbell's story or that makes a conspiracy theory more plausible.

Of course, in showing the evidence for a conspiracy to be non-existent, we have not proved there was no conspiracy. But since there is no documentary evidence, testimony, or forensic evidence proving conspiracy, we are not justified in believing that Goodwin was the victim of a conspiracy.

Does it matter? Ginger Goodwin is, after all, just as dead as if there were an international web of intrigue.

It *does* matter, for events such as these inform our world-view and we may draw powerful lessons from them. Assume for a moment that all the forensic evidence is exactly as conspiracy theorists have claimed. Assume the existence of powder marks, of a shot that entered the back at

put forward a third resolution that made the direction of the conference plain:

Resolved that this convention recommend to its affiliated membership the severance of their affiliation with their international organizations, and that steps be taken to form an industrial organization of all workers.

The conference was voting on nothing less than the creation of a new union, modelled after the IWW dream of one big union of all the workers, a new union that would give voice to the aspirations of workers tired of war and angry with capitalism. It would be the most momentous decision ever taken by Canadian unionists.

Just as the vote was to take place, David Rees, a United Mine Workers of America (UMWA) official from Vancouver Island, demanded the floor on a question of privilege. His voice rising to carry to the corners of the hall, Rees warned the delegates "that there might be spies present." He pointed dramatically to Robert Gosden, who was sitting in the visitor's area. "There he is in the gallery," Rees roared. "He has grown a moustache lately, but it would be well for the delegates to know him." He outlined Gosden's past quickly, and once again the old stories of advocating violence and the poisoning of McBride's coffee were aired. More recently, Rees continued, Gosden "had masqueraded in Fernie lately under the name of Smith, and also at Hillcrest as Brown. In both places he had proven himself a troublemaker."

Elected as a delegate to the Western Labour Conference by the miners at Hillcrest while posing as Bob Brown, Gosden knew he could not submit his credentials under the assumed name for fear someone would recognize the fraud. Instead he slipped into the conference as an observer, but now he was exposed. In Rees's opinion he was "a police spy and a stool pigeon, even an agent provocateur." The delegates, he concluded, should "be guarded as to their statements."

Delegates got to their feet and craned their necks to look at Gosden as the meeting broke out into a frenzy of charges and counter-charges. Another delegate, Walter Head, formerly a miner at South Wellington on Vancouver Island, jumped up to denounce Gosden. During the big miners' strike, he said, "Gosden had tried to stir up trouble and had given certain persons the formula of a composition designed to be spread on the floor of buildings with the result that they would take fire." A delegate from Hillcrest rose to add to the clamour. He backed up some of Rees's accusations, insisting that Gosden had somehow "wormed" his way into the local.

If they thought he would panic or bolt, they misjudged the man who had faced police, politicians, and bullies most of his life. Instead, he stood up in full view of everyone. To Rees's identifying him as Brown, a.k.a. Smith, a.k.a. Gosden, he replied, "Yes, I am here!" and asked for the floor so he could answer the charges made against him. But the hall was in chaos and his request was denied.

Angered at the presence of an alleged spy in their midst, delegates shouted to have Gosden forcibly ejected from the conference. Others

close range, of dumdum bullets. At best this brands Campbell a conscious, cold-blooded murderer; it still does not link him to a high-level intrigue involving Cominco or the Borden government.

Yet the government and business are, in my view, as culpable as if they had pulled the trigger. The government took the country into a war fought to defend imperial privilege. It created the "crime" of pacifism and the category of draft dodger. It sent armed men in pursuit of these "criminals" and used armed force to protect capitalist interests. This is not a conspiracy. It is the way the system is supposed to work. If the word "conspiracy" is to mean anything other than a plan by a group of people pursuing their self-interest – a definition so broad as to be meaningless – it must refer to groups working illegally, outside the usual exercise of power and authority. In sending police after Goodwin, politicians were operating normally. Immorally, of course, but legally, following their usual rules and orders. The real criminality is that they were simply doing their day-to-day regular jobs, maintaining a capitalist order and ensuring the smooth operation of an exploitative system.

The conspiracy theory takes a short-cut through this analysis and blames not the system, but a few villains. At worst, proof of a government conspiracy to murder Goodwin would indicate that, say, the prime minister acted improperly. The solution to that would be to imprison him. But the real problem is much deeper, much more evil, and much more difficult to eradicate.

We do not need a conspiracy to explain Goodwin's death. What we need is to understand that the government and business rarely need to operate in the shadows or illegally to suppress workers' resistance to capital. They can do so openly, because they have, quite legally and openly, already made the rules. Conspiracy theory obscures this understanding and deflects our attention from the real issues. Ultimately, conspiracy theory, for all its intrigue and darkness, provides an oversimplified analysis of society and of the workings of capital and of the state. That is why it is important to correct the misconception that Ginger Goodwin was the victim of a conspiracy. As a simple conspiracy of a few men, his death has no meaning. Such an explanation leads only to the kind of mystification and liberal idealism Goodwin lived – and died – to refute. He was the victim of a particular set of social relations and the institutions created to protect them, and his death is a lesson we cannot afford to have obscured by notions of conspiracy.

pleaded for calm, suggesting he simply be asked to leave. A motion to eject him was made but was voted down; most of the delegates believed that they had nothing to fear from police spies, for their business was legal and public. In the midst of the uproar, Gosden "remained decidedly one of the coolest and least disturbed of those present."[6]

He had heard all the charges before, and again he fought back. In a letter to the *District Ledger*, a Fernie, BC, labour paper favourable to the One Big Union, he denounced the men who attacked him. He was no longer the querulous supplicant asking the minister of justice for help; much of the old fire had returned. "In the interests of unionism and fairplay," he began, "I ask the liberty of a free press and free speech which was denied me at the Western Conference...Perhaps my side of the story may also be interesting to those union men who are in favor of greater solidarity of labour along the lines of industrial unionism."

He then posed a series of rhetorical questions in which he laid out his own history as a radical and unionist. "Who organized the Miners' Liberation League?" he thundered. "Who showed up the rottenness of the UMW of A officials at that time, also renegade Parker Williams?...Who was it that formed the first Industrial association embracing all trades in Prince Rupert? Who was it formed the first Industrial association in Calgary?...Who was it in Hillcrest Local who always advocated more industrial solidarity and who offered his wages to help defray the expenses of the delegates?... At whose house did the wife and children of a boycotted miner find food and shelter when he was blacklisted from Vancouver Island due to his being one of the principal men over whom the strike was called?"

Having established his own credentials, Gosden then went after David Rees and other union officials. Referring to the Vancouver Island strike and the failure to declare a general strike to support it, he asked:

> Who were the leading labor men of the coast who prevented that sol-idarity of labor?... Why did the [Vancouver Trades and Labour] council refuse to protest? Who were that council?... Who are the men today most loud in shouting Industrial Unionism who have blocked every form of labor organization until this last few months? Who were the men most active as UMW of A officials who opposed the Federal Workers Union and helped the authorities?... Who gave the scabs and strikebreakers union cards and allowed their loyal men to wander under false names all over the country?... Who was the official in Hill-crest Local who said, "Brown, if you want a job digging, you have got to quit talking industrial unionism?" Who were the officials who helped the authorities hound Bob Brown out of that camp? Mr. Editor, these are a few of the questions relating to the Western Labor move-ment of the last few years...anytime I am granted a fair hearing, I will give a little of the labor history which will be interesting to those union men who are in favor of Industrial Solidarity and my answers will be capable of verification.

He closed with his characteristic bravado: "He only fears the truth whom the truth will hurt."[7]

But this time Robert Gosden had reason to fear the truth. For the truth was that he was now a spy for the Royal Canadian Mounted Police.[8] He had been on the police payroll since January 1919 and had travelled throughout the mining camps of eastern BC and western Alberta, report-ing from Fernie in early February and from Macleod, Alberta, at the end of February. Later he was sent to Hillcrest, and from there to the Western Labour Conference in Calgary, reporting on labour conditions and union activity in each town under the code name of Agent 10.[9]

THE ONE BIG UNION

In the years immediately after World War One, capital and government were determined to roll back the gains workers had made and to crush the threat to the system. A "red scare" was created in Canada and the US, and militants and radicals were arrested, jailed, and deported in large numbers. The labour movement was attacked in the press, the workplace, and the streets as capital and government prepared to usher in a decade of labour-bashing and harassment.

One of labour's responses to this was the formation of the One Big Union (OBU). While it shared with the IWW the idea of organizing by industry, in other respects the politics of the OBU were a mish-mash of socialism, reformism, and syndicalism, with the syndicalists soon weeded out. Like the IWW before it, the OBU had to fight employers, government, and conservative trade unionists. It was also split by factions; some members wanted the OBU to be more like the IWW, while others wanted it to be an industrial union without a revolutionary vision.

If employers disliked unions, they disliked the OBU more, and they often signed contracts with other unions simply to keep the OBU out. The government infiltrated the union, and craft unions

He was not an undercover police officer, that is, a regular member of the RCMP, trained in Regina and then sent out to work undercover. He was an informer, hired as a casual employee, much as he had been when he was a labourer. These informers were paid according to the amount and quality of their information. The maximum rate of pay was five dollars per day, an excellent wage for someone such as Gosden, perhaps double what he might receive for manual labour. Few records or files were kept on them, and often their identities were known only to the local officers who were their "handlers." In this case, Gosden appears to have reported directly to Inspector J.W. Spalding, commander of the Calgary Sub-District of Division "K," headquartered in Lethbridge. District commanders were not always aware of the identities of secret agents, and municipal and provincial police forces were intentionally denied the information by the RCMP. Indeed, on at least one occasion a secret agent, possibly Gosden himself, was arrested by the Alberta provincial police, who were unaware that he was working for the RCMP. A secret agent was instructed not to reveal his identity if arrested, for as the head of the RCMP, Commissioner A.B. Perry, put it, "an arrest and punishment may often strengthen his position and secure the confidence of the element he is investigating." Likely this accounts for the fact that Gosden appears in the RCMP records as both a secret agent and a radical.[10]

We do not know how Gosden signed up for his loathsome duties. He may have been approached by a member of the RCMP. Certainly he was bold enough and opportunistic enough to simply walk into an RCMP detachment, bluff his way into the office of the ranking officer, and offer his services.

However he made his pitch, his timing was perfect. In December 1918 the federal police forces had been reorganized, with the role of the RCMP expanded considerably to include secret service activities for western Canada. By January 1919 the force had targeted labour and radical groups and begun recruiting informants; six months later, thirty detectives and thirty-five secret agents were employed in western Canada.[11]

There was little to distinguish Gosden from other informants until the Western Labor Conference. He is usually mentioned casually in police reports that only note briefly that "Secret Agent Gosden" was dispatched to one town or another. That all changed in Calgary.

The RCMP was keen to have reports on the Western Labor Conference. At least two agents were there, Gosden and Frank Zaneth, an undercover RCMP officer sent to infiltrate the labour movement.[12] Gosden, however, was believed to have a unique insight into radical politics. Commissioner Perry noted that Gosden "has for many years taken an active part in the Industrial Workers of the World and kindred associations, and is therefore peculiarly competent to discuss the leaders in such movements and their aims and objects." Inspector Spalding added that Gosden had a "most intimate acquaintance with the psychology of the men to whom he refers."[13]

Their assessment was correct. Gosden's lengthy report — five typed, single-spaced, legal-sized

purged OBU members and locals. In Vancouver, moderate unionists such as Percy Bengough and Helena Gutteridge attacked the OBU and helped drive it from the Vancouver Trades and Labour Council. The OBU dwindled to 5,000 members by 1923 and formally folded into the Canadian Labour Congress in 1956. It represented a Canadian approach to radical labour politics and industrial unionism, and provided a forum and training ground for organizers such as Jack Kavanagh, Helen Armstrong, and Ernie Winch, head of the Lumber Workers Industrial Union and later a CCF MLA.

WHEN DID GOSDEN
BECOME A SPY?

Was Gosden a spy for the
Conservatives during the
Vancouver Island coal strike?
The speculation is an interesting exercise in historical
reasoning and inference. We
know that McBride's government did use the provincial
police and private detectives
to infiltrate and report on the
labour movement during the
coal strike, so it is certainly
possible that Gosden worked
for the Tories. Was the man
himself capable of such trea-
sonous work? Given his love
of intrigue and his subsequent
career, undoubtedly.

But how strong is the evidence? The first time the
charge was made publicly was
at the UMWA Convention of
1915. Robert Foster, president
of District 18, spoke on the
history of the big strike. He
attacked the IWW for advocating violence and made reference to an unnamed agitator,
"supposedly working on our
side...but now working as a
janitor for the Government."
Foster said that he had
accused him earlier of being a
spy, but the charge had been
denied. In 1916 at the plugging
commission hearings, Parker
Williams also accused Gosden
of acting as a spy or agent for
the Tories during the Vancouver Island strike of 1912–14,
but neither man offered any
proof. Instead they made an
inference, based on three
premises. Their argument

pages – drew upon his experience with the labour
movement and his knowledge of the OBU
founders, some of whom, such as Jack Kavanagh,
he had worked with some years before. His report
demonstrated many familiar aspects of Gosden's
character. It was perceptive, ranging from an
overview of the labour movement to nuanced
assessments of individuals. It was a blend of fact,
impression, and fantasy, showing traces of bril-
liance and paranoia, keen observation and opportunism. And at the end, it was utterly ruthless.[14]

The report was divided into five sections. The
first described the aims and motives that led to
the Western Labor Conference, as interpreted by
Gosden. It had been called, he maintained, by the
socialists in western Canada, led by those in the
BC Federation of Labour. Its aim was "to try, if
possible, to seize the present chaotic condition
resulting from the war to weld together the different bodies of labor in a common effort to overthrow the present social order and install a Bol-
sheviki regime." He noted that the "Reds" had
been successful in having a large number of
socialists sent to the conference as delegates, and
the executive of the committee formed to organize the OBU were all members of the Socialist
Party of Canada.

The second short section outlined the conference resolution to send organizers across the four
western provinces to convince unionists to leave
the international unions and join the OBU. It was
crucial that workers in what OBU organizers
called the "basic industries," that is, mining, the
metal trades, and transportation, supported the

new union, because these industries represented key sectors of the economy and could shut down the entire country if they went on strike.

The third section of his report purported to give details of secret plans of organization. Again Gosden asserted that the SPC wanted to "stampede organized labor in the direction of mass action, with the idea that it shall finally terminate in social revolution of the Bolshevik type." This would be accomplished by the SPC taking over "prominent and official positions in labor where their socialist propaganda can be the most effective." Once these positions were secured, it "would give the Socialist Party of Canada a standing in the working class communities which they have never had before – both from the standpoint of finance and from the standpoint of safety from the authorities...by the time the One Big Union is actually put into concrete existence the labor movement of the whole country will be absolutely represented by men and women of socialist calibre."

These sections were reasonably factual and accurate, though highly coloured by Gosden's own politics and his alienation from the labour and radical movements. It was certainly true that the conference was dominated by SPC members, and while the OBU attracted syndicalists, socialists, and labourists, SPCers would remain in effective control. But the SPC had not captured the conference, if by that is meant that it had bent rules, silenced opposition, and forced its agenda on unwitting delegates. Given the well-publicized and highly democratic structure of the con-

went like this. First, Gosden made provocative remarks that in their opinion harmed the cause of the miners. Second, he was not arrested or impeded in his movements around Vancouver Island during the strike, despite his provocative remarks in Vancouver and on the Island. Third, Gosden was later hired as a janitor at the legislative buildings; as one commentator put it, he was employed to wash the windows of the men he had threatened with violence, and that implied they knew he was harmless and working for them.

The argument is plausible, but how well does it stand up to investigation? Gosden's rhetoric was not unique; many radicals who were not spies also advocated violence. While Foster and Williams thought Gosden's speech had hurt their cause, the crowd that heard his remarks responded favourably and elected him to the presidency of the MLL; clearly there was some sympathy for his views. It is true that many miners were arrested during the strike, but most of the arrests were directly related to the demonstrations and the subsequent violence against scabs and property. It does not appear that anyone was arrested for making a speech, especially a speech in Vancouver. Indeed, neither Foster nor Williams was arrested despite their activities and speeches during the strike.

The politics of Gosden's accusers shaped their accusation. Foster was explaining to his union why the coal strike that he ostensibly led had been lost. Blaming the failure on mysterious spies was easier than taking responsibility himself. Williams was a socialist who supported the Liberals by 1916. During the plugging investigation he was fighting to preserve a fellow MLA's reputation before a crucial election in which the Liberals were selling themselves as the untainted alternative to the corrupt Tory regime. Williams had been a moderate socialist at best and had always been careful not to appear to be a revolutionary or radical. He was quick to distance himself from radicals and to accuse them of outrageous, outlandish, non-productive tactics. So too was Foster, as the representative of the UMWA. Careful to pose as the voice of reason, of conciliation, of respectability, both Williams and Foster could be expected to attack any radical idea as the work of a secret agent, for the radicals always threatened to displace them at provincial and union elections.

Based on the Nanaimo *Free Press's* coverage of the 1919 Western Labour Conference – where David Rees and Walter Head charged that Gosden was an "agent-provocateur" – my colleague

ference, there was no way for the SPC to take over in that fashion. The party's success was due to its organizational abilities, the calibre and popularity of its leaders, the lack of an organized alternative, and the desire of Canadian workers for some alternative to capitalism. SPC members were the most prominent and the best organized, but their support had more to do with the aspirations of workers than their ability to control events.

Gosden, however, had a longstanding distrust of the SPC. It had been shaped by his Wobbly belief that political action was futile, the relatively conservative response of the SPC to the Vancouver Island strike, the treason of socialist-turned-Liberal Parker Williams, and his own isolation from the movement. By 1919 he was inclined to see any work by socialists as an attempt to pole-vault into positions of power through manipulation and scheming. Nonetheless, there were some grounds for Gosden's comments. The conference was clearly aimed at focusing working-class anger to create fundamental changes, and delegates did vote to send "fraternal greetings" to the "Russian Soviet government," as well as to the Spartacist movement in Germany and to all "definite working-class movements in Europe and the world." Some delegates, most notably Jack Kavanagh, would soon join the Communist Party of Canada. To label the Western Labor Conference and the SPC "Bolshevik," however, was to ignore the many different political tendencies in the Canadian labour and left movements. To suggest the conference was purely the invention of the SPC was to ignore the rising radicalism of Canadian workers. Coincidentally, many in government, business, and the police shared the view that the OBU was imposed on workers by a handful of radicals, although they arrived at their conclusions from a different logic. For them, Canada offered the best of all possible worlds and dissent had to be the work of outside agitators. Whether Gosden was sincere or was simply playing to his paying audience, his conclusions were undoubtedly welcome.[15]

Now Gosden stepped out of his role as spy and observer to provide analysis. The fourth section, titled "Possible Results," was calculated to alarm. The result of the SPC influence would be, he wrote, "that the whole of the country will have been flooded with socialist arguments and literature and every official capacity in the organized ranks of labor will be in their hands, and the Government will be absolutely powerless; because if they attempt to suppress the socialist propagandist at that time, they will directly bring about the thing they seek to prevent, viz. Revolution."

Gosden continued to paint his apocalyptic vision in vivid colours. As the socialists became more successful and revolutionary strikes broke out, he warned, "the more rebellious or impetuous elements within the ranks of the workers will immediately take drastic action, in groups and as individuals...These acts of individuals and groups will range the whole length and breadth of actions called anarchistic, and will be to a large extent spontaneous..."

The socialists would officially oppose this reign of violence and anarchy, for they wished to avoid arrest. But in fact they were "loading the gun which the workers will fire. To put it in a

Allen Seager concluded that Gosden was either directly or indirectly responsible for the explosion at the Ladysmith Extension colliery in August 1913 and that he was "almost certainly on someone else's payroll." My own view is that while Gosden undoubtedly urged direct action and may even have handed out recipes for bombs and incendiary devices, there is no direct evidence linking him to the explosion. The Vancouver Island miners certainly had reason enough and skill enough to dynamite the mine without Gosden's help. He may well have helped inspire the actual perpetrators. But Head's accusation, made some six years after the event, is not backed by any evidence, and no mention of Gosden as an arsonist or advocate of dynamite was made during his legal battles of 1916, when such allegations would have been extremely useful to Williams and the Liberal party. Nor does his advocacy of violence imply he was a spy.

More damning is the account by George Hardy in his memoirs, *Those Stormy Years*. Hardy was a British leftist, active in the IWW in BC during the coal mining strike, and later a highly placed official in the Communist Party in the US and Britain. According to Hardy, an IWW member "had angered the movement by saying at a mass meeting that McBride should get someone to taste his morning coffee and should be careful when going out shooting during the hunting season." The Wobbly, obviously Gosden, later visited Hardy and congratulated him for a speech he had made. He asked Hardy, "How would you like a Government job?" He continued by saying, "I'm working as a janitor in the Government building. I've been requested to inform you that there's one waiting for you if you care to apply to Mr…" Hardy led him on, and the spy added, "You know, to obtain a good job it's not always necessary to be a good booster. They can be got by being a good knocker." Hardy, as the hero of this tale, of course informed the spy that he was not for sale and sent him packing.

If true, this direct testimony would prove that Gosden was a labour spy as early as 1914 and probably when he made his infamous speech in 1913. That would make him not just a spy who passively reported on the strike, but an agent-provocateur who attempted to entrap workers by encouraging them in illegal acts. The remark about being a "good knocker" would also explain how Gosden could reconcile his radicalism with his activities as a spy.

We must, however, ask how reliable Hardy's memory is. The memoirs were written

nutshell, they are a clever, intelligent, well-educated body of men with an ambition to rule the country as they see fit…The mass is the herd and they are the 20th century cowboys." Gosden warned that for the socialists, "the end justifies the means; such being the case they will use any and every means to this end, disregarding this, that, or the other instrument from time to time, as its usefulness to them ceases." The result could only be "absolute anarchy."

Having played to the worst fears of his handlers, Gosden now offered a section of solutions, subtitled "Some of the means which might be employed as a preventive." Here he demonstrated a keen knowledge of the labour movement that borrowed from the Wobbly critique of labour bureaucrats. The heads of established unions would be quick to oppose the One Big Union and radicalism, Gosden argued. "Most of these officials," he pointed out, "receive their finances, directly or indirectly, from their International Headquarters." The internationals were for the most part "absolutely opposed to this form of action, knowing, as they do that it would lead to the loss of their positions as heads of the Internationals, with the salaries, political prestige, etc., which goes with those positions." As a result, the officers would soon use their influence and control of union finances to roll back the OBU and the rank-and-file dissent. The local leaders, who were closer to the rank and file and depended on them for their positions, would "go with the side which in their judgement looks the most likely to win, though preferring to stay with the International if possible, due to the assurance of the meal ticket which comes from that source." The choice for them was clear: "If they do not buck the Red element and defeat them, they will go down to oblivion as officials...the most they could hope for from a victory of the Reds is to play a subordinate part without financial compensation within the unions of which they are now practically masters." This was "galling," and therefore a large majority of the labour bosses could be depended on to fight the One Big Union, even if it meant the destruction of their own unions. His prediction was uncannily accurate.

The obvious tactic for the government, therefore, was to strengthen this conservative element so it could purge the labour movement of the radicals. If "all the machinery of preferment and privilege, of finance, publicity, positions, etc.," could be given to "the conservative forces of labor," and if employers cooperated by giving jobs to "men who stand for conservatism," it would help prevent "the crystallization of the One Big Union."

Gosden had long believed that the socialists were, when all was said and done, cowards. He had proved as much, at least to his satisfaction, while he was president of the Miners' Liberation League and was denounced for his calls for direct action. He now returned to that theme in his report. The most effective response of the government would be one "which plays upon the psychology of the Red element themselves, which is exclusively composed of the SP of C and its adherents." The SPC leaders were, "with very few exceptions...intelligent opportunists." As such, Gosden

more than forty years after the event, and memories fade, intensify, and distort over time. On the other hand, meeting a flamboyant figure who turned out to be a traitor might be a vivid moment that stayed firmly and accurately in place. Can Hardy's recollections be trusted?

Hardy's account does leave some room for doubt. He was mistaken about James Hawthornthwaite's name, rendering it as Hawthenwaite, and states that Hawthornthwaite retired in 1912. In fact, he had been expelled from the SPC for his real-estate dealings and resigned from the party to take up financial speculation in Britain. Hardy makes no mention of Hawthornthwaite's strained relations with the SPC or his later return to the BC legislature, and makes no distinction between the SPC and the SCPBC. Hardy confuses Robert Dunsmuir with his son James, and is mistaken when he dates the Tory rise to power as 1900 rather than 1903. In fact, before 1903 there were no strong party labels in BC, and candidates did not run under a party banner. Hardy refers to the provincial premier as the prime minister and is mistaken about the age of Joseph Mairs, a young striker who died in prison; his dating of events is confused. Hardy's account of the MLL is a little distorted, for while he places himself in the centre of events, he is not much mentioned in the newspaper accounts of the day. These are all small errors, but there are several of them in an account only seven pages long.

How important are these mistakes and lapses? They are, for the most part, small inaccuracies, perhaps inevitable when one reflects on events that happened four decades before. More interesting is Hardy's failure to name Gosden. Gosden was well known in the labour and socialist movement of the time, at least as well known as some of the figures Hardy does name. Did he forget or did he choose not to record the name of a class traitor for posterity? Nor does Hardy mention that Gosden was the first president of the MLL. Hardy must have known this, for Hardy himself was a secretary-treasurer of the League. Did he simply forget or did he leave out mention of Gosden's presidency on purpose? Either way, the failure to note it raises some doubts about the reliability of Hardy's account.

Hardy makes a more substantial mistake as well. From the context of his account, the exchange with Gosden took place in early 1914. It could not have taken place later than August 1914, by which time the strike was over. But Gosden was not employed as a janitor until

continued, "their one weakness consists of the fact that they lack the physical courage of their convictions and they possess the fear of the consequences of their acts. If this fear can be played upon in the right manner, they, as leaders, cease to exist...because their ambition towards leadership and power is greater than their willingness to suffer and sacrifice for revolution. Social Revolution to them is but an ideal which they can paint before the mass, that the mass, believing in that ideal, may carry them on a wave of revolution into the highest places of authority in the land."

In his opinion, the SPC was not building a mass movement because it believed in democracy, but because a mass movement would make it impossible for the authorities to single out the leaders. This contrasted with Gosden's own political beliefs years earlier, when he had called for a militant minority to lead the masses in direct action and sabotage. He seemed to reflect on his own experience when he wrote that the socialists "have carefully excluded from official capacities in this new movement, those types of revolutionaries who are sincere in their convictions and who may be willing, when the acid test of opposition comes, to lead the hesitating mass to revolution, even though it might mean their own death."

The replacement of these sincere and brave revolutionaries by the SPCers, who operated in the shadows and hid behind the masses, meant the socialists had "materially weakened their own possibilities of success." They had also, in Gosden's opinion, given the authorities the tool they needed to stamp out the party and the OBU. Building a mass movement would take time, and until it was successful the movement and the leaders would be vulnerable. If the government acted quickly, it would be possible to turn the socialists into "outlaws instead of heroes in the eyes of the mass." That would in turn give the conservative union leaders, business, and government time to use rewards and pressure to oust the radicals.

How should the government strike against the radicals? The key was "to play on their psychology of fear whilst preventing their becoming martyrs of the cause." How could that be done? Gosden's solution was as simple as it was ruthless. The government should "immediately pick up these different members, one at a time, in such a way that they will automatically disappear from their friends and their activities. They should be picked up secretly and should be safely placed in custody secretly. After one or two of these leaders had been picked up at various points in a mysterious manner, and disappeared just as mysteriously, the unseen hand would so intimidate the weaker and lesser lights that the agitation would automatically die down."

Aware that his plan to kidnap people who had broken no law "may not be in strict accordance with technical law," Gosden argued, as he had so often in very different circumstances, that the end justified the means. The "Reds" were taking advantage of loopholes in the law to organize "the most drastic form of social revolution that one can conceive of." Revolutionary ideas had long been talked about in Canada, as Gosden well knew. The difference now was that "the present condition of

February or March 1915, some six months after the strike. Hardy's account, therefore, could not have happened as he describes it, for he could not have known in 1914 that Gosden would get a janitorial job in 1915. Does this mean Hardy made a simple error of timing? Or does it suggest that years after the strike, relying on an untrustworthy memory, Hardy combined the facts and rumours about Gosden to produce a vivid, but fanciful and misleading episode?

Or might he have crafted the story purposefully for political reasons? When Hardy wrote his memoirs, he had been a member of the Communist Party for more than thirty years and was a high-ranking official and an orthodox Stalinist. His book faithfully repeats the official analysis of the Communist Party and seriously misrepresents the work and politics of all non-CP movements and groups, including the IWW and the SPC. Hardy takes an especially hard line against the IWW and its brand of syndicalism. As a Wobbly in the 1920s, Hardy tried to steer the IWW into the Party. When his efforts were rebuffed, he abandoned the Wobblies for the Communist Party. There one of his tasks was, as he put it, to attack "anarchist and syndicalist prejudices" in the international labour movement. A key part of his argument against the non-Stalinist left was his insistence that these groups were infiltrated with spies and that many well-intentioned radicals were actually helping capitalism by refusing to join the CP.

Thus Hardy's memoirs must be weighed in the context of his political mission to attack all left and labour groups that did not follow the line of the CP. Hardy, like Foster and Williams, is quick to insist that any group that differed from his politics is suspect. His story about Gosden must be considered in the light of his determination to "prove" the inadequacy of every left group outside of the CP and should therefore be taken with a grain of salt.

It is also odd that Hardy appears to have told no one of Gosden's admission that he was a spy and of his attempt to recruit Hardy. In the highly charged days of the Vancouver Island coal strike and its aftermath, a public accusation by Hardy would have been welcomed by many in the labour movement. Presumably it would also have been repeated during the plugging scandal of 1916, for it would have served those eager to discredit Gosden. No one, however, ever mentioned Hardy's accusation publicly. Finally, if Gosden were known as a Tory spy by 1916, would staunch union miner Isaac Portrey have been willing to work with Gosden and to

things, in a social sense, is so ripe for change, that, given a free hand for three months, and the Government of today will go down to utter defeat and the utter annihilation of its personnel. There is no half-way measures can be taken."

"Disappearing" the leaders of the social revolt was the only way to proceed, in Gosden's opinion. Confronting the rebels directly would lead to riots, possibly deaths and martyrs, while bringing "to the front men more courageous than themselves, who would complete the work." Mass arrests and public trials would only garner more publicity and sympathy for the cause. No, the leaders and organizers had to be picked up, "one after the other, at widely different points and at widely separate intervals." This

would put the fear into the hearts of the followers and would confuse the mass whom they seek to weld together: Men would lack confidence in one another, which is an essential factor necessary in revolution; some would say that these men who disappeared got 'cold feet'; others would say that they had disappeared with the funds; others would blame individual capitalists; others would blame the conservative forces of labor; and others again might blame the local or federal police; but none of them would have any tangible evidence upon which to hang a centre of propaganda, and the discussion, suspicion, jealousy, and fear aroused, would be the greatest factor in preventing that solidarity and enthusiasm so essential to the success of this movement.

His analysis of the effects of a campaign of terror was as insightful as it was chilling. It reflected Gosden's own experience in strikes, free speech campaigns, and the Miners' Liberation League, where he had learned both the importance of solidarity and its fragility. It also built on his particular views of manhood and courage that had informed his world-view since the Prince Rupert strike and his denunciation of Shorty O'Donnell in the San Diego jail. Gosden understood that the carrot and stick worked better than the stick alone, and the reforms he had proposed to Harlan Brewster in 1916 surfaced again in his RCMP report. "Side by side with the line of action suggested above," Gosden added, "should be progressive reforms adopted, or widely advertised as being put into operation, to act as a counter argument against revolution. These reforms should be far-reaching, national policies, along the lines of the standardization of hours, minimum wages compatible with the cost of living, big public works of national importance, such as military highways, etc...." The labour movement could easily be co-opted by such reforms, especially if conservative union leaders were given supervisory jobs. A program of public works, Gosden's report ended, "would cure, to a large extent, the fear of unemployment, which is one of the biggest arguments of the social revolutionaries, and it would also prevent State aid for unemployment."

Gosden's report first went to Inspector Spalding, who passed the report up the line, noting that it and other information from other agents

have his wife and children board with him? Would members of the Socialist Party have sent him aid during his perjury trials? Would that fiery impossibilist E.T. Kingsley have chaired a meeting in the Labour Temple that featured Gosden as the chief speaker? Would John Sidaway, an active labour leader and socialist of the day, have noted years later that there was a great deal of sympathy for Gosden during the plugging scandal and the subsequent perjury trials, yet thought it unimportant to mention that Gosden was a spy?

Nor does Hardy appear to have told his story to his friend Bill Bennett, an SPC and CPC member who, like Hardy, was active in the miners' strike. Bennett knew Gosden as early as 1910, and in a 1936 newspaper column he briefly outlined Gosden's shadowy career. Bennett noted Gosden's work in the Prince Rupert strike, the coffee speech, the janitorial job, the plugging scandal, and his spying in 1919, but does not even hint that he was a spy during the coal mining strikes. The fact that Bennett did not repeat Hardy's accusation, even in language veiled to avoid a libel suit, suggests he did not know of it. And that suggests that Hardy did not tell him of the episode. Did Hardy keep the entire incident to himself for forty years? Or did he put it together much later, perhaps

97

creating a composite figure for literary and political reasons?

None of these problems – the small mistakes, the larger mistake of the timing of Gosden's janitorial job, the political motives, the apparent failure to reveal the story for forty years – proves Hardy was wrong or lying. How much doubt do they cast on his allegation? Do they create a "reasonable doubt" or is the balance of evidence on Hardy's side? Probably each reader will draw different conclusions.

Is there evidence to suggest Gosden was not a spy in 1913–15? There is some negative evidence. That is, some proof one might reasonably expect to find is not there. First, to date, no official record of his working for the Tories has been found. No documentary evidence has been found in the attorney-general or provincial police files, though evidence of other spies and of Gosden's later career has turned up there. When the BC Provincial Police in 1932 asked the RCMP whether Gosden had worked for the Mounties, the reply noted that Gosden had been an RCMP agent in 1919 but made no mention of his having worked for anyone else prior to that. The fact that the BCPP had no knowledge of Gosden working for them or the Tories suggests that he did not. But of course, spies live in a nether world of

convinced him that immediate action was necessary. His response to the suggestion the SPC members be kidnapped was ambiguous. He first acknowledged that it "cannot...be considered, being against all principles of British law." There was an out, however: the plan could be considered if "we can be guided by war time conditions." In the meantime, Spalding preferred to adopt another of Gosden's recommendations, "a campaign of education by the Press, and through literature, education, for distribution by the conservative element of labor." Gosden's remarks about getting employers on side were also, Spalding indicated, "worthy of consideration."

As the report made its way up to the commissioner's office it continued to attract attention and comment. A page of notes compiled for the commissioner suggested Gosden's report was "interesting, but to my mind is considerably overdrawn in that he has recommended a drastic line of action, apparently taking the line that these men had actually accomplished something and the masses were ready to do their will." Nonetheless, the writer agreed with Gosden that the "far fetched dreams" of the radicals "is Bolshevism," and suggested "a central propaganda bureau might well be started at Ottawa, cooperating with the newspapers and magazines of the various propaganda organizations" and with "the clergy of the various denominations." The author also understood the link between conservative politics and sexual repression in the Canada of 1919. One valuable way to counter left-wing propaganda, the author pointed out, would be to argue that sexual liberation was part of the radical agenda. Many anti-Bolsheviks believed the Russian revolution had loosened sexual mores and decreed that women were to be shared by all men, just as private property was to be shared by workers. Thus the note concluded, "[T]he recent decree socializing women in Russia should be given the widest publicity amongst the various women's organizations throughout the country."[16]

Commissioner Perry thought Agent 10's report so important that he forwarded it to the office of the prime minister with five pages of comment. Perry agreed with Gosden's views on the purpose of the One Big Union and also agreed that harsh, obvious repression stood the "danger of antagonizing those conservative elements in the labour ranks, and the result might easily be to drive them over to the side of the 'reds.'" Perry had "no desire to be an alarmist" and was "not prepared to say that they are aiming at a revolution in the ordinary sense of that word." Yet he was concerned that the radicals were "influencing a section of labour in the West, and unchaining forces which, even if they so desire, some day they will be unable to control. Here is grave danger to the peace and security of the country." He concluded that nothing drastic should be done, that the best course would be to strengthen the opposition to the OBU in the labour movement.

Despite the caution exhibited by the police, in March 1919 the Department of Justice was asked to consider the legality of holding private

unwritten orders and reports; we perhaps should not expect to find proof, especially in the more casual records of an earlier time.

Other questions come to mind. Is a six-week job as a janitor in the parliament buildings several months after the end of the strike an appropriate or likely pay-off for spying? The province often created part-time, casual, labouring jobs as part of its meagre relief efforts, and there may not be much significance in the fact that Gosden took such a job in the dead of winter in a year of high unemployment. We may also ask if the Liberals would have hired him to work for them in 1916 if he had previously been closely connected to the Tories.

What do we have at the end of this chain of evidence, inference, and speculation? How likely is it, on balance, that Gosden was a spy in 1913–15? I have no better answer than the reader.[33]

trials; clearly someone thought Gosden's plan of holding radicals in secret had some merit. And the history of the OBU demonstrates Gosden's keen perception of the labour movement and the lengths to which labour bureaucrats would go to hang on to their positions. Conservative unionists, business, and the state formed what radicals called an "unholy trinity" to destroy the OBU. While Gosden could hardly take credit for this, his observations and analysis were deadly accurate.[17]

As Agent 10, Gosden once again revealed his ability to thrill and alarm the authorities. His lurid tales of impending revolution, secret organizations, and drastic solutions reflected both his taste for drama and action that characterized his life and his talent for opportunism. Undoubtedly he understood that informers' reports that indicate nothing much is happening do not pay well and do not lead to requests for further information.

The report on the Western Labor Council was the most significant episode in Gosden's career as a spy. Despite being exposed at the conference, Gosden continued to inform on his comrades. In a memo dated 31 March 1919, Gosden reported that some of his predictions were already coming true. The Calgary Trade and Labour Council was split on the question of the OBU, and several UMWA locals were planning to split from the International. He noted with some satisfaction that "it is now war to the knife between the Socialist element and the International Union Officials." At the same time, the socialists were "already extremely nervous realizing the possibilities of their acts coming home to them...fearing that some of their enthusiastic supporters may do something and the Socialists will be held responsible for it. This situation will lead to bitter controversies in the ranks of labour and will result in their ranks being split...This chaos is beneficial to the Government."

Gosden himself worked to create chaos. He attended a meeting at Blairmore and "arranged a hot reception" for the featured speaker, one Lawson, who was the editor of the District Ledger and a strong supporter of the OBU. About four hundred people attended the meeting, but Lawson, according to Gosden, "was paralyzed by fear and his speech was a very poor exhibition and fell remarkably flat. It would pay the Department to permit Lawson to speak everywhere on the OBU if this was his best effort." Hillcrest too was disrupted by Gosden. His letter to the District Ledger, where he had defended himself against Rees's charges, had turned the camps there into "a little inferno...This is well as it has got them all fighting among themselves, preventing solidarity."[18]

Another report, dated 4 June 1919, appears to have been written by Gosden, but does not have his name or code name on it. It does make reference to earlier reports by the same agent that stressed the cowardice of the OBU leaders, and from this and other remarks it is reasonable to conclude that it was indeed written by Gosden. It differs from his other reports in that it contains no facts or observations. Like the earlier report, it called for the arrest of leaders and the deportation of "alien troublemakers" as well as a series of reforms to blunt the edge of the revolutionaries. Unlike the previous report, this one contained a lengthy section of labour and political philosophy. Gosden was aware that it was presumptuous to air his views in a spy's report and acknowledged that "they are not new and many have said the same things, but I have lived this life and know that revolution is inevitable if the violent programme is acted upon on the part of the masses."

The choice for the government was plain, the report concluded. Canada was in the midst of upheaval and change, that was certain. Workers desperately needed reform and improvements in their lives and now were "grasping at any and every straw of hope as a means to ease conditions." Change was inevitable; if the government wanted it "to be peaceful then the basic grievances of the ninety five per cent must be adjusted; if the government wishes it to be violent, then catering to the five per cent will bring it that way." Non-violent change had to be implemented from above, he continued, for "the mass cannot install a more orderly regime even if they were allowed to, because they have not been organized for it, but conditions are driving them to attempt it without the collective training and administrative capacity necessary to such a position."

There was a solution, a way to prevent violent upheaval. Once the OBU was crushed, Gosden wrote, the government should "immediately unionize the whole labour of the country upon a national basis, in industrial unions embracing each industry. This would satisfy labour and make for the highest efficiency in production, creating an intense nationalism and eliminating the stupidity of international unions." He insisted that unions were necessary, and that the old craft unions were "not constructed in line with the evolution of industry." If unions were at present a force for division and conflict, "unionism rightly organized is the very basis of national unity and strength... If this OB Union agitation is handled right, out of it may be built the greatest factor for stable government, with an ever increasing contentment and solidarity of national life, with society so organized that it can immediately conform to any changing conditions, without the present absurd conflicts."[19]

The report is the last one that can be tied to Gosden, whose career as a spy was brief. How can we explain and understand his transformation from radical to informer? It is impossible to know for certain what led to his decision. We can, however, make some informed suggestions and guesses, based on what we know of Gosden's life and his own writings, including his lengthy spy reports. We do know that he differed from other labour spies. The RCMP agent Frank Zaneth, for example, was not a worker who turned against his comrades; he was a policeman whose job was to spy on and entrap radicals. Other famous spies, such as James McParland, who infiltrated the Molly Maguires and later tried to frame Big Bill Haywood and other Western Federation of Miners leaders, were employees of the notorious Pinkerton, Burns, and Thiel detective agencies. Despicable as these men were, they at least had the flimsy excuse that they were following orders. Nor was Gosden like the hapless Canadian Harry Orchard, the half-wit hired by McParland to frame Haywood for the murder of the former Idaho governor Frank Steunenberg in 1905. Orchard admitted killing Steunenberg and others, then, at McParland's urging, gave false testimony in an attempt to railroad union leaders. In return, Orchard had his sentence reduced from death by hanging to life imprisonment.[20]

If Gosden's actions were no more admirable than those of Zaneth, McParland, or Orchard, his motives were more complex. It may be that Gosden was a sociopath, devoid of the emotions and conscience that kept others from such behaviour. But such an explanation is surely too simple. It reduces historical process to individual defects and does not allow us to consider the particular causes that led to Gosden's particular actions. We need to understand the conditions that limited Gosden's life and allowed and encouraged him to act as he did. In examining his life, we get some sense of the complicated braiding of the personal and the political.

Certainly the money was important. Gosden admitted during the plugging scandal that he had gone to work for Scott out of necessity, for dollars and cents. The pay for spying was good money even for a skilled worker in 1919. The type of work probably appealed to Gosden as well. Spying was considerably easier than railway construction or ditch-digging. It also required the use of some of his skills and attributes that could not be used in labouring jobs. He had enjoyed his work with Scott and had taken some pride in performing it with accuracy and thoroughness. Clearly he had hoped that his job would continue, and spying required similar skills.

Viewed from one angle, Gosden was a frustrated intellectual. He was clever, enjoyed writing and public speaking, and loved political debate. Born into different circumstances he might have become a socialist politician or a labour leader. But these pursuits were denied to him. He did not have the white-collar background of James Hawthornthwaite or Ralph Smith. Nor did he have the craft and craft union base of Samuel Gompers or George Bartley, the Vancouver printer who enjoyed a lengthy career as a union official, labour paper editor, and politician.[21] Furthermore, Gosden's own rough life and volatile politics isolated him from the respectable labourists and even the radical socialists who controlled the BC labour movement and its paid positions. Being a spy required the use of his native intelligence in ways that manual labour did not. His lengthy spy reports allowed him to comment on current affairs and to turn some of his brutalizing experiences as a worker and revolutionary into political wisdom.

Gosden also had a love for the limelight. Fencing with politicians and prosecuting attorneys, addressing mass meetings, commanding headlines in the daily press, shocking the middle class, all gave his life more meaning. It was obvious too that he was attracted to intrigue and conspiracy early on, whether that involved formulas for explosives and incendiary devices, elaborate election schemes, or sabotage by a handful of dedicated revolutionaries. Each represented a shortcut for the powerless to obtain power. Involvement in intricate plans, double-dealing, and conspiracy may have provided some adventure, even a higher meaning to his rough life. Working as a labour spy would do all this, with the additional delicious risk of being caught.

Ironically, Gosden's politics probably contributed to his becoming an agent for the police. His days as a Wobbly and his experience with the SPC during the coal mining strike convinced him that parliamentary action was futile. He also came to believe that the SPC and labour leadership refused to take direct action because they were physical cowards who did not share his courage of conviction. This led to Gosden's isolation from the mainstream of the left and labour movements, and this isolation undoubtedly fuelled his beliefs and his resentment. By 1919 his old political foes were poised to take over the leadership of the OBU and the workers' revolt. In his mind, if the SPC captured the new movement, real chances for revolution and progress would be squandered by a handful of politicians who knew little of the life of working people and who would betray the movement when the time came. And of course there would be no place for him in a union or party dominated by the SPC. As a spy, Gosden could deal a blow against the socialists he regarded as cowards and traitors. Even in his reports as Agent 10 we can detect Gosden's faint hope that once the traitors were kidnapped, the real radicals, including perhaps himself, could rise to lead the working class in revolt.

Gosden's report of 4 June 1919 offers another clue to his politics and perhaps to his willingness to act as an informer. In it he urged the government to consult with labour, to address its real grievances, and to find a peaceful way to reform a system that enriched five percent of its population at the expense of the other ninety-five percent. Such reform had to be introduced from the top, for, as Gosden saw it, the mass of workers were not educated or trained to create a new society themselves. In short, reform was necessary but workers could not do it themselves. This belief had been foreshadowed years earlier in Gosden's article on sabotage. Then he had written that it was impossible to win over all the workers to a program that was in their own best interest, for they had already been victimized by the propaganda of boss and state. It was instead necessary for a "militant minority" to act in the name and the interests of the working class.

He was not alone in this belief. By the late 1910s and early 1920s many European left-wing radicals had come, like Gosden, to believe that the masses would never revolt, no matter how desirable a revolution was. Nor could real reform take place through parliamentary democracy, for the state was controlled by capital and even the most earnest revolutionaries, once elected, would be forced to compromise to hold onto power. As an example, they could point to the German Social Democratic Party, the SPD. The SPD was the strongest socialist party in Europe prior to the First World War. It had been successful in electing several of its members to the German parliament, the Reichstag. Once there, however, the party was faced with several dilemmas, many of which had already been faced by the SPC in British Columbia. Should the party stress extra-parliamentary politics by the working class, such as strikes and demonstrations, or would this alienate middle-class voters the party hoped to win over? Should it concentrate on achieving reforms through the system, or would this simply forestall the revolution? Should the party make alliances and compromises with liberals and others, or should it remain loyal to its principles? Would working within the system not make parliamentarians part of the system? Would they not become part of the middle class by virtue of their jobs as politicians? And would that not convince them that revolution was no longer necessary, convince them to abandon working-class politics? The cruelest dilemma was forced upon the SPD by the First World War. The party had long opposed war. Yet when the vote came to supply the Kaiser with the finances necessary to fund the war, nearly all of the SPD's parliamentarians abandoned party policy and voted to support the war effort. For radicals around the world, this was the final proof of the treachery of social democracy and parliamentary politics.

If the masses would not revolt and parliamentary action was futile, what choice was left for the radical? Some were led to advocate individual acts of violence and terror, as had many anarchists around the world in the 1880s and 1890s. Others were attracted to the "vanguard party," advocated by Lenin and the Bolsheviks in Russia, that would build on working-class resistance but guided the masses toward revolution without their participation in strategic decisions. Still others were led in another direction: that of fascism.

In this period, fascism was something rather different than what it came to be by the late 1920s and early 1930s. It offered the promise of a charismatic leader who would appeal directly to the masses. Depending on direct, popular support, the leader would not be beholden to capital or elections that were controlled by capital. Nor would the leader have to make the compromises required by parliament and coalition-building. Fascism, at least in its early theoretical elaboration, outlined a vision of society that would not abolish capital, but would use the state, embodied by the leader who was directly accountable to the popular will, to control capital and to protect and enrich workers. Class conflict would be eliminated, and with it, the need for revolution. The move of many socialists, including Benito Mussolini and the German sociologist Robert Michels, from left to right was not as irrational or inexplicable as it may seem to us today.

Gosden seems to have taken some initial steps in this direction himself. Certainly he regarded the parliamentary compromises of SPC politicians as betrayals of the working class. Parker Williams's move to the right and into the Liberal party was proof of that. Clearly becoming politicians removed workers from the reality of working-class life and encouraged them to abandon the working class for alliances, even friendships, with the middle class. At the same time, the conditions of the masses remained as miserable as ever, but still they refused to revolt. A state that had the power and the will to legislate for the "ninety-five per cent" of the population was one way out of the dilemma. Could the Canadian state play this role? Probably not, but certainly as Agent 10, Gosden spent much of his time outlining ideas and programs that reflected his analysis of the failure of both capitalism and socialism, and his analysis and his solutions paralleled to some extent the debates that other former socialists were engaged in. In that sense, his decision to infiltrate and betray the socialist movement may have been the continuance of his early political trajectory rather than a definite reversal of it.

None of this is meant to obscure the ugly facts of Gosden's career as a labour spy. He turned on former friends and comrades, even suggested they be kidnapped by the police to crush the wave of strikes in 1919. Whatever his politics, he took money for his betrayal and may well have encouraged workers to take actions that resulted in their arrest.

The swirl of politics in this period, in which many radicals groped to find new solutions, does suggest that Gosden, like all humans, was complex, contradictory, and shaped by circumstance. His motivation for betrayal was probably more complicated than just a desire for money. It was a blend of resentment and hope, personal tragedy and immediate need, feelings of betrayal and loyalty, left-wing thought and right-wing opportunism. It combined a love of politics with a love of intrigue, physical courage with moral confusion, desperation with cunning.

As a result, Gosden held several seemingly opposed strands of thought simultaneously. He appeared to see no contradiction between conspiring against workers and advocating reforms for them, and he wove all these different strands into a useful, if inconsistent and self-serving, world-view. We see in this odd ideology the attempt of a bright, self-educated man to make sense of his world, to explain the injustices he saw and lived, and to hold out some ray of hope. It was a world-view that held courage and strength at a premium, for without them one could hardly withstand the class violence employed by bosses and the state. It was also a world-view that allowed him to hate, and surely he had cause to do that. An intelligent man, he was forced to take up near-slave labour and was denied access to the reins of power by the bourgeoisie, the labour aristocracy, and the socialist elite. In his own mind, any betrayal by him of employers, politicos, or the left may have seemed but a pale echo of the betrayals he had suffered. Gosden's radicalism and his constant references to manhood, his love of intrigue and the sense of power it gave, all stemming from his class experience, combined in such a way that taking money for spying on his fellow workers seemed expedient and justified. Far from being shocking, Gosden's perfidy may well have been, for him, a logical and consistent step to take. The same conditions that created a disdain for bourgeois morality and respectability and fuelled an uncompromising, if temporary, revolutionary sentiment, ultimately led to a self-serving ethos that could accommodate any betrayal or immoral activity.

Even the IWW recognized the dual nature of the class experience of its members. When author John Graham Brooks suggested that the revolutionary union attracted "the most unselfish and courageous, together with the self-seeking and the semi-criminal," the IWW reviewer noted that "we cannot quarrel with this statement."[22] It may be an appropriate observation to make of Robert Gosden.

CHAPTER 5

"The Ruling Class is Absolutely Insane"

Whatever his motivation, Gosden's career as a spy was a short one. It was over by 1921 according to one source, by 1922 according to another. He was of less use after he was exposed early on and because after 1920 the amount of strike activity and labour militancy decreased considerably. The "unholy trinity" did its work well. Conservative labour leaders, much as Gosden predicted, fought back against the radicals and the OBU, often working with employers to purge them from the workplace and the labour movement. In Vancouver the conservatives preferred to sell off the Labour Temple rather than have control of it fall to the OBU; in Alberta they refused to recognize OBU contracts and union cards, and crossed picket lines and cut sweetheart deals with bosses. The business sector launched an open assault on the labour movement, using blacklists, yellow-dog contracts, firings, and minor reforms such as workers' councils, improvements in conditions, and stock options.

The government deported, arrested, and harassed labour activists, and the economy sagged with the end of war production. The resulting depression made it more difficult for unions to organize, as workers now feared for their jobs and were less likely to protest poor wages and conditions. The need for labour spies was still apparent, but it was less urgent. And by 1921 the police were less interested in the IWW, the OBU, and the SPC. They were turning their attention to a new political organization: the Communist

BLACKLISTS, YELLOW-
DOG CONTRACTS, AND
WELFARE CAPITALISM

After the labour revolt of 1919 to 1920, capital and the state fought back. Business used force to break unions, roll back wages, and attack the left. Two of its weapons were the blacklist and the yellow-dog contract. The blacklist was a record of workers who were active in the union or had advocated unionism. Employers would compile lists and share them with each other so all could avoid hiring men and women who might be "troublemakers." If employers thought blacklisting was just taking care of business, for workers it meant they could be denied a job for exercising their legal rights to freedom of speech and to form and join unions.

The yellow-dog contract was an agreement drawn up by the boss that prospective employees had to sign before being hired. The contract would state that the worker did not belong to a union and would not join a union while employed by that company. If workers later decided to join a union, they could be fired for breaking their contract with the employer.

Employers also devised a number of ways to make the ground for unionization less fertile. For example, some employers set up insurance or health plans; many created stock option plans that

Party of Canada. Gosden became yesterday's man; he had few connections with the CPC and was less able to comment on the new party.

There is some evidence that Gosden was not considered a reliable source after his initial report on the Western Labor Conference, and this likely shortened his career. The amount of hard material he produced was rather slim; his June 1919 report was largely a rewrite of earlier reports, and much of the information he passed on could be obtained by reading the newspapers. He was, as Commissioner Perry indicated, prone to alarmism, either because he was inclined to intrigue and exaggeration or because he hoped overstating the danger would keep him on the payroll. Gosden's additional political commentary and analysis was not much appreciated. His supervisor, J.W. Spalding, noted that "while he furnished much useful information, he was ever ready to advance theories and deductions on a given situation when he pictured possibilities that were unlikely of fulfillment and in fact did not materialize." While Gosden's analysis was "not altogether without foundation," Spalding, like Perry, believed Gosden was "somewhat of an alarmist" who "likes to prophesy, and should he happen to be in a measure correct, takes great satisfaction in saying 'I told you so.'" Spalding concluded that Gosden could be depended on to give useful information in certain circumstances, but that he was "too restless and unstable for regular employment." Another officer considered Gosden "untrustworthy," believing that "his reports were found to be unreliable and in some cases false." In short, the same traits that made Gosden unlikely to find regular employment or a position in the labour movement also made him a poor spy.[1]

By 1922 Gosden was back in Vancouver, over forty years old, still with no career, stable job, or home life. He turned to the spiritualism he had rejected so vehemently while in California, perhaps for some of the same psychological reasons he had earlier turned to radicalism and to espionage. He became particularly interested in Theosophy and became a follower of the English reformer and mystic Annie Besant. Started in 1875 by the Russian émigré Helena Petrovna Blavatsky, the Theosophical Society set out a convoluted creed that freely blended millenarianism, eastern mysticism, pyramid worship, the power of personal will, and belief in spirits, fairies, and superior beings from Atlantis. It was a strong movement in the 1910s and 1920s, and in Europe and North America it attracted numerous political reformers of all stripes. Phillips Thompson, a journalist who had been active in the Knights of Labor and the Socialist Party of Canada, was an ardent Theosophist. So too was Vancouver labour leader Helena Gutteridge.

Gosden's tirade against mysticism in California in 1912 may have been a screen to hide his own fascination for it. Probably living with Ethel Cuthbertson, who had a keen interest in the occult, fuelled his curiosity. By 1919 he was deeply immersed in occult studies, a passion that he maintained until his death.

The appeal of this mysticism to someone like Gosden is not so hard to understand. These move-

allowed their employees to purchase shares in the company. Some improved workplace conditions by designing pleasant washrooms, putting in cafeterias that supplied cheap meals, and making work stations more comfortable. Others worked to create a "team spirit" by starting up company baseball and hockey teams, organizing company parties and picnics, and setting up workers' committees, controlled by the employer, to discuss grievances with management. These various schemes are known collectively as "welfare capitalism." The intent was to have workers believe that changes could come from the benevolent employer rather than from their own effort and struggle.

While some of these reforms undoubtedly made workers more comfortable, welfare capitalism was not created to benefit workers. It was created to keep unions out and protect bosses and profits. In that sense it was a cynical ploy rather than a genuine attempt to make life better for employees. Bosses gave workers what they thought was needed to keep the union out; workers were not allowed to decide for themselves what they needed. Nor were these changes made by all employers; in many workplaces, conditions did not change at all. Whatever improvements were made, workers paid for them by having to work harder and longer as wages dropped and the pace of production speeded up in the 1920s. Worse, whatever the employer gave, he could – and often did – take away. Without a union, workers had no way to build on these improvements and could not defend them if the boss rolled them back. Nor did welfare capitalism touch the real problems workers faced. It did not allow workers to extend political democracy to the workplace or win better wages or shorter hours. At best it replaced the foreman's scowl with the hypocritical smile of the personnel manager.

Welfare capitalism is still around today. It is especially popular in the service and restaurant sectors, where wages are low and unions are beginning to organize. Some employers win a great deal of favourable publicity by highlighting their medical plans, stock options, and snazzy uniforms, but these are not new ideas. They date back at least to the 1920s, and their aim today is the same as it was then: to keep unions out.

ments promised to reveal hidden wisdom to the special band of followers and provided forums for discussion and social activities. Intricate ritual and murky, complex doctrines gave adherents a sense of power and special knowledge, while the suggestion that one's lot could be improved through personal action and willpower is as seductive today as it was then. To a man such as Gosden, the mysterious world of Theosophy offered an escape from the harsh reality of life as a migrant worker and gave him opportunity to exercise his mind in study and debate. Theosophy also offered a critique of modern science and social thought that could easily be grafted onto the revolutionary's critique of capitalism and parliamentary democracy. Indeed, since these mystical movements maintained that the modern world was built on false principles of materialism, linear logic, and empiricism, Theosophists could argue that their analysis was more fundamental and more radical than that of the socialists who accepted so much of the bourgeois world. Thus Theosophy offered Gosden a slightly different mixture of secret knowledge, hidden power, intrigue, and excitement than what he had found in radical politics and espionage.[2]

It was through the spiritualist movement that he met the woman who would be his companion for the next sixteen years. Isabella Bunyan had been widowed when her husband was killed overseas in the First World War, leaving her to raise two sons under the age of five on the meagre government pension. Like many people, she turned to Theosophy when conventional religion seemed to offer no explanation for the chaos and destruction of the war. She had another reason to investigate mysticism. The Canadian government had told her that her husband was killed on 16 June 1916, but she received a letter from him dated 17 June. In her grief she refused to believe that there had been a simple error of dates made by her husband or the government, and spent years trying to unearth a non-existent conspiracy. She also attempted to communicate with her husband through seances and other mystical means.

She met Robert Gosden through another mystical group, the British Israelites, and they took up residence together at 120 East 67th Avenue, at Sophia Street, in south Vancouver. At that time the area was largely bush and farmland. Isabella refused to marry Gosden, for it would mean the loss of her widow's pension, and Gosden was too unreliable to count on for steady income. When he worked, he was lavish with money, but too often he was unemployed or working for low wages as a gardener, cement worker, labourer, or semi-skilled carpenter. Gosden helped raise her sons, John and Bill, who regarded him as their step-father. Gosden taught them basic carpentry, warned them of the dangers of smoking, and encouraged them in their studies. He enjoyed rough-housing with the boys, and he bought them rifles, took them hunting, and taught them how to shoot and make bows and arrows. Gosden would tell them stories of his days riding the rods, about the Mexican revolution, and about Joe Hill and Frank Little.[3]

At home, Gosden liked to read, to grow vegetables and flowers, and to make wine. Around 1924 or 1925 the family moved to 6659 Cullo-

RELIEF CAMPS

The "boom and bust" cycle has always been part of the capitalist economy and probably always will be. Depressions are the "bust." A depression is an extended period of slow, or no, growth in the economy, resulting in increased levels of unemployment. That's the official definition. But such definitions hide the reality of jobs lost, poverty, and the turmoil that families and individuals face.

When the Great Depression began in 1929, many business and political leaders believed it was nothing more than a seasonal slow-down. When unemployment worsened, however, it became clear that the depression was a crisis. At times during the decade, the official unemployment rate was over 30 percent; the unofficial rate was undoubtedly higher. Few in business or politics had any idea how to fix the system. Just as they do now, corporate heads and politicians insisted anyone who wanted work could find it and that cutting government spending to balance the budget was more important than providing people with relief.

The tight budgets and fiscal restraint only made the depression worse, for without jobs and money, people could not purchase goods. As demand for goods fell, more businesses were forced to fire people. That meant higher unemployment, fewer people to purchase goods, and the spiral continued.

Typically, governments decided to treat symptoms and not the disease itself. The symptom that worried them the most was the large number of unemployed men who, as time went on, organized to protest the depression and the lack of action.

The spectre of organized protesters in the cities terrified the government. The response of Conservative Prime Minister R.B. Bennett in 1932 was to create the relief camps. The camps were usually far from city centres, and the men were housed in hastily built barracks, fed in mess halls, and supervised by the Department of Defence. They were put to work on labour-intensive projects: clearing brush, building stretches of road to nowhere, landscaping the Peace Arch, putting up government buildings, even building golf courses for the wealthy. They were paid twenty cents a day, roughly enough for two packages of cigarettes. The work was dreary, monotonous, and often useless. Jobs that could have been done easily and quickly with machines were done with shovel and wheelbarrow, pick and hoe. Formally, no one was forced to go to the camps, but refusing to go meant one would be denied relief benefits. Over

den Street. The house was on two city lots. That left plenty of room for the family dogs, and one lot was turned into a garden. Roast beef or roast pork was a staple for Sunday dinner. The boys found part-time jobs a few blocks from their home, cutting alder trees on land that would later become the Langara golf course. In 1932 Gosden pre-empted forty acres of land on the Sunshine Coast between Gibson's Landing (later renamed Gibsons) and Port Mellon, and with the help of John and Bill he built a rough cabin on it. Accessible only by water, it was the first property he had owned, and he was inordinately proud of the land and the shack. While Isabella visited the place occasionally, it was his getaway, and it remained rough, furnished simply and plainly.[4]

He was still friends with Owen Paulson and Ethel Cuthbertson, who both visited him and Isabella. Paulson married Beryl Gillis in 1926, and this apparently disappointed Ethel, who had hoped to marry Paulson herself. Beryl Gillis was the daughter of William Gillis, a rum-runner who, along with his son, was murdered in 1924 by three men who hijacked their cargo. Their boat, the Beryl G, was named after Beryl Gillis, and the grisly murder made headlines in British Columbia. Beryl was welcomed in the Gosden/Bunyan household and, like Ethel and Isabella, was fascinated by mysticism, spiritualism, and the occult.[5]

But Gosden's love of intrigue and politics did not disappear. With the onset of the depression in 1929, governments were unprepared to deal with mass unemployment. Welfare was primarily the responsibility of municipalities, but the communities were ill-equipped to look after those who desperately needed help. Vancouver was particularly hard-hit, for its relatively benign winters attracted those who had to sleep outside in hobo camps or "jungles." As conditions worsened, many Canadians again turned to socialism and to communism to try to find solutions. Terrified by the prospect of angry young men, provincial and federal authorities came up with a scheme of relief camps, designed to take men out of the cities and put them to work on government and private works. That, however, made it easier for labour organizers to unite the men, who now protested against the poor camp conditions as well as unemployment. As a result, authorities were keenly interested in locating and removing "troublemakers."

Once again, Robert Gosden was quick to take advantage of the situation. He made his way to the string of relief camps at Deroche, BC, about

170,000 men passed through the camps between 1932 and 1936.

The camps were designed to end political protests and to provide near-slave labour for government and private industry. If they succeeded in the second objective, they failed in the first. The camps brought together large groups of men and forced them to live and work in squalid conditions. Soon the camps themselves became the target of protests, and the men created the Relief Camp Workers' Union to push for real work and real wages. In April 1935, thousands left the BC camps and made their way to Vancouver. There they supported themselves by "tin-canning," that is, asking people on the street for donations and help. The protesters marched in the streets, snake-

Crowd gathers at Granville and Hastings in the aftermath of the police attack on the Post Office sit-in.

danced through the Hudson's Bay Company store in downtown Vancouver, and occupied the city museum and library. After two months of such actions, they decided to go to Ottawa to speak directly with Prime Minister Bennett. As many as a thousand men left Vancouver on 3 June on the On-to-Ottawa Trek, riding on freight trains. The Trek was hastily but well organized. Supporters gave the men food and shelter along the way, and the Trek gathered momentum and trekkers as it moved east.

Bennett, however, determined to stop it at Regina, where a Liberal government was in power and where the RCMP was headquartered. The Trekkers were kept off the trains and herded into the Regina Exhibition Grounds while eight delegates were allowed to meet with Bennett. The meeting soon broke down, and Bennett ordered the leaders of the trek arrested. Police moved into the Exhibition Grounds and with tear gas and clubs started the Regina Riot. One policeman was killed, probably shot by a fellow officer, and scores of Trekkers were injured, but the publicity only hardened public opinion against Bennett. The relief camps became a political issue, and the Liberal William Lyon Mackenzie King ordered the camps closed when he became prime minister in 1935.

thirty kilometres west of Harrison Hot Springs. There he prepared lengthy reports that he later gave to the district engineer of New Westminster, who forwarded them to the BC attorney-general's office. The tone of the reports echoed that of his earlier ones for the RCMP; if anything, they were more alarmist, and they strongly suggest that Gosden had moved significantly to the right.

He provided a list of names of men who "in the event of a show-down...should be rounded up" and hinted that he had information on "a minority more secret, dangerous, and irreconcilable." He was not prepared to give these names, he claimed, as it would serve no purpose unless the authorities were prepared to act. In fact, Gosden was probably pretending to hold back information in the hope of being hired by the police. He warned, much as he had as Agent 10, that a firm hand was needed, even though the organizers had not advocated violence. Jailing "the very mediocre leaders" only gave them "notoriety and hero worship." He attacked the government for its meagre relief schemes, charging that it was "committing political suicide and forcing on anarchy and bloodshed." Gosden was outraged by what he believed was a relief system that forced

thousands of men, fathers of families, taxpayers and home builders...to exist upon a miserable dole of about four dollars worth of groceries carried home in a sack each week, whilst thousands of young able-bodied men, many of them aliens, and a good percentage revolutionists, who pay open allegiance to a

116

foreign country and its plans of world conquest, sworn enemies of our constitution, are being fed, housed, and looked after upon the best of food and sanitary facilities possible, with cooks to feed them, flunkies to wait upon them, bull cooks to warm their sleeping quarters, carry the fuel, warm the water for their shower baths, and call them up in the morning, yet, when asked to give service in useful labor for this, they refuse and practically tell your Government and the starving taxpayers who feed them to go to hell.

His long rant, filled with anti-immigrant sentiment and red-baiting, shows no sympathy for the unemployed. In part it reflected the view of the old Wobbly who detested the state rule of the Bolsheviks and understood that in some measure the Canadian Communists were shaped by Moscow. More importantly, it reflected the change in his own condition. No longer the young radical, Gosden seems resentful and bitter that the unemployed of the 1930s appeared to have it softer than he did in the 1910s. And now, a taxpayer and home builder himself, he was outraged.

His second report continued the theme. In it he insisted, "your Government will fail if you allow one physically sound person to get food without reasonable service." Again he suggested the arrest, jailing, and deportation of the men on his list, and again he railed against "malcontents" and "foreigners." Gosden added that the RCMP should be requested to assist the provincial police, "because for purely psychological reasons the mounties are

Protests over unemployment did not end when the camps were closed, however. As the depression worsened in the fall of 1937, more and more unemployed flowed into Vancouver. Again they supported themselves with tincanning and tag days. When the city banned panhandling, the men had no way to survive.

On 11 May 1938 over 1,200 protestors took action. They divided into three groups and took over the Vancouver Art Gallery (now the Carnegie Centre at Hastings and Main), the Georgia Hotel, and the main Post Office (now the Sinclair Centre). Led by Steve Brodie and other On-to-Ottawa Trek veterans, the men occupied the buildings and refused to leave. They held the Georgia Hotel for ten days, then left when they were given relief vouchers. But the protestors remained in the art gallery and post office. People brought them food and supplies, sometimes passing it up in baskets hauled in by ropes dropped from windows. The protestors organized classes and lectures inside the buildings and sang songs.

On the morning of 20 June the men left the art gallery. At the same time, city, provincial, and federal police surrounded the post office, where 600 men remained inside. The protestors debated whether they should surrender and be arrested or stay inside. They voted to remain inside and continue the protest. The police flooded the building with tear-gas bombs, then sent in riot squads armed with batons. Windows were smashed as protestors fought to get air and tried to defend themselves against the police attack. Eyes streaming, gasping for breath, they were dragged outside and herded down to Cordova Street by mounted police with riding whips. When Brodie was forced outside, he was clubbed by two policemen until an RCMP sergeant noticed the beating was being filmed and intervened to stop it.

The brutal police attack angered many in Vancouver. Nearly 20,000 people gathered in the city to protest the police action; another 2,000 marched in Victoria. The photographs of the men, especially the picture of Steve Brodie beaten and bleeding, became a symbol of the unemployed resistance.

Did the unemployed protests accomplish anything? Unquestionably their actions led to the closing of the relief camps and the defeat of R.B. Bennett. More importantly, they laid a foundation for political action during World War Two. When the war began in 1939, the economy heated up, just as it had during World War One. Again workers organized into unions – this time in the new industrial

feared more by the bohunk type." If his advice was not followed to the letter, Gosden warned, "your camps will burn and your commiserate [sic, probably commissariat] will be looted." He concluded by hinting he had more secret information he could divulge, and offered his services to government. These would require his "being given carte blanche action of movement as I might need." He was available to meet with government officials, he said, but warned that "whatever actions are taken must be carried out promptly if peace and order are to reign."

The reports were passed up the line, and Sergeant W.A. MacBrayne of the BC Provincial Police was sent to investigate the camps and interview Gosden. MacBrayne found no cause for alarm. Many of the men on Gosden's list had already left the camps, while no record could be found of others. Some men had been ordered out of the camps for refusing to work, but on the whole, MacBrayne believed the situation was well in hand. He then spent two hours with Gosden, where he learned of Gosden's earlier work for the RCMP. He believed that Gosden was probably trying to secure protection or employment from the police, despite his "Socialistic leanings." He doubted that too much attention should be paid to these leanings, for MacBrayne had "noticed in the past in connection with agents that they possibly unconsciously air their socialistic views especially if they are mixing with that element." Gosden had "very sound" ideas about undercover work, MacBrayne concluded, and "if reliable, would make a good undercover man."

Was he reliable? The BC Provincial Police contacted the RCMP to find out. His old handler, J.W. Spalding, now commanding Saskatchewan District, acknowledged that he had worked for them before but concluded that he had been unreliable and untrustworthy as an agent. Spalding noted that Gosden had sent duplicate copies of his Deroche reports to the RCMP. That was "an indication that he would like to secure service with us, but the fact he has furnished us copies of his reports that rightly belong to the BC Government shows his unreliability." Superintendent S.T. Wood, commanding BC District, added that after leaving the RCMP, Gosden had been "mixed up in a case of obtaining money by false pretences and later was arrested for attempted arson, the case against him being dismissed." Wood noted parenthetically that a "local Barrister of Vancouver, Mr. Gordon Wismer, is well acquainted with Gosden and his activities." This is particularly interesting, for Wismer was a member of the Liberal party and would, in the following year, become the MLA for Vancouver Centre, the riding held by M.A. Macdonald until 1921. Wismer was, by 1925, part of the "Vancouver machine" and was widely regarded as a corrupt politico who, together with J.W. de Beque Farris, was responsible for handing out liquor licences to Liberal cronies. Wismer later became BC's attorney-general in the Pattullo government and perfected a political machine that journalist Blair Fraser in *Maclean's* magazine suggested shared with a Montreal riding "the gamiest reputation in Canada." While it has not been possible to trace Gosden's

unions of the Congress of Industrial Organizations and the Canadian Congress of Labour – and again they won many of their demands.

Throughout the war, Canadians increasingly supported reform, labour, and left-wing candidates in federal and provincial elections. Fred Rose, a member of the Communist Party, was elected to the House of Commons in 1943 and again in 1945; the CCF elected eight MPs in 1940 and twenty-eight in 1945. The CCF became the official opposition in British Columbia and Ontario and became the government in Saskatchewan in 1944.

This support for the left, coupled with Prime Minister King's vivid memories of the revolt of 1919 and the depression protests, pushed the Liberals to create significant reforms during the war and after. Unemployment insurance, welfare, expanded post-secondary education, health care, federal intervention in the economy, protection for trade unions, and other reforms were drafted. Without the threat of militant action in the streets and at the polls, it is unlikely these measures would have been put in place. In this way, the sacrifices of the unemployed resistors in the 1930s undoubtedly created the public and political will for important changes in the Canadian economy and body politic.

For many years, when British Columbians talked about William Bennett, they did not mean W.A.C. Bennett or his son Bill. William Bennett, often called "Ol' Bill," was an organizer and writer for the Communist Party of Canada, and his weekly column, "Short Jabs," ran in a number of CPC newspapers.

Bennett was a contemporary of Robert Gosden, born in Greenock, Scotland, in 1881. He trained as a barber and joined the Scottish Labour Party in 1897, where he opposed Britain's Boer War. Bennett emigrated to BC in 1907 and set up a barber shop in the skid-road district of Vancouver. He soon joined the Socialist Party of Canada, where he was an admirer of E.T. Kingsley and a contributor to the party's paper, the *Western Clarion*. In the 1912 provincial election, Bennett ran as a Vancouver City candidate for the SPC but did not win.

The relative collapse of the SPC during the First World War, the tumult of the Winnipeg General Strike, and the success of the Bolsheviks drew Bennett to the CPC when it was formed in 1922. A delegate to the founding convention of the Workers' Party of Canada, he was a regular party speaker and commentator.

In 1935 he helped found the *BC Workers' News* and soon began his "Short Jabs."

relationship with Wismer, the two undoubtedly had much in common and perhaps found each other useful on occasion.[6]

It has been impossible to learn whether Gosden was hired by the police, and even his politics in this period remain a puzzle. The depression clearly caused many to forget their principles: David Rees, the UMWA delegate who had denounced Gosden as a spy at the Western Labor Conference, was suspended from the CCF for taking a job as foreman in a relief camp. Gosden's step-sons and friends remember that he sympathized with the CCF and that he knew the party's leader, Ernest Winch. There is some evidence that he corresponded with the CCF. But he still met regularly with politicos from the Conservative and Liberal parties, usually at Vancouver's White Lunch restaurant, and still, according to his step-son John, "making money off of both of them."[7]

In 1936, however, Gosden again attracted some public attention, and this time his politics seemed clear enough. Communist journalist Bill Bennett singled out Gosden in the CPC newspaper, the *BC Workers' News*. Bennett, who had known Gosden since about 1910, devoted a large part of one column to attacking him for working for local political and radio personality Tom McInnes. McInnes was the son of Thomas R. McInnes, BC lieutenant-governor from 1897 to 1900. Closely connected with the right-wing Shipping Federation, a group of shipping companies and other employers, McInnes Jr. formed the reactionary Nationalist Party of Canada in the 1930s and devoted newspaper columns and radio broadcasts to attacking the left and the labour movements of the day. Often accused of being a fascist, McInnes was certainly on the hard right and frequently espoused racist views. According to Bennett, Gosden was employed as "bodyguard to the fascist radio-orator." Gosden was, Bennett continued, "an individual with the most unsavory reputation that ever blackened the labor movement of this province." Taking the standard CP line on the Wobblies, Bennett characterized the IWW as "that conglomerate of religious enthusiasts and political confusionists" and noted that Gosden was one of its leaders. He criticized the coffee speech and claimed Gosden had been Macdonald's "first lieutenant" in the plugging scandal. He inflated the fifty dollars Gosden claimed he received to several thousand dollars and suggested that Gosden had been given the janitor's job by Richard McBride as a reward. He outlined the Western Labor Conference accusations and concluded that Gosden was now part of the Nationalist Party "riff-raff ready to prostitute their manhood for the measly dish of pottage the lords of society hand out to them for doing the dirty, scabby, strike-breaking work. Judas got 30 pieces of silver. Whatever McInnes gets, Gosden certainly does not get more than 30 pieces of copper."[8]

There is no record that Gosden responded to Bennett's column in subsequent issues of the BC *Workers' News*. There is no further information on Gosden until 1938, when Isabella Bunyan died, age fifty-six, on 4 July. The memorial service was given by the Theosophical Society. Gosden and

The column continued through several Party newspapers, including *The People*, *The Advocate*, and the *Pacific Tribune*. Bennett had an earthy, punchy style with which he commented on labour, politics, current events, and other topics from an orthodox CPC position. In 1936 he wrote *Builders of British Columbia*, an overview of the province's labour history that is still useful and interesting today.

Bennett died in Vancouver on 31 December 1949. In 1951 his friend and fellow CPCer Tom McEwen published *He Wrote for Us: The Story of Bill Bennett, Pioneer Socialist Journalist*, a short biography that quotes from many of Bennett's columns and outlines the CPC position on labour and politics.

the boys, now in their twenties, had to leave the house, and Gosden probably returned to his pre-emption in Gibson's Landing for a time.

By 1944 he was living in West Vancouver at 2463 Marine Drive, in a house owned by another widow, Mrs. C. Mabel Smith. They were together for a number of years, and when Smith moved to 3494 Marine Drive in 1947, Gosden moved with her. During these years the city directories list his occupation as gardener. By 1950 Smith and Gosden appear to have separated. Sometime between 1950 and her death in 1966, age eighty-two, Smith moved to 2196 Argyle Avenue with her daughter Joyce but without Gosden.

Around 1950 he began a relationship with Helena Margaret Hesson. Helena was the daughter of Alexander Roger and Elizabeth Ellen Hesson, both Vancouver pioneers. Alexander came to Vancouver in 1887 and prospected for gold in the Yukon Gold Rush. He ran a Cordova street grocery store for several years, and in 1904 purchased Victoria's Leland Hotel. Elizabeth Ellen emigrated to Soda Creek, BC in 1885, and then to Vancouver. The two had seven children, five girls and two boys.

Helena Hesson was born in Victoria in 1889, and was raised in Vancouver. She taught native children in Soda Creek for a year, then returned to Vancouver to finish her training at the Vancouver normal school. Her next teaching job was in a classroom in a house at 599 W. 19th Avenue. The school, known as DL 472, had only one room for twenty-five boys and girls, all under ten years old. Later, Hesson taught at Shaughnessy Elementary School. She taught first and second grade throughout her career, and was granted a second class teaching certificate in 1912. She earned $750 that year, probably more than Gosden earned as a labourer. Her salary went up regularly, and she moved to Edith Cavell Annex in 1920.

Hesson stayed at Cavell until 1925, when she transferred to Oak Street Elementary. Five years later, she returned to Cavell. The onset of the depression, however, meant that business lobbied to slash public salaries. Hesson's was cut in 1931, cut again the following year, and yet again in 1933. In all, Hesson saw her annual income lowered by nearly 30 per cent over three years. By 1936, when she transferred to Aberdeen Elementary, the economy improved somewhat, and Hesson's pay was increased to about

$1,600, still far short of her pre-depression earnings. Not until 1942 would she regain her pre-depression salary. She transferred to Kerrisdale Elementary in 1938 and then to Lord Selkirk Elementary in East Vancouver the following year, where she remained until 1949. She married Bob Gosden on 18 June 1949, two weeks before she officially retired.[9]

Helena invested her salary in property, and owned buildings that she rented out. When she and Gosden married in 1950 or 1951, they moved to a house she had purchased in Gibson's Landing, at 627 Marine Drive. Ironically, Gosden's old foe David Rees also retired to Gibson's Landing, though it is not known if the two men ever met there. Gosden kept his shack on the pre-empted land and often retreated there. Oddly enough, given his earlier life, many who met the Gosdens in this period thought he was quiet and unassuming, even dominated by his wife.[10]

Gosden became more interested in the occult over time, attending seances and exploring Theosophy and other mystic religions. He was an early survivalist who was always encouraging people to cache food. He believed the world economy was likely to collapse at any moment and that it would be necessary to have food and weapons stockpiled if one was to survive. He followed his own advice: he kept grain and canned goods hidden on his pre-emption and carried a sword cane. His love of intrigue stayed with him as well. In 1951, age sixty-nine, he sent a letter to John Cates, BC minister of labour responsible for native Indian affairs and land claims. He claimed he had found an old British dispatch case, long hidden in the woods, that contained an early treaty document between natives and government officials. He gave detailed instructions on how to find the case, emphasizing that he was not seeking publicity but that a quiet reconnoitre might prove useful to the government. If the denial of a desire for publicity seems rather out of character, the old themes of hidden knowledge and intrigue remain as clues to his earlier experiments in espionage.[11]

His politics continued to veer to the right. Among his papers were three pages of notes, quoting newspapers and Hansard, on the evils of public debt. In language that borrowed from the right-wing anti-Semitism of Major C.H. Douglas, the founder of Social Credit, Gosden warned that Abraham Lincoln's issuance of paper money led to the Americans being "controlled by Interna-

COMMUNIST PARTY OF CANADA

By 1921 the left was in disarray again. Parliamentary socialism had failed; radical socialism and syndicalism had been crushed after the 1919 revolt; even the new One Big Union was foundering. What could be done to continue the struggle?

For many radicals, the success of Lenin and the Bolshevik Party in seizing control of the Russian Revolution in 1917 seemed an appropriate model. In June 1921, delegates in Guelph, Ontario, founded the Communist Party of Canada. It was based on the Bolshevik model of a "party of a new type." This meant several things. First, the party would pursue a radical, not a reformist, program, while still taking part in parliamentary politics. To ensure it remained revolutionary and did not devolve into reformism, a leadership cadre would be created. Second, the party would follow the principle of democratic centralism; that is, there would be open debate until a decision was made, then strict obedience to the party decision. That would end the schisms that had hurt the IWW and other groups. If this sounds undemocratic to Canadians, we might recall that this is the way the Canadian cabinet and parliamentary system work. Finally, there would be both an open, legal party and a secret,

tional Finance (i.e. Barney Baruch and Co.)." Baruch was a Jewish-American financier and advisor to the US government during both world wars, and he was a favourite target of anti-Semites. Gosden also made references to the "Protocols of Zion," probably the notorious *Protocols of the Elders of Zion*. This was a book faked by agents of the Russian czarist regime and passed off as a real document, allegedly written by Jewish conspirators, that outlined a Jewish plot to take over the world.[12]

And yet Gosden continued to have some sympathy for working-class politics. He sometimes reflected on his life as a migrant worker and would on occasion recite poetry that he had learned on the road years before. One was a poem scratched on the wall of the San Diego jail by a man named Hawkins, imprisoned with Gosden for his role in the free speech fight:

> *We are the people who God has forgot,*
> *And here we sit, or lie,*
> *In this vile Bastille we will rot,*
> *Or from starvation die,*
> *If this poor, sleepy, wooden-shoed town*
> *Don't give us the right to speak*
> *Or mount a soapbox where we like*
> *On any damned old street.*
> *They've stacked their cards for the cutthroat game*
> *And we put up the stake.*
> *Play we must and play we will,*
> *Until the last heart breaks.*
> *We'll stay till Christ comes back on earth*
> *To gather up the meek.*
> *Or we'll put this old town on the bum,*
> *Just for the right to speak!*[13]

The work of Robert Service, whom Gosden claimed to have met, was a favourite, but it was not the familiar, humourous verse of "The Cremation of Sam McGee" that he had committed to memory. Instead, it was the hard-edged poem "The Men That Don't Fit In." Maudlin and sentimental, it may well reflect Gosden's appraisal of his own life:

...He is one of the Legion Lost;
He was never meant to win;
He's a rolling stone, and it's bred in the bone;
He's a man who won't fit in.[14]

Gosden still talked about the need for a workers' revolution and thought the collapse of capitalism was inevitable and desirable. He kept with him until his death postcards of Wesley Everest and Joe Hill, the famous Wobbly martyrs. After the murder of the well-known organizers, these postcards were issued by the Industrial Workers of the World to commemorate them and to raise money for the union. On the back of a picture of Joe Hill, Gosden had written,

"Lest we Forget," Bobby Burns said.
A man is thought a knave, a fool,
A bigot plotting Crime
Who for the advancement of his kind
Is wiser than his time.

For him the gibbet shall be built
For him the stake prepared
For him the hemlock shall distil
For him the axe be bared.

underground party. That would protect the party from repression by the authorities.

The legal party was organized as the Workers Party of Canada in February 1922. The new party attracted radicals from many different groups, including the Wobblies, the SPC, the SPD, and the One Big Union. The Communist Party of Canada quickly affiliated with the Communist International, or Comintern, led by the Soviet Union, and at least in its official policy it followed the decisions and programs of the Comintern. When Stalin became the leader of the Soviet Union, this meant the Canadian Party followed the twists and turns of his foreign policy and often acted as an apologist for Stalin's crimes and mistakes.

The CPC's contribution to the labour and left movements and its effectiveness are still hotly debated. What cannot be denied is the leading role Party members had in organizing industrial unions in the 1930s. Annie Buller and Rebecca Buhay in the Industrial Needle Trades Workers, Harold Pritchett in the International Woodworkers of America (IWA), Harvey Murphy in the International Union of Mine, Mill, and Smelter Workers (Mine-Mill), and Arthur "Slim" Evans in the Relief Camp Workers Union are just a few of the people who helped form new unions and organize workers that the craft and conservative unions would not go near. Organizing is difficult work anytime; in the depth of the depression it was nearly impossible. But organizers in the CPC took on the job and reminded workers that unions were especially necessary when times were hard. Its work was crucial to the organizing of Vancouver's longshoremen in the 1930s and to the success of the IWA. Even those union organizers who later left the Party owed some of their success to lessons they had learned in it.

In 1936, when the fascist Franco launched a coup d'état against the democratically elected Spanish government, the CPC, along with other groups such as the CCF, recruited people to join and support the International Brigade. This was a volunteer force that gathered people from around the world to go to Spain to defend the legal government and fight fascism. The Mackenzie-Papineau Battalion, named after two leaders of Canada's 1837 Rebellion, was formed later and took part in some of the heaviest fighting of the Spanish Civil War.

The Party often clashed with the Co-operative Commonwealth Federation. In its quest for electoral success, the CCF tried to appeal to labour, the middle class, and business with its moderate program. Often that meant

Him shall the scorn and hate of men
Pursue with deadly aim
And envy, malice, hatred, lies,
Shall desecrate his name.

So *"Adios Joe,"* El Capitan Musiciale, la Union Industriale Travaro del Monde

He wrote to Aneurin Bevan, British Labour MP and health minister, in 1957, outlining his adventures as a radical. His original letter cannot be found, but Bevan's reply gives some indication of its content:

I was most interested to read your reminiscences about Jack London and your own struggles for our movement. Unfortunately there isn't enough time to conduct really heart to heart correspondence in the way I would like to, but letters such as yours are most encouraging.

Gosden also left about twelve pages of autobiographical sketches that talked proudly about his meetings with another IWW martyr, Frank Little, in 1912, and with the anarchist organizer Lucy Parsons. The accuracy of his accounts, entitled "Heard Round the Coffee Tables in the White Lunch at Midnight" and "A Reminiscence of Long Ago, Overheard in the White Lunch: 'Local Colour,'" is thrown into doubt by his recounting a later meeting with Frank Little, years after Little's murder, in a seance and by his casting one of the sketches as a story told to a reporter by someone else. Yet Frank Little did take part in the Mexican revolution and Lucy Parsons did speak in

Vancouver, and it is certainly possible that Gosden met both of them. Perhaps as significant is the fact that he believed it important to write about them late in life. The stories are evocative, and one ends powerfully with the underscored words:

These Joe Hills and Frank Littles in their countless thousands, are working and helping to complete what they died for, and you will meet them, sooner than you may think, for remember, they cannot be killed now, but they

A postcard of Joe Hill kept by Gosden.

sacrificing labour so the CCF would appear balanced, respectable, and responsible. In the 1940s the CCF decided to raid or take over unions led by the CPC so it would have access to union dues and would not face the competition of the CPC at election time. In a series of purges aided by business and government and the hysteria of the Cold War, the CCF removed the CPC leadership from most of the unions and federations in which it had a foothold. The Party held on in a few unions, notably in BC in the United Fishermen and Allied Workers Union (UFAW), but it was weakened and over time became much less influential.

The CPC was active in the peace movement and in civic politics. It was particularly successful in Vancouver, where in 1947 it supported Effie Jones and the Civic Reform Committee. Jones nearly won the mayoralty race against the business-supported Non-Partisan Association. In the 1960s and 1970s, Bruce Yorke, Bruce Erickson, Libby Davies, and Harry Rankin would sit on the city council and would owe some of their support to the work of the CPC.

The Communist Party made many contributions to the cultural life of BC workers. In 1952, for example, Harvey Murphy, the BC head of Mine-Mill, asked the famous African-American singer Paul Robeson to sing at the union's convention. Robeson was closely connected to the US Communist Party, and the American government used a little-known law to refuse to allow him to leave the United States. The union, however, organized an outdoor concert at the Peace Arch on 18 May 1952. From the back of a flatbed truck parked two feet inside the US border, Robeson sang to a crowd of 40,000 in the parkland landscaped by relief camp labour nearly twenty years before. He returned three more times to sing at the Peace Arch; by the last time, the US government finally relented and allowed him to leave his own country.

The CPC started People's Co-op Bookstore, an alternative bookstore, still thriving today, that stocked books on labour, politics, and culture that mainstream stores rarely carried. Party newspapers were often lively and informative, even though they followed the official line faithfully. Writers such as William Bennett and Hal Griffin produced important books on BC labour and politics from a radical perspective, and Party members were active in the folksong revival of the 1950s and 1960s.

The CPC has been criticized from the left and the right, and much of this criticism is deserved. Its leadership was often dogmatic and quick to follow the Party line

can and do help the cause of progress...The ruling class are now absolutely insane, and are committing social suicide which is the Karma they have earned.[16]

Until the end of his life, Gosden kept to an odd credo that blended right-wing conspiracy theory, mysticism, and left-wing politics. While he still had strong views about capital and labour, he appears to have had little involvement in politics after the 1930s. As an observer, however, he would have seen many parallels with the years of his own involvement as activist and spy.

In both periods, an economic depression was followed by a world war. During the Second World War, workers moved to the left, joined unions, and went on strike in greater numbers, just as they had done during the First World War and for many of the same reasons. And after both wars, capital, the state, and conservative union leaders and reform politicians were generally successful in stopping the workers' revolt.

In the 1940s and 1950s, however, the methods they used were different. Prime Minister Mackenzie King was determined that the chaos of 1919 would not be repeated. Long before the war ended, his government put policies in place to ease the transition to the peace-time economy. Ironically, the Liberal programs echoed the spirit, and even some of the specific details, of the suggestions Gosden made to Harlan Brewster in 1916 and to Robert Borden in 1919.

In particular, King and the Liberals created a social safety net that included unemployment insurance, a national welfare system, increased spending on housing and education, the family allowance, the Canada Pension Plan, and other measures. The government did not grant these measures because they were just. On the contrary, the Liberals were pushed to the left by working people who made it clear, by voting for left-wing candidates and going on strike, that they would no longer support political parties that listened primarily to business. If the Liberals were to stay in power, King concluded, they would have to walk a fine line. They had to provide enough reform to win popular support while avoiding any real restructuring of the economy. Unemployment insurance was a good example of his political manoeuvring. In the 1930s, workers demanded unemployment insurance that was funded entirely by business. King did provide unemployment insurance, but collected money from business and workers to pay for it. Business grumbled at having to pay anything at all, but in the years of post-war prosperity its contributions, little though they were, were enough to blunt the demand for more radical change.

Gosden would have recognized another post-war strategy as well. While capital and the state did not repress workers as violently as they had in 1919, they did purge the labour movement of radicals. The red scare and McCarthyism that swept Canada and the US were aimed as much at domestic labour and the left as they were at the Soviet Union. The alleged threat of communism was a handy pretext to attack the left leadership of unions such as the IWA and Mine-Mill and to

laid out in the Soviet Union. It could be opportunistic in politics, though no more so than the Liberals, Conservatives, or CCF; its ties to the Soviet Union made many suspicious and allowed the government to red-bait the entire labour movement. Yet without the CPC, labour in BC would have stalled in the 1930s. In many ways, the Party was more significant than the CCF, for it provided inspiration, training, and focus for three generations of activists who would create new industrial unions and organize the unemployed and the unorganized.

INDUSTRIAL UNIONS SINCE THE 1930S

Militants connected to the Communist Party of Canada created and rejuvenated industrial unions in the 1920s and 1930s under the umbrella of the Workers Unity League. Perhaps the most important of these CP unions in British Columbia were the International Woodworkers of America (IWA) and the International Union of Mine, Mill, and Smelter Workers (Mine-Mill).

In the United States the battle for industrial unionism began again in 1935, with the creation of the Committee for Industrial Organization. This was a committee of the AFL, but it soon proved too radical and too interested in organizing so-called unskilled workers. After the AFL purged the committee, it renamed itself the Congress of Industrial Organizations (CIO) and created unions for workers in the mass industries of automobile manufacturing, steel, textiles, lumber, and others. Canadian workers soon followed suit. In 1940 the All-Canadian Congress of Labour merged with Canadian sections of the CIO to form the Canadian Congress of Labour (CCL).

By the 1950s, craft and industrial unions finally found common cause as attacks by business and the government, and changes in industrial production, made craft distinctions less important and less

smash unions such as the Communist-led Canadian Seamen's Union. In the last case, the Canadian government deemed an American union led by the gangster Hal Banks preferable to a Canadian union.

Gosden would also have appreciated how conservatives in the labour movement and the CCF worked with capital and the state to purge leftists and channel labour into reformism. This confirmed his prediction in 1919 that much of the dirty work could be left to the officials of the labour movement, who would protect their own positions by going after the radicals.

He likely would have applauded a final measure in the post-war period: the regulation of industrial relations. The law had always been used to control labour. Often that meant calling out the militia. Over time, however, that was recognized as counter-productive, for repression could lead to radicalism. The approach taken by King was more sophisticated. Instead of resisting unions, the state would recognize them but take away their most effective weapons.

The initial instrument to accomplish this was Privy Council Order 1003, passed in 1944. Together with subsequent federal and provincial legislation, PC 1003 established the industrial relations framework still in place today. While unions had been legal since the passage of the Trade Unions Act in 1872, employers did not have to recognize unions or bargain with them. Thus many strikes, including the 1912 strike against Canadian Collieries and the Winnipeg General Strike, were waged to try to compel the employer to begin negotiations. PC 1003 eliminated this cause of strikes by forcing employers to recognize legally constituted and certified unions that were democratically chosen by employees. If a union organized workers, employers now had to bargain with the aim of achieving a collective agreement.

Later legislation limited the actions employers could take to thwart an organizing drive by declaring some tactics illegal. These unfair labour practices included hiring or firing workers, increasing or decreasing pay, threatening workers, making promises, changing the conditions of work, and speaking about the alleged pitfalls of unions. The law acknowledged that the employer was more powerful than unorganized workers and tried to create a more even playing field during an organizing drive. New laws also provided security for unions once they had organized a work place. For example, the dues check-off gave unions a steady source of income, and the union shop made union membership a condition of employment, which prevented the employer from hiring people who would not join the union.

As a result of these legal protections, union membership shot up in the post-war years. Before the Second World War, the unionization rate in BC fluctuated between 6 percent and 13 percent, with a momentary peak in 1919 of 22 percent, which slid down to 10 percent the following year. War-time conditions saw the number climb to 29 percent, and with the passage of PC 1003, it continued to climb to a high of 55 percent in 1958. Companies such as Cominco,

useful. The CIO merged with the AFL in 1955; the CCL merged with the Trades and Labour Congress to form the Canadian Labour Congress (CLC) in 1956. In recent years, many craft unions have merged and now resemble industrial unions. And even industrial unions are broadening their base: the Canadian Auto Workers (CAW) organize office workers and restaurant workers as well as autoworkers, while the IWA has changed its name to Industrial Wood and Allied Workers to indicate that it has expanded its mandate to include workers in retail stores and restaurants.

which had resisted unionization for years, were now organized and engaged in collective bargaining.

But unions paid a price for this legal protection. They were now subject to discipline by the state: unions that did not play by the rules would not be recognized under the law and would not be protected by it. That encouraged the labour movement to abandon radical ideas and radical tactics. The newly won collective agreements set out wages and conditions, but left most other issues to management. How work was done, company policy, technological change – all of crucial importance to workers – were viewed as decisions for management and could not be taken up in negotiations. The battle now was simply for a bigger piece of the pie. That the pie itself might be rotten, as Wobblies, socialists, and communists had argued, was no longer considered.

Most important, the new industrial relations system limited worker militancy and strike action. Bargaining could only take place when a contract had expired. That gave employers ample opportunity to prepare for a strike by stockpiling, putting on extra shifts and overtime, and training management to take over during a strike. Strikes could only be called after a vote and a drawn-out process of arbitration and conciliation. Since solidarity and militancy are often difficult to maintain, stretching out the process gave employers an advantage. Grievances could no longer be handled by strike action. Instead, they went to a formal grievance procedure. Again that gave the advantage to employers, for production continued while they argued with the union and arbitrators. Unions lost much of their power to force employers to settle quickly.

The system worked well enough for some workers in the relatively prosperous years after the war. As the economy worsened in the 1970s, however, employers set out once again to roll back wages and increase profits. The protections of the industrial relations system now entangled and frustrated workers, for employers took advantage of the law to stall organizing drives, limit strikes, and decertify unions. The rate of unionization dropped fairly steadily from 1977 on, and it has proved difficult to organize the poorly paid workers in the service and food industries. Gosden the Wobbly would have predicted this and advocated sabotage and direct action as ways to help labour secure its rights. Gosden the labour spy would have approved of both the social reforms and the curtailing of radical thought. What Gosden the older man would have thought remains a mystery.

On 11 April 1961, Robert Gosden, age seventy-eight, died in Gibson's Landing of stomach cancer. His death was not reported for three days, as Helena hoped that mystical incantations might revive him or at least set his spirit free. His friends held a small memorial service in Vancouver, conducted by the Reverend Phillip Hewett, a Unitarian minister who often undertook such duties for people involved in non-traditional religions and politics. Gosden's ashes were scattered on the land he had preempted in Gibson's Landing, near the rough shack he and John and Bill Bunyan had first put up in the 1930s. Helena outlived him for seventeen years, dying in Burnaby on 1 May 1978.

What is the historical significance of Robert Gosden? His story is interesting, but perhaps no more so than many lives. It is a useful story for the light it sheds on several aspects of labour history. First, it gives us some insight into the world of the migrant male worker in the early years of the twentieth century. In sharp contrast to the romanticized notions of the hobo and tramp, Gosden's life story boils with rage. It is the rage of the oppressed, of those who are damned to a life of harsh toil. It is a rage Gosden shared with many other Wobblies, and it is something that is often neglected when we study labour history. It is easier and more palatable to recall the humour of the Wobblies, the wry songs and cartoons, the jokes and stories.

The song by Haywire "Mac" McClintock, "Hallelujah, I'm a Bum," is a good example of that genre. McClintock parodied a popular hymn, "Hallelujah, Thine the Glory" or "Revive Us Again." The chorus of the parody is still well-known: "Hallelujah, I'm a bum, Hallelujah, bum again; Hallelujah, give us a handout, To revive us again." But McClintock also wrote a poem in 1916 that echoes Gosden's anger and forces us to remember the stark reality the working class faced. Titled "Hymn of Hate," it reads, in part –

We hate you with hand and heart and head, and body and mind and brain,
We hate at the forge, in the mine and mill, in the field of golden grain...
We shall keep our hate and cherish our hate and our hate shall ever grow,
We shall spread our hate and scatter our hate till all of the workers know.
And The Day shall come with a red, red dawn; and you in your gilded halls,
Shall taste the wrath and the vengeance of the men in the overalls.[17]

Gosden's rage was shared by the Wobbly Jim Seymour, who expressed it in his 1913 poem "The Dishwasher." Alone in the kitchen, he railed against a capitalism that "makes me a dullard in brain-burning heat," while he looked "at rich viands, not daring to eat." Seymour wrote of the "grease-laden steam," of the "foul, indescribable muck" into which he plunged his "red blistered hands." He dared the "leeches," the "overfed parasites," to

...look at my hand.
You laugh at it now, it is blistered and coarse,
But such are the hands quite familiar with force;
And such are the hands that have furnished your drink,
The hands of the slaves who are learning to think,
And hands that have fed you can crush you as well
And cast your damned carcasses clear into hell![18]

Gosden is important because he reminds us that oppression was not simply a word for those workers who built the infrastructure of BC's economy: it was a harsh, grinding, degrading, daily reality. It was a world that was manifestly unfair, and Gosden's life demonstrates just how unfair it was, even to someone who appeared to have the advantages of gender and racial privilege.

It was also a world that teaches us hard lessons about class and politics. Gosden could not have plugged an election or become a labour spy if government and business had not created the circumstances of political corruption and repression. His own crimes paled beside those of his political masters and the capitalists who exploited him and countless others.

Gosden's references to manhood are also instructive. Gender is constructed. That is, ideas about what is appropriate behaviour for men and women are not inevitable or preordained. They are fashioned by humans in particular sets of circumstances, and they change over time. Gosden's ideas about masculinity, about what it meant to be a man, reflected his own experience as a migrant, unskilled labourer. In an informal, unexamined way, he contributed to the making of what one historian has labelled "virile syndicalism" and another "Marxist masculinity."[19]

Throughout his life, images of sexuality and power were entwined: the California idealists he met in 1911 were "emasculated"; the stool pigeon Shorty O'Donnell was dared to "stand on his legs and be a man"; Parker Williams lacked the manhood to be a revolutionary, while socialists in the OBU did not have the courage of their convictions and refused to take up violence to advance the revolution, which made them unmanly, cowards, and class traitors all at once.

This vision of masculinity differed greatly from that held by respectable labour leaders and socialists. In their world of relative stability and affluence, masculinity included such respectable virtues as forthrightness, temperance, and forbearance. A man told the truth and could be depended on; he stood up and spoke his mind and was responsible for what he said and did. "The Recipe for a Union Man" printed in the Vancouver Trades and Labour Council newspaper, the Independent, called for

>...an ounce of gumption
>Just a grain of sand.
>A little independence,
>Some manly spirit, and
>Mix them well together
>With patience – if you can.
>Add to it unselfishness –
>And you have a union man.[20]

For Gosden, however, the virtues of honesty and responsibility were excuses for moderate and cowardly behaviour. Gosden's radicalism from 1910 to 1913 signified his refusal to be ground down without a fight, a fight in which every weapon was judged by its tactical, rather than its moral, worth. His call for sabotage, direct action, and violence set him apart from the reformism of labourists and parliamentary socialists on the terrain of class politics and gender relations.

Gosden's story also gives us some glimpses of the shadowy world of the labour spy. It demonstrates one man's slide from principled revolutionary to confused police agent, and if it does not elicit sympathy, it may lead to understanding. His motives were contradictory and complex, but perhaps they suggest ways to fathom the apparent illogic of right-wing movements among working people. They may provide a warning for a present-day left-wing that prefers its politics well-dressed and polite. If people like Gosden are dismissed because they are angry and violent, they are likely to find refuge on the right, which will always reward them and use them for its own purposes.

Finally, Robert Gosden reminds us that workers are as important in our history as the politicians and business owners who are more usually studied in newspapers and history books. Not all have the political significance of Bob Gosden. After all, few had the opportunity to brush shoulders with Duff Pattullo when he was a neophyte alderman in Prince Rupert, to speak on platforms with men such as Parker Williams and Jack Kavanagh, to be attacked by Liberals ranging from Harlan Brewster to John Oliver, and to help topple politicians such as M.A. Macdonald. Few are offered the opportunity to betray their fellow workers for coin of the realm. And yet this unskilled worker shaped the politics of BC in crucial and dramatic ways.

He was the exception, not the rule. Nonetheless, he also reminds us that working people, usually unknown, shape history, not as individuals but as part of a collective. If Duff Pattullo had been struck by lightning in 1911, the history of BC would have changed little, and his death would have mattered as little as that of Harlan Brewster in 1918. Someone else would have taken his place and would have found that the premier of BC was subject to much larger forces of history that he could do little about. One of those forces was, and is, the resistance of working people to the daily oppression they face. Anonymously, sometimes unknowingly, their actions in their day-to-day lives provide the wealth of the province, and their resistance provides the basis of much of its history. Robert Gosden stands in for the millions of men and women in BC and Canada whose lives go largely unrecognized and unwritten. Revolutionary, reactionary, mystic, spy, he was as unique and complex – and typical – as any. Understanding his story helps us understand, to some small degree, the working people who make the province and history.

Helena Hesson Gosden is at left and Bob Gosden is second from right.
The other two people in this photo from the 1950s are unknown

CHAPTER 6

On the Trail of a Labour Spy

SOME THOUGHTS ON DOING LABOUR HISTORY

How did I track down Robert Gosden? It was a combination of luck, digging, and assistance from several friends and colleagues. Details of where material was found are in the endnotes that begin on page 172, but a discussion of how it was found and used may be of interest to people who want to write labour history for their unions or coursework at college and university.

I first heard of Robert Gosden in 1985, when I began my Master of Arts degree in history at Simon Fraser University. My MA thesis was on the Industrial Workers of the World. Their radicalism and dedicated opposition to capitalism were exciting. In part I wanted to study the Wobblies because of my own experience as an unskilled worker in a number of jobs ranging from dish washing to construction labour to bridge-tending. I had become pretty disillusioned about conservative trade unions, none of which were interested in organizing the places I worked.

Someone once remarked that all historians write autobiography. What he meant was we each ask questions of the past that are important to us and in some way reflect our own lives, ideas, and experiences. Looking at the Wobblies was not an attempt to come to terms with my own past, but my own experience led me to think about and ask certain kinds of questions about work, unions, and social democracy.

My supervisor, Allen Seager, had come across Gosden in the course of his own research. He had read a Nanaimo *Free Press* account of the Western Labor Conference that detailed how David Rees had denounced Gosden as a spy, and he had found a newspaper story about Gosden encouraging Steveston cannery workers to think about sabotage. Seager subsequently published an article in the journal *Labour/LeTravail* where he argued that Gosden was probably working as a spy for someone during the 1912–14 Vancouver Island coal strike, and he suggested I keep an eye out for Gosden.

As part of the research for my thesis, I read theVancouver daily newspapers such as the *World*, the *Province*, the *Daily News-Advertiser*, and the *Sun*. I also read the labour newspaper the *BC Federationist*, the Socialist Party of Canada's *Western Clarion*, and the iww newspapers *IndustrialWorker*, *Solidarity*, and the *Industrial Union Bulletin*. Some were available on microfilm or as originals at theVancouver Public Library (VPL), the University of British Columbia (UBC), and Simon Fraser University (SFU) while others had to be ordered through Inter-Library Loan (ILL). Getting material from ILL took from two to four weeks. Going through theWobbly papers, I discovered Gosden had a few articles and letters printed in the *IndustrialWorker*, the iww paper published in Spokane and Seattle.The first of these talked about the Prince Rupert strike. Others called for workers to sabotage and to be more militant and revolutionary. From these I learned about his arrests in Prince Rupert and the San Diego free speech fight. Allen Seager and I had several discussions about Gosden, wondering if he had been a spy. I stoutly defended Bob, arguing that his calls for sabotage were not proof that he was an agent-provocateur. I maintained that his articles showed that he was a real revolutionary, precisely the kind of person one would expect to find in the Wobblies. In fact, I was happy to find such a radical at work in Canada. We agreed to disagree, and I forgot about Robert Raglan Gosden.

In 1987, the MA finished, I went to Memorial University of Newfoundland to take my PhD. Greg Kealey was my thesis supervisor, and he was working on a history of the RCMP and its domestic spying on radicals and labour organizations. Graduate students are notoriously short of money, and I was happy to be hired as an editorial assistant for the labour history journal *Labour/Le Travail*. One of my duties was proofreading, and one of the first pieces I proofread was a research note by Kealey on the early years of the RCMP's spying. It was an interesting article, but I sat bolt upright when I came across an excerpt from an RCMP officer in Alberta dated 1919. Reporting to his superior, the officer remarked that he was going to send special agent Robert Gosden into Hillcrest to report on developments. So Seager was right: Gosden was a spy, at least in 1919, when he was at the Western Labor Conference, if not in 1912. He was also on a list of known Bolsheviks compiled by the police. Greg and I applied under the Freedom of Information Act to see what other material the RCMP archives might hold. The request turned up nothing: there were no records of Gosden left. Our search ended, and Seager, Kealey, and I went on with other projects.

My PhD thesis was on the development of bureaucracy in the early BC labour movement. In 1988 I returned to Vancouver and started my research. I spent months in the Vancouver City Archives and in Special Collections at UBC, reading union newspapers and minutes, reports, and statistics.

I spent some time in the Angus MacInnis collection at Special Collections, a rich depository of all kinds of material on the labour and left-wing movements of British Columbia. I found little of immediate use for my thesis, but enjoyed reading the wonderful anecdotes, reminiscences, and stories. One particularly interesting collection consisted of the notes made by the Co-operative Commonwealth Federation (later the New Democratic Party) activist and MLA Dorothy Steeves. Steeves wrote a biography of early socialist and CCF leader Ernie Winch, and in the early 1960s she spoke to many old-time labour and left-wing figures as part of her research. She had extensive notes from her interviews, and I spent an enjoyable afternoon going through the accounts of these men and women who had played such a vital role in the history of the province. Here were the stories of strikes won and lost, elections fought, political ideas debated and hammered out, told by the very people who took part in them. In her notes she mentions that one of the people interviewed, John Sidaway, suggested that she go interview Bob Gosden, who lived somewhere in West Vancouver, married to Helena Hesson. Bob was a good radical, he said, but unfortunately got tangled up in that political scandal of 1917.

What political scandal? I asked. Could there be more on Gosden? Might there be enough information to put together the story of this radical, sabotage advocate, and spy? That night I pulled out my copies of Margaret Ormsby's *British Columbia: A History* and Martin Robin's *The Rush for Spoils: The Company Province, 1871–1933*. Together these two books provide the story of BC's political history with verve, detail, and analysis that more recent accounts cannot touch. But as far as I could tell, there was no political scandal of 1917. Ormsby did talk about a by-election in 1916 in which men were brought up from Seattle to vote illegally – the so-called "plugging scandal." Robin mentioned the incident briefly, characterizing it as a plot involving "rowdies...thugs and renegade Wobblies." Could Gosden be one of those "renegade Wobblies"?

I checked Robin's footnotes and found that the references to the incident came from the *Canadian Annual Review* for 1916. The CAR was a quirky publication, put together from 1901 to 1926 by John Castell Hopkins, who combed Canadian newspapers for stories and items that he would edit and comment on. It is an idiosyncratic source that reflects the pet peeves, gripes, and causes of the editor, and it is still a useful series to consult. It was extremely useful in the search for Gosden, for there Hopkins told the story of the plugging scandal in greater detail and mentioned one of the renegade Wobblies by name: Robert Gosden.

I finally had a real lead. Using the CAR article as a guide for dates, I looked at the daily press for news of the plugging scandal and Robert Gosden. Since the scandal and the subsequent investigation by the government was of great interest to newspapers and politicians, there were several stories that mentioned Gosden, sometimes in great detail. He was called as a witness and questioned about his involvement with the election fraud, and in the course of the investigation he gave a great deal of personal information, including details of his early life in Canada and his involvement with the IWW and the Vancouver Island miners' strike of 1912–14. Here I read about Gosden's different jobs, from ditch-digging to construction, his travels from Glace Bay to San Diego, and his political adventures from the IWW to the Liberal party.

The newspapers told me something else about Gosden as well. As part of my research for my MA thesis I had read the book *Those Stormy Years,* communist George Hardy's memoirs of the years he had spent in British Columbia. I remembered a story Hardy told about a militant who, during the Vancouver Island coal strike, made a speech warning the premier about tasting his coffee and how that militant, now working as a janitor, had later asked Hardy if he wanted to spy on labour organizations in return for a comfortable job. In the newspaper stories on the plugging scandal it was revealed that Robert Gosden was the radical who had hinted darkly at assassinating the premier. From the *CAR* I had learned that Gosden had been employed as a janitor in the parliament buildings. Hardy's reminiscence was a strong suggestion that Gosden was a spy.

Or was it? I went through the newspapers to find a record of Gosden's speech and discovered the discrepancies in Hardy's story mentioned above. It was too early to damn Gosden, I thought.

I now had a good deal of material. It still wasn't enough for an article; at best I had seven or eight pages of material, centred on his involvement in the plugging scandal and ending in 1919 with his working for the RCMP. I put Gosden away and continued to work on my PhD thesis.

But writing a thesis can be boring and frustrating. I continued to look at the Gosden material and tried to find more material on him whenever I needed a break. I looked in the city directories of Vancouver and found out where a Robert Gosden lived and what he worked at in the 1930s. City directories, available at the VPL and Vancouver City Archives, as well as some university libraries, list people by name and by address, and they list occupations. But it still didn't add up to much. I kept my eyes open when I read the labour newspapers and when I searched the records of cemeteries as part of my thesis research. Some cemetery records are now available over the Internet, but when I was doing my research in 1989, I ended up going in to the Vancouver City Archives and to the Fraserview Cemetery itself to search for Gosden: nothing. My thesis research took me to the BC Archives and Records Service (BCARS) in Victoria, where I searched through the attorney-general's papers, BC Provincial Police files, and papers of the premier's office. In the premier's correspondence file I found the letter from Gosden to Harlan Brewster shortly after his election

in 1916, but this was of limited value. I tried to get Gosden's death certificate from the department of Vital Statistics, but the records are arranged
by date of death. Without knowing roughly when Gosden died, I would
have to pay for a records search, and this I could not afford.

I continued to read about spies, and one of the most useful articles was
that by Stan Horrall, the RCMP archivist. In his article, he wrote of "Agent
10" who had attended the Western Labour Conference. I talked to Greg
Kealey about Agent 10, and he forwarded a copy of Agent 10's report that
he had found in his research, the one in which the agent suggested the
government could end the wave of strikes by making the socialist leaders
disappear. Since I knew Gosden had been at the convention, I asked Mr.
Horrall if Gosden might be Agent 10. He was rather skeptical, as we had
no direct proof. He supplied me with a great deal of fascinating information on the structure of the early intelligence service, but nothing on Gosden. Once more, the trail had grown cold.

On a whim, I wrote letters to the newspapers, asking if any readers
knew anything of Robert Gosden or his wife, Helena Hesson. A week or
so after the letters were published, I received a telephone call from Ann
McLeod, a woman who had worked with Helena. Both women were
teachers in Vancouver at Lord Selkirk School in the 1940s, and Ms
McLeod had known Hesson and Robert Gosden for a time. She knew that
the two had married sometime in the 1950s, that they had lived on the
Sunshine Coast, and that Gosden had died some years after that. Ms
McLeod had visited Helena often when Helena went into a nursing home
in Burnaby, and she told me the name of the nursing home and that
Helena had died in 1978.

Was this a lead? It seemed remote. It was more than ten years since
Helena had died, and probably twenty years since Gosden's death. It was
unlikely they would even keep records on clients long deceased. What could
a nursing home tell me about these people anyway? But I was curious and I
wanted a break from writing my thesis. I called up the nursing home and
spoke with someone in its records department. They still had the records on
Helena. The records consisted largely of bills, payments, and treatments, and
these could not be released to me. They would be of little value in any case.

There was, however, a contact number from 1978, and they could give me that. I took the number down and thanked them for their help.

The number seemed like another fruitless lead. What were the odds that the same people lived there or were even alive? I certainly didn't want to bother people needlessly. And yet, it was the only thing I had to go on. My partner, Annette, checked out the number in old telephone directories. She found out it was registered to the same people, the Arthurs, from the 1970s to the present. It was a number in Gibsons. I dialed the number and explained to the man who answered who I was and what I was doing. Then I asked him, "Did you know a man named Robert Gosden?" There was a pause, and he replied, "I knew Bob Gosden well. He died in my arms."

I was stunned. When I recovered the power of speech I asked if we could get together. He said he would be delighted, that we could take the ferry to Gibsons and he would meet us there. Annette and I went over as soon as we could and spent a wonderful afternoon with Leon and Gwen Arthur. Both had known Gosden and Hesson, and they told us many stories about them. We had tea and cookies and some of Mrs. Arthur's homemade bread as they described how Bob had been a survivalist and a nudist, how he had known Robert Service and Jack London, and what he was like as a friend. Gosden had even left Mr. Arthur some tapes and some material he had written, along with some photographs of Gosden and postcards of famous Wobbly martyrs. Mr. Arthur was kind enough to give me the pages of written material, the photos, and the five reels of tape.

I was thrilled. I had perhaps six hours of tapes and reminiscences written by Gosden himself! This might be enough material for a book. I could see the opening scene of the movie in my mind: Gosden, played by Harrison Ford, riding the rails from Prince Rupert to Vancouver, stopping off at a hobo jungle to give a fiery speech to the men huddled around a fire... Maybe I could even get a bit part, nothing too elaborate, perhaps "second picketer" or "cheering worker." I made a mental note to call a friend who was a lawyer to see what my legal rights were and thought I'd better get an answering machine so I wouldn't miss Steven Spielberg's call.

I read through the papers that night. There was a letter from British Labour MP Aneurin Bevan, thanking Gosden for his letter and noting his appreciation of the stories of meeting Jack London and fighting for social-ism in BC. More useful were Gosden's reminiscences where he talked about taking part in the Mexican revolution, listening to the anarchist Lucy Parsons speak in Vancouver, and meeting Frank Little in 1912. This was great stuff and confirmed my sense of Gosden as a revolutionary who became a spy rather than a simple informer from the beginning. Then, in the middle of his story about Frank Little, my enthusiasm crashed.

After he and Little split up, they never saw each other again, Gosden wrote, and he was saddened to learn later of Little's murder. But, he con-tinued, he did speak with Frank once more: at a seance. He knew it was Frank, because the spirit told him the same joke Little had when they parted in 1912.

I was crushed. All of this information, uncorroborated and supplied by a man who admitted to believing in seances and talking to the spirits of the dead. Maybe I could do the rest of the research with a Ouija board. In the end, Gosden's mysticism became part of the story, but at the time, I was disappointed. Gosden was not the most credible of witnesses to begin with, and now I wondered if any of his stories were true.

Perhaps the tapes would be more useful. I called SFU's Instructional Media Centre and arranged to meet with its audio wizard, Kurtis Vanel. He carefully set up the old tapes, which were in some danger of breaking, and we started to listen. I was hunched over the tape recorder, notepad and pencil at hand. This was the moment of truth: I would actually hear Gosden's voice from the past.

Kurtis started the tape rolling. The first sounds were chaotic and I struggled to make sense of them: clattering, banging, static. Then I heard a voice: "Please pass the potatoes, Bob," it rang out. Could this be code? I leaned forward, one ear tilted towards the speaker. More noise, more voices, then suddenly it was clear. Gosden had put his tape recorder, new-fangled and rare in the 1950s, under the dining room table and was tap-ing a meal with several of his friends. Probably everyone with a tape recorder has done this at one time, and Gosden's exercise was no more useful than anyone else's. We went through the tape, sampling portions. Surely the other tapes would be better.

They weren't. No revelations, few stories, nothing that shed light on Gosden and his life. There were long discussions on the principles of Theosophy, more tapings of dinners and of parties, a couple of stories of childhood pranks, and that was it. For my purposes, the tapes seemed to be a bust. Finally, at the end of one of the tapes, Gosden recited three poems, including one written during the San Diego free speech fight. They were interesting, and Gosden's voice was impressive, but they didn't shed much light on the man. I went back to my thesis.

I did have a few other places to search. The Arthurs had told me the year of Gosden's death, and I could now request the death certificate. I sent off a cheque and the filled-out form to Vital Statistics. This information can now be ordered over the telephone and the fee paid by credit card (in 1999, the number was 1-800-663-8328). The BCARS Internet website (www.bcars.gs.gov.bc.ca) has a link to an on-line search for death records as well, but the information is limited. The certificate told me a few things: Gosden's birthday, place of birth, surviving relatives, and the like. Unfortunately, the place of birth was given as "England" and no surviving relatives were listed. But I now had the very end of the story as well as the very beginning.

The Arthurs also told me about Gosden's step-son, Captain John Bunyan, the son of Isabella Bunyan. He was a retired BC Ferries captain who lived on the Sunshine Coast. I found his telephone number, got in touch, and Annette and I visited him. He had wonderful stories to tell of Gosden, about his quick wit and native intelligence, his love of the occult, and his fatherly relationship with Captain Bunyan. It was a side of Gosden I hadn't expected to find. He was compassionate, charming, thoughtful: none of what I expected in a man who was an informer.

The interviews with the Arthurs and Captain Bunyan made it possible to flesh out Gosden. It also made my work more difficult, for now he was a human, with all of our strengths and weaknesses. It was easier to write about him when he was two-dimensional, a simple black-and-white figure who could be denounced for his treachery. Listening to people who knew him made Gosden more complex and more interesting. He was a spy, certainly, but not just a spy.

After the tapes and the interviews, I read up on the background of many of the events of Gosden's life. I ordered books, articles, and theses on the San Diego free speech fight, the Mexican Revolution, Theosophy, the IWW, and sabotage. This was essential to understand Gosden in the context of the times and social movements. I wrote to other historians who studied the BC Provincial Police, coal mining in Nova Scotia, where Gosden first took part in labour struggles, and other subjects.

I got a little farfetched at times. Gosden claimed he had stolen horses from the Hearst ranch, so I wrote the appropriate police department to ask if they had any records. They didn't, but I learned something about police procedure and records. It was also useful to learn how to find police departments. I met with several retired members of the BC Provincial Police. The Provincial Police had done a great deal of work infiltrating labour movements and I thought some of them might have come across Gosden. They hadn't, but I had a fascinating afternoon listening to them talk about their history. The journal *Labour/Le Travail* has a "Notebook" section that lists conferences, new books, and other items of interest to labour historians. I put in a query asking if anyone had information about Gosden. This attracted the attention of Roger Stonebanks, a journalist with the Victoria *Times-Colonist* with a keen interest in BC labour history. Roger was working on a book on Ginger Goodwin, the famous BC labour organizer and socialist who was shot by police in 1918. Roger had come across Gosden in the course of his own research and was gracious enough to share his information with me.

Other pieces of information drifted in from colleagues and friends who were now alerted to look for Gosden. A fellow I had gone to SFU with, Ira Chaikin, found Gosden's letter on the dispatch case containing an early treaty while doing his own research on Native land claims. David Bright, working on Calgary labour, found the newspaper reference to Gosden and Owen Paulson in that city. Greg Kealey forwarded details from his research on the RCMP.

At this point it seemed useful to begin writing. It was relatively easy, at first, for I had a rough chronology to follow: his birth, the struggles in Prince Rupert, San Diego, and other places; the 1916 election scandal; the

1919 spying, and of course his death in 1961, with some stops along the way. But it wasn't clear what the focus should be. I didn't have enough for a full biography, and it was the spying that seemed most interesting. I wanted to find out why someone would go from being a radical and revolutionary to an informer. Was there enough material to understand his motives? Perhaps it didn't really matter; perhaps what was important was what he did, not why he did it. I kept on writing, trying to tell a story and show the material causes of his behaviour.

As I wrote, I read other books on labour and continued to teach and to think about the Gosden material. A crucial part of the story was his role at the Western Labor Conference: was Gosden Agent 10? Spies and informers tend not to leave records, while their masters prefer to keep what records there are secret. While many RCMP records have been made available to historians under the Freedom of Information Act, they are scrutinized and censored before being released to remove information that would identify agents and informers. Agent 10's report does not identify the author as Robert Gosden, and the attached comments of RCMP officers have deleted the spy's name. There are few things more frustrating than reading a letter that says, "In his report, BLANK says..."

Stan Horrall, the official RCMP historian, documented RCMP surveillance of the western labour movement in a groundbreaking and fascinating article in the *Canadian Historical Review* in 1980. Working from RCMP files and sources, Horrall deduced that there were at least two spies at the Western Labor Conference. Rees's denunciation of Gosden, and RCMP Commissioner Perry's comment that Agent 10 had been in the IWW and other radical organizations, led a number of researchers to surmise that Gosden was indeed the author of the notorious report.

Stan Horrall, in a letter to me, maintained that while Gosden was certainly a good candidate for Agent 10, there was no direct evidence and he preferred to remain cautious. Authors James Dubro and Robin Rowland, in their biography of Frank Zaneth, later suggested that Gosden "probably" was Agent 10. Greg Kealey subsequently argued that Gosden was "almost certainly" Agent 10, while Daniel Francis in *National Dreams: Myth, Memory, and Canadian History*, stated without reservation that Gosden was Agent 10.

As the conjecture was repeated, it seemed to become more true, although there was no more evidence to prove Gosden was Agent 10. Historians do build on each other's work, and in fairness, the question of Gosden's spying was not the main focus of any of their work. It was plausible Gosden was Agent 10, even probable, and the blurring of probability into "fact" did no harm and helped along historical narratives that wanted to make other points.

In a biography of Gosden, however, whether he was Agent 10 was a crucial question. There was ample RCMP evidence that he was a spy, but none that labelled him as Agent 10. Unable to find definitive proof, I resisted the urge to overstate my argument. In the interest of historical precision and accuracy, I fudged the issue, suggesting Gosden was probably Agent 10 and if it could not be proved that he had written the report, it was at least a fair indication of the mind-set of informers. This was highly unsatisfying, but was preferable to pushing the evidence too far.

In the meantime, I continued to talk about Gosden to friends and colleagues and made a point of asking them to keep their eyes open for references to him as they pursued their own research in government and public archives. I had looked at the BC attorney-general's correspondence at BCARS and had found some items from 1916 pertaining to the perjury trials. I continued to search through the 1920s, and finding nothing, stopped looking. A former student of mine, Andy Parnaby, was working in the provincial archives on a completely different topic and was looking at correspondence to and from the attorney-general's office in the 1930s. There he found a series of letters between the attorney-general, the BC Provincial Police, and the RCMP that mentioned Gosden. He passed them on to me. He had found a crucial document. Responding to a request from the Vancouver division of the RCMP for information on Gosden, Assistant Commissioner J.W. Spalding mentioned in passing that Gosden had been employed by the RCMP in 1919–20 and was "identified as S.A. No. 10." There was the missing connection and the rest is, well, history.

Another former student, Todd McCallum, also shared his research and ideas with me. His MA thesis on gender and the One Big Union was an important influence on my thinking about Gosden and masculinity. From the 1970s on, many historians began to be interested in the history of gender, that is, the way ideas and standards of behaviour for men and women are created and used. It seemed to me that Gosden's life had something to say about this. I went over the material again and highlighted those sections where he talked about masculinity, manhood, and what it meant to be a man. I did not think this was the only, or even the most important, thing to understand about Gosden, but it was one vital strand to pursue.

Todd also found references to Gosden in the course of his own research. He was particularly ingenious and thorough. He found a report from a labour spy that had no name or agent number on it. But Todd thought it sounded like Gosden, and he pointed out a sentence in the report that mentioned a letter the spy had had published the week before in the Fernie District Ledger. I looked at the Ledger and found that Gosden had indeed written the letter. This gave me two new pieces of evidence: the letter and another report that could be tied directly to Gosden. Todd also found a second report, one that does not name Gosden or Agent 10. But it did talk about the cowardice of the SPC members, and, as I note in Chapter 4, it is logical to assume it was by Gosden.

Both Todd and Andy were important in another way. Both were willing sounding boards. We swapped theories and ideas about Gosden, many of which have found their way into the narrative.

I pulled together the material for a conference in Austin, Texas, in 1995. Several people there made useful suggestions, as did people at another conference in St. John's, Newfoundland. Eventually, the paper became a thirty-page article, published in Labour/Le Travail. My friend Sean Cadigan thought there might be a book in the story. I said I really didn't think so, but Cadigan kept after me. I teach labour history at SFU and often give workshops in the subject to people in the labour movement. I had been asked several times if there was a good book on BC labour history, an introduction to the subject, and I had to reply that while there were some excellent books on BC labour, none was really an introduction. Cadigan suggested I write a series of sidebars to outline early BC labour history to accompany the story of Robert Gosden.

I talked to Rolf Maurer of New Star Books about it. New Star is BC's pre-eminent labour/left book publisher. Started in the 1970s, it continues to publish books that are politically provocative. The press had published my first book, a history of the IWW in BC, and Rolf had been bugging me to write a comprehensive history of the BC labour movement. We had lunch, and I pitched the Gosden book. To my surprise, he liked the idea, and I thought about turning the article into a book.

As I returned to my notes and files and newspaper clippings, I realized there was more material than I had put in the article. Scholarly articles are written in a certain style; too much speculation is frowned upon. And length is an issue: at thirty pages, the article was just about the maximum size, and a great deal of stuff had to be left out. A book aimed at a more general audience can take more chances, and I re-read my research looking for details and other stories I could incorporate. While going over the newspaper accounts of the plugging scandal, I came across the references to Mrs. Cuthbertson. On a hunch I looked up her name in the list of radicals published in the RCMP *Security Bulletins*. There was a Mrs. Cuthbutson, living in Alberta. Perhaps it was the same person. I also played the tapes of my interview with Captain Bunyan, who had died in the intervening years. In the tapes he talked about Owen Paulson. The name had meant nothing to me at the time, and Captain Bunyan had only mentioned him in passing, but now I had the Alberta newspaper reference from David Bright. Captain Bunyan's interview mentioned Gosden had moved to Alberta with Owen Paulson and Ethel Cuthbertson, and that Paulson had married Beryl Gillis. This gave me some important details about that period in their lives and opened up another side of Gosden's life. Originally I was uninterested in his personal life; for me, the burning questions were about his radicalism and his spying, about simply finding out who he was and what he did. As those questions were resolved, I became more and more interested in his life apart from his public career. Details on his personal life, however, were even more difficult to prise out than those on his spy career, and not being able to flesh that part out is my chief regret with the book.

How I wished I could have spoken with Captain Bunyan now that I had this new information! I called his brother William. I hadn't spoken to him before, as he had told his brother he didn't remember anything. He did, however, give me a great deal of useful information. I contacted Owen Paulson's son, also named Owen Paulson. I found him by looking up his father in BCARS' on-line death records. That gave me the date of death of an Owen Hustler Paulson. One of my graduate students, John-Henry Harter, went through the newspapers around that date and found the obituary notice for Paulson. It revealed that he had a son, Owen, and two daughters, Ethel and Pauline, and listed their married names.

This method did not work in all cases. Ethel Cuthbertson's daughter was named Helen according to the Bunyans. They believed her married name was Provis. I entered that into the BCARS site and found nothing. Had she died after the cut-off date for the BCARS entries? Had she re-married and taken another name? Had she moved away? Died somewhere else? Perhaps she was still alive.

The telephone directory for BC is on the Internet; I plugged in her name but found nothing. I entered the other names. There was only one Owen Paulson, and I phoned him. He was the son of Owen Paulson, and indeed he did remember Bob Gosden. Again, our talk gave me some insight and details into both men. Sadly, his mother, Beryl Paulson, nee Gillis, had died three years earlier. If I had made the connection between Gosden and Paulson and Gillis when I first spoke to Captain Bunyan, I would have been able to speak with her and perhaps found out more about all of them. That was the last step in the research. It was time to write.

Tracking down Gosden was fun. Entering the shadowy world of the spy, even eighty years later, was exciting. It was also tedious. I spent long hours going through records only to realize nothing was there. Whenever I looked for Gosden, he would disappear, appropriate behaviour for a spy. When I gave up, something would turn up, unexpected and unpredicted.

But knowing when to stop is as important as knowing where to start. I expect there is more to be found on Robert Gosden, although it is increasingly difficult to find people who knew him. I stopped looking for information, not because I thought I had everything but because I knew I could not hope to get everything. I could put together a reasonable account of his life and times, even though I knew it wasn't complete. No book is ever finished; at most, one just runs out of time. Somehow, I suspect that Robert Raglan Gosden has a few more surprises for historians.

Are there any general lessons that may be useful for people interested in writing labour history? I think so. There is a great deal of labour material in BC archives and museums. It can be found in several different ways. One is to go to one of the archives and ask for help. It is important that you know something about your subject first. The more you know, the more useful the archivists and librarians can be. If you say only that you're interested in labour, they may well reply that they have several metres of material on labour. If you start at the beginning and work your way through, you will spend years finding out nothing. If, on the other hand, you've done some reading and thinking and ask about metal trades in BC, they may point you to the minutes of the machinists' union or to the Metal Trades Council records. Asking the right question is perhaps the most difficult part of writing history. You need to think about what you are interested in and then find out what kind of materials exist to help you answer your questions. Often it is not possible to answer the question you want to ask. In that case, it is necessary to rethink the question, keeping in mind the sources that do exist.

Other labour materials can be found by searching computer indices and card catalogues. Be creative: one archive may file material under "labour," another under "trade unions," a third under "industrial relations." Talk to the archivists, but do your homework. Archivists are highly trained specialists, and they cannot teach every researcher how to look up basic information. Many archives publish finding aids and guides. One that is particularly helpful to labour historians is the *Guide to the Archival Research Collections in the Special Collections and University Archives Division* of the University of British Columbia Library.

A great deal of material is available on the Internet. One good place to look is the BC History Internet/Website, which at the time of this writing can be found at http://victoria.tc.ca/resources/bchistory.html. This site provides links to several archives, including BCARS (formerly the Public Archives of BC), Special Collections at UBC, and the Vancouver City Archives. You will also find indices, search engines, and finding aids here.

The actual material is not on-line, but it is possible to do a great deal of research about the collections from here. By searching the catalogues you can find out what union minutes and records exist.

Newspapers are invaluable. They pose problems for researchers, of course. They are not politically neutral and, in Gosden's day, were often closely aligned to a political party. Coverage of the plugging scandal, for example, varied depending on whether the paper was Liberal or Conservative. The Liberal *Sun* often ignored the scandal, while the Liberal *Times* used every editorial trick it could to attack Gosden. The Conservative papers, the *Province* and the Victoria *Colonist*, used every opportunity to embarrass the Liberals.

Newspapers are also impossible to use unless you can pinpoint the dates you need with some accuracy. The BC Legislative Library Newspaper Index can be extremely useful in pinpointing dates. The index is a microfilmed guide to newspaper stories, put together by researchers at the BC Legislative Library in Victoria. Originally it was a card catalogue, with newspaper stories deemed useful to Members of the Legislative Assembly listed by name and subject. It is not a comprehensive index: stories not thought to be of use to legislators are not included, and the issues that concerned earlier generations of politicians are not always of interest to contemporary historians. Nor is it complete; there were several stories on Gosden that were not noted in the index. Nonetheless, it is a useful place to begin newspaper research. University libraries and the VPL have the index on microfilm.

Labour history is often about strikes. One way to find information on strikes and lock-outs is to look at the *Labour Gazette*. This was a publication of the federal government, started in 1900. Correspondents across Canada sent in information on labour disputes, unions, strikes, and lock-outs. The *Gazette* lists the number of strikes, the number of people involved, the number of days lost, the unions and companies involved, and who won. The *Gazette* is not perfect. The coverage varies widely, depending on the correspondent; it is not a definitive list of strikes, but it is a place to begin. Once the strike is found, you can then go to the newspapers and look for stories on and around the dates in the *Gazette*.

Royal commissions are another important source for labour historians. Federal and provincial commissions for BC have examined industrial relations, conditions of work, and specific unions and strikes. Much of BC's labour history has been explored in MA and PhD theses, and many of these are listed in the bibliography in this volume. Theses are useful, not just for the information they contain but also for their references. Going through their footnotes and bibliographies reveals a wealth of material and research clues.

Writing the Gosden book gave me some general lessons on writing history as well as researching it. One is that it can be a mistake to see research and writing as two separate operations. Often people allot several days for research, then plan on several days of writing. This is rarely the best way to proceed. It is better to do some research, then write up what you have. This will force you to put the raw research material into order, to make sense of the data, and to find out what else you need to learn to continue. Writing clarifies ideas. More, every sentence you write puts limits on what can be done; it forces you to think about the logic and opportunities of the material, to think about what should come next. That is, the order and analysis of the research is not always self-evident from the research itself. Only when you apply your intelligence to the raw material does it become history. It is your job to impose some order on the chaos of the past, but you must be sensitive to the research. If you separate writing from research, you are liable to miss nuances and ideas in your rush to get each stage done. It is important to think about your research, and the earlier the better; the best way to think about it is to write it out. Nothing is fixed forever. You may well change your mind and go back and rewrite. The point is, if you have written nothing, there will be nothing to think about and nothing to rewrite. I'm not sure it would have occurred to me to write on masculinity if I had simply gathered up everything on Gosden and decided to stop reading and researching in order to write. When I started finding material on Gosden in 1985, discussions of gender were just beginning to appear in journals. When I wrote a draft of the article in 1995, it was impossible to think about Gosden without considering gender. While ten years is a pretty long time from idea to article to book, the principle is the same when you are writing over a much shorter time span. There is a great deal of information out there, and researchers may be aware only of fragments. The themes and orders of the research material that are first apparent to writers may seem less interesting or important as they read and learn more about the subject. So it is important to think of research and writing as connected rather than as separate tasks.

Think about other ways to investigate the subject if the obvious ones fail. Work on more than one project at a time, or on different parts of a project, so you can shift your aim if necessary. Read, research, and write; think about what you are doing and think about different ways to approach the subject. Pay attention to details, but don't get bogged down in them. Understand the big picture and read widely in the secondary literature. Pick a topic you like, because even the most interesting topic will get boring sometimes. If you don't like it at all, you'll soon find ways to avoid it.

Keep accurate notes, and only write on one side of your note paper. If you write on both sides, one day you will be sorting through your notes, looking for a crucial fact, and you will forget to look on the back. You will spend hours looking for this reference and will get angry because you know it is there somewhere. You will then feel really stupid when the note turns up because you drop the stack of papers and it flips over. This has happened to me and to most of the researchers I know. Learn from our experience.

Write down the full reference for all the books and articles and theses you look at. Otherwise you will search in vain for them later. Be very nice to the archivists. They hold our past, and your future as a historian, in their hands.

Oral history is an important part of the modern historians' craft. There are several books on the subject that the researcher should consult. One of the best is Paul R. Thompson's *The Voice of the Past: Oral History*. A few practical tips: Use a tape recorder and take notes at the same time. The tape recorder will give you a complete record, but your notes will let you process information, think of new questions, and record subjective information the machine will not pick up. Don't try to write out the interview in your notes: the machine will do that. But hit the high points, jot down questions you think of, note expressions and your impressions of the material. Test your equipment several times before you go to the interview and make sure you know how to use it. A tape recorder intimidates many people. If you seem confident around it, this will help the person you are interviewing. Test the range of the microphone so you know where to place it during the interview. Take lots of extra batteries and tapes, many more than you think necessary. Know how to change the batteries and tapes quickly and smoothly. Let your subject do the talking. Don't be too urgent to ask the questions you think are most important. It is more useful, and respectful, to let the subject come to the topics in his or her own way. Remember that the things you most want to learn may be of little interest to the person you are interviewing. Think about what you could tell an interviewer who wanted to learn about your parents. You might have great stories of happy holidays or family tragedies; you are less likely to know about the politics of their workplaces.

Remember that when you talk to people, they may not be able to help you as directly as you wish. For example, none of my interview subjects knew that Gosden had been a spy. Yet they had a great deal of important information to share. Be clear about your interests and what you are doing – you cannot mislead people about your work – but don't alienate people. The Arthurs and Captain Bunyan had fond memories of the man, and if I had simply launched into a torrent of questions about "Gosden the stool pigeon," they might well have decided not to talk to me. I told them what I had found and asked them to comment on Gosden. Do some homework. Don't just show up and expect your interview subjects to fill you in on everything. The more you know, the better your questions will be. Talk to your interview subjects about themselves, as well. This may be of great use to you. Then again, it may not, but it is a way of showing respect for the subject as a human and not just as a "resource."

How one writes labour history depends very much on one's audience. University and college students writing essays and theses need to make an argument. A narrative is important: readers need to know what has happened. But a university course requires more than that. Students need to do more than tell the story of a strike or a union or labour activist. They need to explain cause and effect and explain why the subject is significant. Academic historians do not just entertain or seek to inspire people with stories from our past. They seek to explain the past, to understand not just that events happened but why they happened and what the consequences were.

In my classes, for example, many students have written about BC's coal miners. Papers that only outline the story of Robert Dunsmuir and the crushing of several miners' strikes do not take us any further than the work that has already been done by authors such as Allan Wargo and Lynne Bowen. That organizing miners was hard and often unsuccessful is an argument, but it is not a very good one, for that has been obvious for years. A cursory reading of the literature teaches students that much. A good paper goes beyond the obvious story and the simple arguments. More sophisticated arguments or questions might be: did ethnic and gender differences hamper or help organizing efforts? What role did miners' wives and children play? If conditions were so terrible, why did mining families come to BC? Why was Robert Dunsmuir a worse employer than the New Vancouver Coal Mining and Land Company, which operated coal mines in virtually the same location and time and faced similar conditions? A student might pick up one common theme in the mining literature and explore it more thoroughly. One argument, repeated often by historians, is that Vancouver Island coal mines were the most dangerous in the world. While this statement is often made, there hasn't been much detailed comparison to prove that it is true or explain, if it is true, why they were so dangerous.

With each of these topics, a labour historian will start with a story and a detailed reading of the work already done by historians and will then go on to ask questions that take us beyond what is already generally known, by combining knowledge in new ways. To make sense of what historians have written, it is important to understand historiography.

HISTORIOGRAPHY: WHY THE PAST KEEPS CHANGING

In writing history, it is vital to read the work of other historians, not just to gather information, but also to see how others have interpreted the past. As you read, remember that historians are not objective, uninvolved reporters who simply uncover the facts. They do not report the past; they interpret it and, in some sense, create it. They ask questions of the past, influenced by a world-view that has been shaped by their lives and their studies. The questions they ask, the frameworks of explanation they use, the choices they make about what is important and what is trivial, the causes and effects they examine, are as individual and different as the historians themselves. Understanding history, then, is not just about understanding what happened or memorizing dates; it is also about understanding how historians have interpreted the past. That is historiography, which may be defined as "the study of the writing of history."

How can the reader figure out where a historian should be placed in the historiography? One way is to ask questions about the material. What is emphasized? How are controversial issues and politics handled? To whom is the author most sympathetic? Most critical? What are the general principles the author subscribes to? Where should the author be placed on the political spectrum? What explanations does the author give for historical change? Does the author support the status quo or challenge it?

One important question is, who has been left out of the account? Much of our history simply ignores working people. Typically, historians have concentrated on the powerful – kings, queens, prime ministers, presidents, the wealthy, and military leaders. Peter C. Newman, for example, has written a great deal about the Hudson's Bay Company, but very little about the workers who performed most of the tasks and made up the majority of people in the company. For those interested in the history of working people, some important questions about historiography are basic. Does the author even talk about workers? How does the author write about relations between bosses and workers? Is capital presented in a glowing or a realistic light?

Within the field of labour history itself there have been several different ways to interpret the past. These have evolved to reflect the strength of different political tendencies, current events, and the refinement of historical thought. The first book-length study of BC labour was William Bennett's *Builders of BC*, published in 1937. Bennett was a communist, and this perspective brought to his work some particular strengths and weaknesses. As a communist, he was convinced that the real builders of the province were not "real estate sharks, timber barons, mine speculators, fishery pirates, oil brokers, stock gamblers, and political heelers" who came to BC "to batten like leeches on the workers." His book did not ignore these historical actors, but rather cast them as the villains. Working people were the heroes in his view, and Bennett outlined their struggles, their victories, and their defeats.

Bennett's politics also led him to understand that the histories of First Nations, Chinese, and Japanese workers were vital to the history of the province, and this too set him apart from other historians, who assumed that BC was a white man's province.

Like most of his contemporaries, however, Bennett assumed that labour history was almost exclusively the history of men; if he was advanced in his treatment of race, he rarely seemed to consider the role of women. His politics also coloured how he described other labour and left groups. For example, he virulently denounced the Wobblies, whose anarchism was fundamentally opposed to the hierarchical politics of the CP.

More tellingly, Bennett distorted the CP's recent past to dovetail with shifts in the party's politics. By 1936 the CP was trying to build a popular front with the CCF and moderate labour unions. This reflected Stalin's belief that the primary threat to the Soviet Union was Nazi Germany and Fascist Italy. Between 1928 and 1935, however, Stalin had believed that France and Britain, long hostile to communism, were more likely to launch a war against the Soviet Union than Germany or Italy. In those years, Communist Parties around the world were instructed to attack other groups on the left and to call for revolution in the hope that the resulting chaos would make it more difficult for the capitalist countries to wage war. In Canada, the CP had been extremely hostile to the CCF and moderate labour unions. Little of this, however, is documented in Bennett's book. The unwary reader would conclude that the CP had always been eager to work with social democrats and labourists.

Other historians made other choices about what to include and what to ignore. In 1967 came the second book on BC labour history, Paul Phillips's *No Power Greater: A Century of Labour in BC*. The book was published by the BC Federation of Labour and the Boag Foundation, an institute closely tied to the NDP, to help celebrate Canada's centennial. Read one way, the book is a factual chronology of the labour movement that outlines in a straightforward way the creation of unions, the large strikes, the labour legislation, and the political action of the labour movement. Read more critically, the book is generally sympathetic to the contemporary "mainstream" of the labour movement, that is, the moderate leadership of the BC Federation of Labour and the NDP.

As a result, the book is largely uncritical of the labour movement and does not outline in great detail the racism and elitism of the early craft unions. The book virtually ignores the role of the Wobblies and the Communist Party in creating new, radical unions that were highly critical of labour reformists and social democrats, even though one could plausibly argue that these groups were much more influential than the CCF until the late 1940s. The book treats the purge of communists from the labour movement almost as a natural evolution, when in fact the anti-communists or "Whites" were supported by business and government and engaged in dirty tricks and dubious tactics to get rid of the "Reds." Nor does the book mention the movement for Canadian unions that began in the early 1960s. This is because the BC Federation of Labour and the international unions affiliated to it bitterly opposed these new organizations. Efforts to organize women and white-collar workers, both constituencies that were not well-represented in the traditional labour movement, also get scant attention. This perspective was shaped by the desire of the victors – the CCF/NDP and like-minded labour leaders – to tell their story, and by the sources – the official minutes and newspapers of the movement – that Phillips drew upon.

In the 1970s, three important books on western Canadian labour history were published: A.R. McCormack's *Reformers, Rebels, and Revolutionaries: The Western Canadian Radical Movement, 1899–1919* and David Bercuson's *Confrontation at Winnipeg: Labour, Industrial Relations, and the General Strike* and *Fools and Wise Men: The Rise and Fall Of The One Big Union*. The three books drew upon earlier work on industrial relations and the relatively new school of regional history to inform their study of labour in the west.

Industrial relations experts had long been interested in labour history, chiefly to discover the causes of strikes in order to find ways to avoid them. The study of regional history, on the other hand, began in the 1950s as the university history profession expanded and authors such as W.L. Morton and Margaret Ormsby, born in Manitoba and BC respectively, argued that Canada had to be understood as a community of regions. Each region had a unique history that was not identical to that of Ontario, which too often served as the model for national history.

Bercuson and McCormack took these perspectives and applied them to labour history. They focused on large strikes, radicals, and political parties and concluded that the dependence on the resource economy, especially mining; the rugged nature of the frontier; and the late development of industrial and social reform meant that western Canada developed differently from eastern Canada. Economic expansion came more quickly, cities sprang up overnight, class divisions were more pronounced, and employers and the state were more repressive. Bercuson and McCormack suggested that radicalism had flourished in the absence of moderate reform. The exceptional conditions of the western industrial frontier led to an exceptional labour history, they argued, one in which workers were more radical and more militant than their contemporaries in the east.

Their focus on the region led to excellent pioneering work in Canadian labour history as Bercuson and McCormack brought to light the nearly forgotten history of western Wobblies, socialists, and unionists. Their prose was lively and they demonstrated that both western Canada and labour were essential to understanding the nation. Ultimately, however, western exceptionalism proved to be a dead end as a historical theory. It assumed what it had to prove: that western workers really were more radical than those in the east. As other scholars were soon to demonstrate, this assumption did not stand up to scrutiny. Subsequent historical work documented radicalism and strike activity in the east and showed that western radicalism was not as widespread as some initially believed. The Vancouver labour movement, for example, developed much as eastern urban movements had; even the coal miners of Vancouver Island were shown to be divided over questions such as socialism and industrial unionism.[1]

The focus on the region also meant that BC labour history was insulated from the radical changes that were being pioneered by other Canadian labour historians. Inspired by the British Marxist historian E.P. Thompson and his classic study *The Making of the English Working Class*, and by the work of the US historians Herbert Gutman and David Montgomery, a new generation of Canadian historians outside BC were approaching labour history with a very different perspective. Most had taken part in the student radicalism of the 1960s, and as a result of their experience they asked new questions of the past. They sought to explore not the famous strikes or moderate labour leaders but the working class as a whole. That meant examining all aspects of workers, not just their membership in unions and participation in strikes. In particular, it meant investigating the culture and experience of workers and working-class families. It meant examining how work was actually done to understand what it meant to be a worker and how that experience shaped resistance. It meant understanding how class struggle took place on a day-to-day level, sometimes collective and obvious, as it was in strikes, sometimes individual and hidden, as it was in family strategies of work and budgeting and sabotage. It meant examining the recreation and informal lives of workers. Finally, it meant treating radical opposition to industrial capital not as an aberration or misguided effort but as a reasonable response to a system based on exploitation and injustice.

This new labour history soon displaced the older historiography. In BC, however, few historians took up the new ideas. As a result, in the late 1970s and 1980s the labour history of Ontario, Quebec, and the Maritimes tended to overshadow BC labour history, and it was the work of historians such as Greg Kealey, Bryan Palmer, Craig Heron, David Frank, and Ian McKay, who studied Ontario, Quebec, and the Maritimes, that framed the important debates and questions.[2]

This new labour history, often called working-class history to indicate its wider concerns, was much more inclusive than the old labour history. Yet like any history, it could not be all-inclusive, and it reflected the concerns and world-views of the historians. These included an emphasis on the nineteenth century and on skilled workers. It also meant that these male historians did not pay much attention to women. Historians such as Linda Kealey and Bettina Bradbury, however, did take up the history of working women.

That was one area that did receive significant attention from BC historians. In *Not Just Pin Money: Selected Essays On The History Of Women's Work In British Columbia*, published in 1984, and *In Her Own Right: Selected Essays on Women's History in British Columbia*, published in 1980, several authors made it clear that labour history could not just be the story of men. Few of the articles adopted the theoretical approaches of the new labour history. Instead, the authors made use of ideas from women's history to create a fruitful synthesis. More recently, *British Columbia Reconsidered: Essays On Women*, edited by Gillian Creese and Veronica Strong-Boag, and including several of the essays from the two earlier collections, continued this tradition, though with less emphasis on labour history as such.

A book by BC historian Rolf Knight asked other questions about who had been excluded from the historical record and from labour history. Historians who studied Natives, especially Robin Fisher, had assumed that with the decline of the fur trade and the increase in white settlement, Natives were excluded from the new capitalist economy, they argued. Knight's *Indians At Work: An Informal History Of Native Labour In British Columbia, 1848–1930*, demonstrated convincingly that Natives quickly adapted to capitalism and indeed were crucial to it. Much of the work done on the debate since is little more than a footnote to Knight's book, and few of his critics match his theoretical sophistication or scope.

By the mid-1980s, theses and articles on BC labour history influenced by the new school of labour/working-class history began to appear. A collection of articles, *Workers, Capital, and the State in British Columbia: Selected Papers*, edited by Rennie Warburton and David Coburn, included the work of historians and sociologists such as Gillian Creese, Allen Seager, and James Conley who worked in the new historiographical tradition. This work was soon followed by articles and theses that explicitly engaged the new ideas of class, culture, experience, law, gender, and ethnicity. BC historians were also engaged in writing a third stream of labour history, sometimes called the "new institutionalism," that retained a focus on unions but insisted that class struggle, class experience, gender, ethnicity, the role of the state, and other topics be written as part of that history.[3]

Today, BC's academic labour history is as theoretically sophisticated as

its counterparts in other regions. The challenge now is for labour historians to expand and synthesize this body of knowledge, take an active role
in shaping the debates in the writing of history, and write labour history
that is accessible to the people who make it.

Non-academic historians have also written labour history. Lynn
Bowen's work, especially *Boss Whistle: The Coal Miners of Vancouver Island Remem-*
ber, brings to life the story of Vancouver Island's coal miners and their struggles. It draws on the memoirs and interviews of miners and their families,
focusing on the 1912–14 strike. In 1990, Susan Mayse's biography of Ginger Goodwin was another popular book that signalled a return to an old-
fashioned labour and regional history. Both books are lively, well-
researched, and important. But they share a liberal perspective in which
history is a progressive development from bad conditions to better ones.
The terrible conditions miners faced are viewed as an abuse of the system
rather than the very essence of capitalism, and the past is studied because it
reminds us that things used to be worse. This is a political message that the
writers might not intend to present, but their choice of how to interpret the
past leads them in this direction. A more sophisticated popular history,
Working Lives: Vancouver, 1886–1986, by the Working Lives Collective, was published for Vancouver's centennial. Short entries examined Vancouver's
unions, strikes, and questions of the work process, ethnicity, and gender.

In general, popular historians rarely discuss historiography explicitly or
make their political allegiances plain. They often see their role as telling a
good story, so much of their work is livelier than that of academic historians. Done well, it gives readers a better feel for what it was like to live in past
times. Unlike academic history, however, it rarely makes an argument about
historical development and change; we learn what happened, but not why.
As a result, the writer's point of view or interpretive framework is not so
obvious. Indeed, some popular historians deny they have *any* point of view;
they're just telling a story. But since they still must make judgments about
what to include and what to leave out, these choices inevitably reflect their
political beliefs. Often these political beliefs are difficult to spot because
they reflect the mainstream views of contemporary society and thus do not
appear controversial or contentious. Precisely because they are not obvious

or unsettling, we need to be especially careful to analyze the politics of those authors who deny they have a political agenda.

As well, since all the facts cannot be known or presented in a history, all historians make judgments about what is important, what is trivial, what is interesting, and what is dull. So though popular historians may claim they don't have a viewpoint, they do make assumptions about events that shape their theme and their writing.

WRITING THE HISTORY OF YOUR OWN UNION OR LOCAL

Many unions have written their own histories, often to mark an anniversary or event. Frequently researched and written by union members themselves, these histories are important for union officers, members, and the general public. They provide an institutional memory for the union and teach new members about the struggles that shaped the organization.

David Frank, in a short pamphlet titled *Making Your Own History*, has outlined several useful ideas for trade unionists who want to write the history of their union or local. Many of the following suggestions come from his pamphlet and from my own experience with writing labour history.

It is important that the official history have a theme. Too often these books only document a series of strikes, motions, or issues that seem unconnected and disjointed. A theme does not have to be specific or profound. It might be something like the organization's evolution from a narrow craft union to a larger, more inclusive union, or the ability of the union to sustain itself against attacks from employers. Popular history may not require an argument in the way academic writing does, but it does need a theme, an idea that ties the narrative together. Without a theme, the historian is merely presenting facts, and a list of facts makes history seem like a collection of random events. The job of the historian is to create some order out of the chaos. This order is subjective, sometimes even arbitrary, but it is an inescapable part of the historian's job. Failing to provide connections and interpretations is failing to help others understand the past, even if they understand by disagreeing with the writer.

The first step in writing the history is to form a small committee or labour history working group. The group should include younger and older workers, women and men, workers of different ethnicity, and people from the different jobs and sites the union represents. This helps ensure that different perspectives are covered.

The next step is to identify the records and papers that exist and where they are. The union might keep these, or they may be deposited in an archive; some may be held by individual union members and former officers. The records might include union minutes, correspondence with the locals and headquarters, membership lists, convention records, newspapers, pamphlets, even posters and photographs. These need to be identified and found.

Other archives and museums in the area may have material that will be useful. They may have information on the union, the businesses the union organized, the work places, the community, and the economy. Unions do not exist in a vacuum, and understanding the context is important.

Talk to the officers of the union, from the local to the headquarters. Many unions have research departments or research officers, and they may be able to help you. If there is a history of the union, for example, this will help with writing the history of a local. Union officers may be able to contact former members and officers, provide funding, help with specific requests for union correspondence, and make it easier to get access to company records.

The working group should talk with a labour historian. While historians probably won't know much about a specific local or union, they can provide background information. They can also provide important tips on doing research, finding materials, and writing, and these tips may save a great deal of time. University and college historians may be able to do some research or find students who are able to do some of the legwork. Students can be hired as part of co-op programs or as independent researchers, and this too may save time.

Interviewing union members, young and old, is a crucial part of labour history. Sometimes their memories are the only existing record of important people and events; other times, their recent experiences are the ones that will be of most interest to current members. The working group can devise questions and topics and do the interviews; volunteers from the union, especially retired members, can also do the work. Deciding who should be interviewed is important, for the diversity of the union should be represented. Rank-and-file members should be interviewed as well as officers. Members can make their own tapes and send in the information or can write down their memories and ideas. The taped interviews should be transcribed as soon as possible, for it is extremely difficult to write from tape recordings. The union staff may be able to do this work.

The working group will have to decide how to organize the material. It may want to tell the story chronologically, starting at the beginning and working up to the present. It may want to organize the history by theme: organizing, negotiating, technological change, strikes, benefits won, and the like. Some sense of where the union is going and what challenges it faces can be valuable.

Writing can be difficult work, and it may make sense to divide the project into smaller sections that individuals can work on. Sitting down to write a 200-page book is daunting; sitting down to tell the story of a single strike is a little easier. Or the working group may want to designate a single writer. In either case, regular discussions with the group are good for morale and for ensuring that different viewpoints and experiences are included.

For union members, understanding their history reminds them that the union was built by people like them, not superheroes or geniuses. It reminds them that the history of labour is the history of struggle, and that struggle shaped the present. Understanding that helps us understand the present and lets us make better decisions. It does something else as well. It reminds us that the past was not inevitable. It was contested and fought for, and no one knew what the outcome would be. The past was not fixed; that means that our future is not fixed. Understanding labour history helps us understand that working people will shape our future. And that is an important, revolutionary idea in a time when capital and the state tell us there are no alternatives. There are, and it is up to us to make them. A place to start is by learning our history.

CHAPTER 1: "THE WORKERS CAN DO NO WRONG"

1 Gosden's death certificate from the Division of Vital Statistics, Victoria, B.C., gives his birthdate as 6 July 1882. In testimony during his trial for perjury in June 1916, however, Gosden gave his age as 35, making his birth year 1881. This is the date given by his stepson, Captain John Bunyan (interview by the author, 16 August 1989). Captain Bunyan also believed that Gosden fought in the British Army during the Boer War, as did Gosden's friends, Leon Gordon Arthur, Gwen Arthur, and Alan Schwab (Mr. and Mrs. Arthur, interview by the author, 29 January 1989; Alan Schwab, interview by the author, 30 September 1998). I have not been able to check this. Also in testimony at the 1916 trial, Gosden denied under oath playing any role in events at Glace Bay, stating that while there he "was only studying labour conditions" (Victoria *Daily Colonist*, 7 June 1916). Historians David Frank of the University of New Brunswick and Ian Mackay of Queen's University, who have studied the Glace Bay events in detail, have no information on Gosden (letters to the author, undated). The Victoria *Daily Times*, 6 June 1916 and 9 November 1916, reports Gosden's testimony on birthplace and travels, while the Victoria *Daily Times* of 9 November 1916 and the Vancouver *Daily News-Advertiser* of 10 November 1916 list his occupations. Gosden told the Arthurs and Mr. Schwab that he had met Jack London and Robert Service.

2 *Industrial Worker*, 6 August 1910.

3 *Industrial Worker*, 28 November 1911.

4 Robin Fisher, *Duff Pattullo of British Columbia* (Toronto: University of Toronto Press, 1991), p 99; Prince Rupert *Optimist*, 6 January 1911.

5 Prince Rupert *Optimist*, 24 January 1911.

6 Prince Rupert *Optimist*, 9 January 1911.

7 Prince Rupert *Optimist*, 23 January 1911; also Prince Rupert *Optimist*, January to May 1911; Patricia Wejr and Howie Smith, eds., *Fighting for Labour: Four Decades of Work in British Columbia, 1910–1950*. Sound Heritage, Volume Four. (Victoria: Provincial Archives, 1978), pp 8–11.

8 Paul Phillips, *No Power Greater: A Century of Labour in BC* (Vancouver: BC Federation of Labour and Boag Foundation, 1967), p 53; Fisher, *Pattullo*, p 101; Prince Rupert *Optimist*, 13 March 1911. Folklorist Philip J. Thomas notes the reference to Foley, Welch, and Stewart in *Songs of the Pacific Northwest* (Saanichton: Hancock House Publishers, 1979), p 102. The *Rainbow* would become notorious for its role in the *Komagata Maru* incident. In 1914 a group of approximately 375 Sikhs chartered the Japanese ship *Komagata Maru* to take them to Canada. They were mounting a legal challenge to a Canadian regulation that barred East Indian immigration. The ship arrived in Vancouver in May 1914, but immigration authorities refused to let the passengers disembark. They were kept on the ship for two months as they appealed their case. The *Rainbow* was brought in to intimidate and pressure the passengers. When the legal case was lost, the *Komagata Maru* and its passengers returned to India, where twenty of the Sikhs were killed in an altercation with the authorities.

9 Gosden's letter and other details of the PRIA are from the *Industrial Worker*, 6 April 1911.

10 Wejr and Smith, *Fighting for Labour*, pp 8–11; *Industrial Worker*, 27 April 1911; Victoria *Colonist*, 7 June 1916; Vancouver *Province*, 6 June 1916.

11 *Industrial Worker*, 27 April 1911, 12 October 1911.

12 *Industrial Worker*, 27 April 1911.

13 Industrial Worker, 12 October 1911.

14 Gosden told John Bunyan and the Arthurs that he had ridden with Villa and that he had been arrested and imprisoned for running guns to the rebels. It has not been possible to determine if horses were stolen from the Hearst ranch in this period. Police records for San Luis Obispo County have not been retained, and according to Detective Sergeant Gary L. Hoving of the sheriff-coroner's office of the county, "Even if the incident had been documented, it would have probably been seen only as a journal entry" (letter to author, 6 September 1989). The autobiographical sketch is in the possession of the author. Its reliability is not enhanced by a fact of error – Huerta assumed the presidency in 1913, not 1912; by its construction as a story "heard round the coffee tables in the White Lunch [a cafe in Vancouver's skid road district] at midnight"; and by the central point of the story, which is that the author later spoke with Frank Little at a seance some years after Little's death. For IWW involvement in the Mexican Revolution see Lowell L. Blaisdell, The Desert Revolution: Baja California, 1911 (Madison: University of Wisconsin Press, 1962); John M. Hart, Anarchism and the Mexican Working Class, 1860–1931 (Austin: University of Texas Press, 1974), pp 157–60. The historian Gibbs M. Smith has concluded that though Joe Hill denied taking part in the Baja revolution, it is likely that he in fact was among the Wobblies who fought for the cause there. Smith, Joe Hill (Salt Lake City: Peregrine Smith Books, 1984), pp 53–55.

15 Industrial Worker, 2 November 1911.

16 For details of the IWW free speech fights, see Melvyn Dubofsky, We Shall Be All: A History of the Industrial Workers of the World (Chicago: Quadrangle Books, 1969), pp 173–98. For the Vancouver and Victoria fights see Mark Leier, Where the Fraser River Flows: The iww in British Columbia (Vancouver: New Star Books, 1990), Chapter 3. "Fellow Workers and Friends": iww Free Speech Fights as Told by Participants, Philip Foner, ed. (Westport: Greenwood Press, 1981), is a fascinating collection of articles, letters, and diaries written by people who took part in a number of these struggles.

17 See Dubofsky, We Shall Be All, pp 189–96, and Philip Foner, The Industrial Workers of the World, 1905–1917 (New York: International Publishers, 1965), pp 194–206, for the events of the San Diego free speech fight.

18 Industrial Worker, 19 June 1912.

19 These excerpts are from the Industrial Worker, 3 July 1913. The IWW itself split on the issue of sabotage, and Walker Smith was removed from the editorial board of the Industrial Worker late in 1913 by Wobblies opposed to sabotage, or at least to the open advocacy of it in the union's official press. By 1914, however, sabotage was an officially sanctioned tactic, and Smith's editorials were published by the IWW in pamphlet form. So too was a speech on the subject by Elizabeth Gurley Flynn. The famous IWW leader Big Bill Haywood was purged from the executive board of the Socialist Party of America in 1912 in part for his refusal to renounce sabotage. See Philip Foner, Industrial Workers of the World, pp 160–65, and Dubofsky, We Shall Be All, pp 162–65, for the union's debates over sabotage.

20 Industrial Worker, 31 October 1912.

21 Victoria Times, 9 November 1912, dateline San Diego, reports that Gosden was arrested and convicted but does not specify the charges. The Times of 6 June 1916 reports Gosden as stating that he spent nine months in county jail in San Diego awaiting trial for violating the ordinance against speaking in the street. A Robert Gausden is noted as being charged with assault with a deadly weapon as well as blocking the street, and received

either a suspended sentence or a discharge in *The History of the San Diego Free Speech Fight* (San Diego: The Industrial Workers of the World, 1973), p 187.

22 *Industrial Worker*, 21 November 1912.

23 Vancouver *Province*, 5 August 1913. I am grateful to Allen Seager for bringing this reference to my attention. See James H. Walsh, "IWW 'Red Special' Overalls Brigade," cited in *Rebel Voices: An IWW Anthology*, Joyce Kornbluh, ed. (Ann Arbor: University of Michigan Press, 1972), p 48.

24 The most in-depth analysis of the 1912–14 strike is Alan J. Wargo, "The Great Coal Strike: The Vancouver Island Coal Miners' Strike, 1912–1914," unpublished BA graduation essay, University of British Columbia, 1962. For a popular account see Lynne Bowen, *Boss Whistle: The Coal Miners of Vancouver Island Remember* (Lantzville, BC: Oolichan Books, 1982), pp 131–98. See also John Norris, "The Vancouver Island Coal Miners, 1912–14: A Study of an Organizational Strike," *BC Studies* 45 (Spring 1980).

25 Victoria *Times*, 7 June 1916, 10 November 1916; Vancouver *Province*, 6 June 1916, 10 November 1916.

26 *BC Federationist*, 7 November 1913, 14 November 1913, 5 December 1913.

27 Vancouver *Sun*, 9 December 1913. The *BC Federationist*, 12 December 1913, gave an abbreviated version of the speech that did not include direct reference to shooting. It did contain the coffee warning. It may be that the *Sun* report put words in Gosden's mouth, for later accounts of the speech focused on the coffee remark.

28 The Vancouver *Sun*, 9 December 1913, observed the crowd size and response. The letter supporting Gosden was printed in the *BC Federationist* on 19 December 1913. It has not been possible to determine where or when Gosden was made president of the MLL. As noted, he was executive chair before the speech and resigned from the presidency on 23 January 1914. There were editorials decrying the threats in the Vancouver *Sun* of 9 December 1913 and Victoria *Times*, 10 December 1913. Robert Foster is quoted in the *BC Federationist*, 19 December 1913. Gosden's resignation and election to the vice-presidency are reported in the *BC Federationist*, 30 January 1914.

29 Victoria *Times*, 12 May 1916.

CHAPTER 2: "I HAVE NO MORAL CONCEPTION OF PARTY POLITICS"

1 *Industrial Worker*, 15 December 1910; Leier, *Where the Fraser River Flows*, pp 121–23.

2 Victoria *Times*, 12 May 1916, 6 June 1916, 9 November 1916, 10 November 1916.

3 Victoria *Times*, 12 May 1916, 5 June 1916, 6 June 1916, 7 November 1916; Vancouver *Province*, 6 June 1916, 7 November 1916, 10 November, 1916; interview with John Bunyan.

4 Victoria *Times*, 11 May 1916.

5 Victoria *Times*, 11 May 1916.

6 Gosden to Brewster, A-G Correspondence, Letters, index, 1916–1937, GR 429, Reel B2520 in the BC Archives and Records Services (hereafter, BCARS). Emphasis is in original.

7 Brewster to Gosden, A-G Correspondence, Letters, index, 1916–1937, GR 429, Reel B2520 in BCARS.

8 Coverage of the plugging committee is in the Vancouver *Province*, 11 May 1916, 15 May 1916, 1 June, 1916, 8 November 1916; Victoria *Colonist*, 12 May 1916; Victoria *Times*, 11 May 1916, 12 May 1916.

CHAPTER 3: "OPPOSED TO ME IS A STRONG AND POWERFUL ORGANIZATION"

1 Vancouver *Province*, 12 May 1916.

2 Vancouver *Province*, 25 May 1916; Victoria *Colonist*, 3 June 1916.

3 Victoria *Colonist*, 12 May, 1916, 7 June 1916; Vancouver *Province*, 15 May 1916, 16 May 1916, 6 June 1916; Victoria *Times*, 6 June 1916.

4 Vancouver *Province*, 16 May 1916; Victoria *Colonist*, 8 June 1916.

5 Vancouver *Province*, 15 May 1916, 2 June 1916; Victoria *Times*, 9 November 1916; Vancouver *Daily News-Advertiser*, 10 November 1916.

6 Victoria *Colonist*, 7 June 1916; Vancouver *Province*, 7 June 1916.

7 Victoria *Times*, 7 June 1916; Victoria *Colonist*, 8 June 1916; John Sidaway interview, Angus MacInnis Memorial Collection, Dorothy Steeves Collection, Box 52, File 52–13, Special Collections, UBC.

8 Letters Inward Register, 1916, GR 1326, B2520, BCARS.

9 Victoria *Times*, 6 June 1916; Vancouver *Province*, 7 June 1916.

10 Vancouver *Province*, 6 June 1916, 10 November 1916; Victoria *Times*, 5 June 1916, 6 June 1916, 8 June 1916; Victoria *Colonist*, 7 June 1916.

11 Victoria *Times*, 8 June 1916; Victoria *Colonist*, 8 June 1916.

12 Vancouver *Province*, 12 September 1916; Vancouver *Daily News-Advertiser*, 12 September 1916; Victoria *Colonist*, 12 September 1916.

13 Victoria *Colonist*, 8 October 1916.

14 Victoria *Times*, 9 November 1916, 11 November 1916; Vancouver *Province*, 10 November 1916, 11 November 1916, 13 November 1916.

15 Vancouver *Province*, 13 November 1916; Victoria *Times*, 13 November 1916.

16 BC *Federationist*, 22 December 1916. I am grateful to John-Henry Harter for finding information on Bursill's newspaper career.

17 Gosden to Minister of Justice, 8 December 1916, RG 13 14 2, Volume 207, File 1891, National Archives of Canada. Thanks to Greg Kealey for forwarding this to me.

CHAPTER 4: "THE UNSEEN HAND WOULD INTIMIDATE THE WEAKER"

1 Interview with the Arthurs; interview with John Bunyan; RCMP to BC Provincial Police, 1932, GR 1323, B2300. F-L-125-1, BCARS.

2 Calgary *Herald*, 16 April 1918. I am grateful to David Bright for this reference.

3 David Bercuson's *Confrontation at Winnipeg: Labour, Industrial Relations, and the General Strike* (Montreal: McGill-Queen's University Press, 1974, revised edition, 1990) is the most recent book-length account of the Winnipeg General Strike. It should be read in conjunction with Gregory S. Kealey's "1919: The Canadian Labour Revolt" in *Labour/Le Travail* 13 (1984), as well as the articles Bercuson attacks in the afterword to his revised edition.

Also see Craig Heron, ed., *The Workers' Revolt in Canada, 1917–1925* (Toronto: University of Toronto Press, 1998) and James Naylor, *The New Democracy: Challenging the Social Order in Industrial Ontario, 1914–1925* (Toronto: University of Toronto Press, 1991).

4 Gregory S. Kealey and Reg Whitaker, eds., *rcmp Security Bulletins: The Early Years, 1919–1929* (St. John's: Canadian Committee on Labour History, 1994), p 383.

5 *Verbatim Report of the Calgary Conference, 1919*, Glenbow Archives.

6 *Verbatim Report of the Calgary Conference; Nanaimo Free Press*, 15 March 1919; James Dubro and Robin Rowland, *Undercover: Cases of the rcmp's Most Secret Operative* (Markham: Octopus Publishing Group, 1991), pp 44–45; *Fernie District Ledger*, 28 March 1919.

7 *Fernie District Ledger*, 28 March 1919.

8 The force was called the Royal Northwest Mounted Police until 1920. I refer to it as the RCMP throughout to avoid confusion.

9 S.W. Horrall, letter to the author; National Archives of Canada (hereafter, NAC), RG 18, Volume 829, p 181; RG 18, Volume 2170. Greg Kealey has kindly provided me with the primary material. See also Kealey's "The RCMP, the CSIS, the PAC, and Access to Information: A Curious Tale," *Labour/Le Travail* 21 (Spring 1988), pp 215–16, for reports mentioning Gosden. Gosden's name appears in two lists, "RCMP Personal Files Register" (p 383) and "RCMP Subject Files Register, 1919–1929" (p 455), in Kealey and Whitaker, *rcmp Security Bulletins: The Early Years, 1919–1929*. John Bunyan confirmed that Gosden lived with Owen Paulson in Pincher Creek, Alberta, in 1919. Efforts to find personal or personnel files on Gosden under Access to Information have turned up nothing. The story of proving Gosden was Agent 10 is given in Chapter 6.

10 I am grateful to S.W. Horrall, former head of the Historical Section of the RCMP, for this information (letter to the author, 1989); J.W. Spalding to Officer Commanding "K" Division, 20 March 1919, in Borden Papers, Volume 104, File Oc519 (A) 1, NAC; J.W. Spalding to Officer Commanding "E" Division, RCMP, 15 April 1932, A-G Correspondence, GR 1323, B2300, F-L-125–1932, BCARS; Gregory S. Kealey, "The Surveillance State: The Origins of Domestic Intelligence and Counter-Subversion in Canada, 1914–1921," *Intelligence and National Security*, 7, no. 3 (July 1992), pp 194–95, 201; Kealey and Whitaker, RCMP *Security Bulletins*, pp 383, 455.

11 For the role and structure of the RNWMP, see S.W. Horrall, "The Royal North-West Mounted Police and Labour Unrest in Western Canada, 1919," *Canadian Historical Review* 61 (1980), pp 169–90; and Gregory S. Kealey, "The Surveillance State," pp 179–210, and "The Early Years of State Surveillance of Labour and the Left in Canada: The Institutional Framework of the RCMP Security and Intelligence Apparatus, 1918–1926," *Intelligence and National Security*, 8, no. 3 (1993), pp 129–48.

12 For Zaneth's fascinating career as an RCMP undercover agent, see Dubro and Rowland, *Undercover*.

13 A.B. Perry to Maclean, 2 April 1919, and "Report of SA No. 10, 19 March 1919," Borden Papers, Volume 104, File Oc519 (A) 1, NAC. Greg Kealey kindly supplied me with this report and the letters and documents attached to it, including Spalding's letter.

14 The following quotes are taken from "Report of SA No. 10, 19 March 1919."

15 David Bercuson, *Fools and Wise Men: The Rise and Fall of the One Big Union* (Toronto: McGraw-Hill Ryerson, 1978); David Akers, "Rebel or Revolutionary? Jack Kavanagh and the Early Years of the Communist Movement in Vancouver, 1920–1925," *Labour/Le Travail* 30 (Fall 1992), pp 9–44.

16 See Todd McCallum, "The Strange Tale of Tom Cassidy and Catherine Rose, or, Free Love, Heterosexuality, and the One Big Union," *Journal of the Canadian Historical Association*, 1998.

17 Perry to McLean, Borden Papers; Greg Kealey, "The Surveillance State," footnote 80; Department of Justice, Access Request A-8800018, File 641 / 1919, for the request for an investigation into the legality of private trials.

18 "Report of SA No. 10, 19 March 1919" and Perry to McLean, Borden Papers.

19 Todd McCallum brought the June report to my attention. He found it in the Mary Jordan Papers, P4199, file 9, at the Public Archives of Manitoba.

20 For Frank Zaneth, see Dubro and Rowland, *Undercover*; the careers of James McParland and Harry Orchard are outlined in J. Anthony Lukas, *Big Trouble: A Murder in a Small Western Town Sets Off a Struggle for the Soul of America* (New York: Simon and Schuster, 1997); Melvyn Dubofsky, *We Shall Be All*, pp 97–104; and Stewart H. Holbrook, *The Rocky Mountain Revolution* (New York: Henry Holt, 1956). Other accounts of labour spies may be found in Jean E. Spielman, *The Stool Pigeon and the Open Shop Movement* (Minneapolis: The American Publishing Company, 1923); Leo Huberman, *The Labor Spy Racket* (Originally published in 1937. Reprint, New York: Monthly Review Press, 1966); Gary M. Fink, *The Fulton Bag and Cotton Mills Strike of 1914–1915: Espionage, Labor Conflict, and New South Industrial Relations* (Ithaca: ILR Press, 1993).

21 For an examination of labour careers in early Vancouver, see Mark Leier, *Red Flags and Red Tape: The Making of a Labour Bureaucracy* (Toronto: University of Toronto Press, 1995).

22 *Industrial Worker*, 8 May 1913. Brooks's book is *American Syndicalism: The IWW* (New York: Macmillan, 1913).

23 Robert Foster's remarks are taken from the Verbatim Report, Twelfth Annual Convention of the District Number Eighteen of the United Mine Workers of America, 15-24 February 1915, UMWA Papers, File 23, Glenbow Archives. I am grateful to Roger Stonebanks for this reference.

CHAPTER 5: "THE RULING CLASS IS ABSOLUTELY INSANE"

1 Spalding to Officer Commanding "E" Division, RCMP, 15 April 1932, A-G Correspondence, GR 1323, B2300, F-L-125-1-1932, BCARS. Spalding was at this time the Assistant Commissioner Commanding Saskatchewan District. S.T. Wood, Superintendent Commanding BC District, RCMP, to Commissioner, BC Provincial Police, 15 April 1932, also at BCARS.

2 For the Theosophical Society and Madame Blavatsky, see James Webb, *The Flight From Reason* (London: Macdonald, 1971), especially Chapter 3. A brief overview of the movement is given by Jay Kinney in "Deja Vu: The Hidden History of the New Age," in *The Fringes of Reason*, Ted Schultz, ed. (New York: Harmony Books, 1989), pp 22–30. Theosophy in Canada is examined by Michele Lacomb in "Theosophy and the Canadian Idealist Tradition," *Journal of Canadian Studies* 17 (1983), pp 100–20. See also Ramsay Cook, *The Regenerators: Social Criticism in Late Victorian English Canada* (Toronto: University of Toronto Press, 1985), pp 167–69, 172–73. In *The Making of the English Working Class* (Harmondsworth: Penguin, 1975), E.P. Thompson has commented on the attraction millenarian movements held for political radicals and speaks of the "chiliasm of despair" in his chapter "The Transforming Power of the Cross." Eugen Weber gives an overview of recent French literature on the issue in "Religion or Superstition?" *My France: Politics, Culture, and Myth* (Cam-

bridge: Harvard University Press, 1991), pp 103–36. Logie Barrow examines the connection between spiritualism and socialism in *Independent Spirits: Spiritualism and English Plebeians, 1850–1910* (London: Routledge and Kegan Paul, 1986), while its connection to feminism is explored in Ann Braude, "Radical Spirits": Spiritualism and Women's Rights in Nineteenth Century America (Boston: Beacon Press, 1989). BC activist Helena Gutteridge's membership in the Vancouver Co-Masons Inner Light Lodge, Number 399, a Theosophy branch of the Masons, may be found in the Vancouver City Archives (Additional Manuscripts 831, Volume 1, File 1, and Volume 2, File 2). For Canadian socialist Phillips Thompson's advocacy of Theosophy, see the *Western Clarion*, 24 April 1903, and Cook, *The Regenerators*, pp 167–69, 172–73. John Bunyan revealed that Gosden was involved with the Theosophy movement by 1919 and continued his research into paranormal and occult phenomena throughout his life. Gosden set numerous occult symbols into the sidewalk at his house in Gibson's Landing, BC, in the 1950s and early 1960s (interview with John Bunyan and interview with Mr. and Mrs. Arthur).

3 John Bunyan and Bill Bunyan, interviews by the author. John joined the Navy League (rather like Sea Cadets today) and went to sea at age thirteen on a fisheries patrol vessel. Later he became a master mariner and a captain on the BC Ferries run between Horseshoe Bay and Gibson's Landing. Bill became a machinist who worked at mining and construction camps across BC.

4 Interviews with John Bunyan, Bill Bunyan, and the Arthurs. The Vancouver city directories for 1931, 1933, 1934, 1936, 1937, and 1938 list Gosden's occupations as cement worker and labourer and list him as a resident in the different houses owned by Isabella Bunyan, widow.

5 Interviews with John Bunyan, Bill Bunyan, and Owen Paulson. See Eric Newsome, *The Case of the Beryl G* (Victoria: Orca Books, 1989), for details of the hijacking and murder of Beryl Gillis's father and brother.

6 Fisher, *Duff Pattullo*, p 176; Martin Robin, *The Rush for Spoils: The Company Province, 1871–1933* (Toronto: McClelland and Stewart, 1972); Martin Robin, *Pillars of Profit: The Company Province, 1934–1972* (Toronto: McClelland and Stewart, 1973), p 94.

7 Minutes of the CCF Provincial Executive Council, 7 July 1935, in the Angus MacInnis Memorial Collection, Box 45, File 5, UBC Special Collections, for Rees's suspension; Minutes of the BC CCF Executive Council, 3 May 1933, Angus MacInnis Memorial Collection, Box 45, File 9, for a note that Gosden had written to the CCF; interviews with John Bunyan and the Arthurs.

8 *BC Workers' News*, 2 October 1936. For more on McInnes see John Stanton, *Never Say Die! The Life and Times of John Stanton, A Pioneer Labour Lawyer* (Ottawa: Steel Rail Publishing, 1987), and *Vancouver Province*, 12 February 1951.

9 Hesson's first name appears in some written sources as Helena and in others as Helene. Since people who knew her called her Lena, I have chosen to refer to her as Helena. Details of Hesson's teaching career were supplied by the Vancouver School Board. I would like to thank Lucie Gambino and Dr. Avis for their help with this. Hesson's family, career, and salary were reconstructed from the *Annual Reports of the Public Schools of the Province of British Columbia* (Victoria: King's Printer) and the Vancouver City Directories. *Annual Reports of the Public Schools of the Province of British Columbia* (Victoria: King's Printer); Helena M. Hesson Fond, Add. Mss. 2115, City of Vancouver Archives. I am grateful to Juanita Nolan for this research.

10 Interviews with John Bunyan, the Arthurs, and Richard Kennett, who purchased land from Helena Gosden; information from Vancouver city directories.

11 Gosden to Cates, 9 December 1951, GR 1071, Box 2, File 8, BCARS. I am grateful to Ira Chaikin for bringing this document to my attention.

12 Gosden typescript, in author's possession. This material was kindly supplied to me by the Arthurs.

13 As recited by Gosden, tape in author's possession (supplied by the Arthurs).

14 Recited by Gosden, tape in author's possession.

15 Recited by Gosden, tape in author's possession.

16 Gosden's materials, in author's possession.

17 Cited in Kornbluh, Rebel Voices, pp 29–30.

18 Kornbluh, Rebel Voices, pp 77–79.

19 Francis Shor, "Masculine Power and Virile Syndicalism: A Gendered Analysis of the IWW in Australia," Labour History 63 (June 1992), pp 83–99; McCallum, "'A Modern Weapon for Modern Man.'"

20 Independent, 8 August 1903. For other descriptions of labourism and masculinity, see Ava Baron, "An 'Other' Side of Gender Antagonism at Work: Men, Boys, and the Remasculinization of Printers' Work, 1830–1920," in Work Engendered: Toward a New History of American Labor, Ava Baron, ed. (Ithaca: Cornell University Press, 1991), pp 47–69; Shirley Tillotson, "We may all soon be 'first-class Men': Gender and skill in Canada's early twentieth century urban telegraph industry," Labour/Le Travail 27 (Spring 1991), pp 97–125; Christine Burr, "Defending the 'Art Preservative': Class and Gender Relations in the Printing Trade Unions, 1850–1914," Labour/Le Travail 31 (Spring 1993), pp 47–73, and "Class and Gender in the Toronto Printing Trades," PhD dissertation, Memorial University of Newfoundland, 1992; Leier, Red Flags and Red Tape (Toronto: University of Toronto Press, 1995), pp 135–42.

CHAPTER 6: ON THE TRAIL OF A LABOUR SPY

1 In addition to the books by McCormack and Bercuson, for examples of western exceptionalism see David Bercuson, "Labour Radicalism and the Western Industrial Frontier," and Daniel Drache, "The Formation and Fragmentation of the Canadian Working Class, 1820–1920." For some of its critics see Gregory S. Kealey, "1919: The Canadian Labour Revolt"; Bryan D. Palmer, "Listening to History Rather than Historians: Reflections on Working Class History"; and James Naylor, The New Democracy. Ian McKay and David Frank have written a great deal on mining in Nova Scotia, while works by western historians such as Robert McDonald, Jeremy Mouat, John Belshaw, and Mark Leier have suggested that the radicalism of BC workers has been somewhat exaggerated.

2 I examine some of the reasons for this in "W[h]ither Labour History: Regionalism, Class, and the Writing of BC History," BC Studies 111 (Autumn 1996), pp 61–75; see also the comments by Bryan Palmer, Veronica Strong-Boag, and Robert McDonald, and my response, in the same issue.

3 Some of the historians who have published books or articles in these categories include Linda Kealey, Janice Newton, Robert McDonald, Allen Seager, Jeremy Mouat, Stephen Gray, Gordon Hak, Andrew Parnaby, and Todd McCallum.

BIBLIOGRAPHY

Akers, David. "Rebel or Revolutionary? Jack Kavanagh and the Early Years of the Communist Movement in Vancouver, 1920–1925." *Labour/Le Travail* 30 (Fall 1992).

Baron, Ava, ed. *Work Engendered: Toward a New History of American Labor.* Ithaca: Cornell University Press, 1991.

Barrow, Logie. *Independent Spirits: Spiritualism and English Plebeians, 1850–1910.* London: Routledge and Kegan Paul, 1986.

Bercuson, David. *Confrontation at Winnipeg: Labour, Industrial Relations, and the General Strike.* Montreal: McGill-Queen's University Press, 1974, revised edition, 1990.

————. *Fools and Wise Men: The Rise and Fall of the One Big Union.* Toronto: McGraw-Hill Ryerson, 1978.

————. "Labour Radicalism and the Western Industrial Frontier." *Canadian Historical Review.* 58:2. (June 1977).

Blaisdell, Lowell L. *The Desert Revolution: Baja California, 1911.* Madison: University of Wisconsin Press, 1962.

Bowen, Lynne. *Boss Whistle: The Coal Miners of Vancouver Island Remember.* Lantzville, BC: Oolichan Books, 1982.

Braude, Ann. *"Radical Spirits": Spiritualism and Women's Rights in Nineteenth Century America.* Boston: Beacon Press, 1989.

Brooks, John Graham. *American Syndicalism: The IWW.* New York: Macmillan, 1913.

Burr, Christine. "Class and Gender in the Toronto Printing Trades." PhD dissertation, Memorial University of Newfoundland, 1992.

————. "Defending the 'Art Preservative': Class and Gender Relations in the Printing Trade Unions, 1850–1914." *Labour/Le Travail* 31 (Spring 1993).

Campbell, Peter. "'Making Socialists': Bill Pritchard, the Socialist Party of Canada, and the Third International." *Labour/Le Travail* 30 (Fall 1992).

Cavanaugh, Cathy and Jeremy Mouat, eds. *Making Western Canada.* Toronto: Garamond, 1996.

Cook, Ramsay. *The Regenerators: Social Criticism in Late Victorian English Canada.* Toronto: University of Toronto Press, 1985.

Drache, Daniel. "The Formation and Fragmentation of the Canadian Working Class: 1820–1920." *Studies in Political Economy* 15 (Fall 1984).

Dubofsky, Melvyn. *We Shall Be All: A History of the Industrial Workers of the World.* New York: Quadrangle Books, 1969.

Dubois, Pierre. *Sabotage in Industry.* Harmondsworth: Penguin, 1977.

Dubro, James and Robin Rowland. *Undercover: Cases of the rcmp's Most Secret Operative.* Markham: Octopus Publishing Group, 1991.

Fink, Gary M. *The Fulton Bag and Cotton Mills Strike of 1914–1915: Espionage, Labor Conflict, and New South Industrial Relations.* Ithaca: ILR Press, 1993.

Fisher, Robin. *Duff Pattullo of British Columbia.* Toronto: University of Toronto Press, 1991.

Flynn, Elizabeth Gurley. *Sabotage*. Published by the IWW in 1915. At the time of printing, the entire pamphlet was available on the IWW website (http://www.iww.org.sabotage/so.html).

Foner, Philip. *The Industrial Workers of the World, 1905–1917*. NewYork: International Publishers, 1965.

———, ed. *"Fellow Workers and Friends": IWW Free Speech Fights as Told by Participants*. Westport: Greenwood Press, 1981.

Gutkin, Harry and Mildred Gutkin. *Profiles in Dissent: The Shaping of Radical Thought in the Canadian West*. Edmonton: NeWest Press, 1997.

Hardy, George. *Those Stormy Years: Memories of the Fight for Freedom on Five Continents*. London: Lawrence and Wishart, 1956.

Hart, John M. *Anarchism and the Mexican Working Class, 1860–1931*. Austin: University of Texas Press, 1974.

Heron, Craig, ed. *The Workers' Revolt in Canada, 1917–1925*. Toronto: University of Toronto Press, 1998.

The History of the San Diego Free Speech Fight. n.a. San Diego: The Industrial Workers of the World, 1973.

Holbrook, Stewart H. *The Rocky Mountain Revolution*. New York: Henry Holt, 1956.

Horrall, S.W. "The Royal North-West Mounted Police and Labour Unrest in Western Canada, 1919." *Canadian Historical Review* 61 (1980).

Huberman, Leo. *The Labor Spy Racket*. Originally published in 1937. Reprint, New York: Monthly Review Press, 1966.

Kealey, Greg. "1919: The Canadian Labour Revolt." *Labour/Le Travail* 13 (1984).

———. "The RCMP, the CSIS, the PAC, and Access to Information: A Curious Tale," *Labour/Le Travail* 21 (Spring 1988).

———. "The Surveillance State: The Origins of Domestic Intelligence and Counter-Subversion in Canada, 1914–1921." *Intelligence and National Security* 7, no. 3 (July 1992).

———. "The Early Years of State Surveillance of Labour and the Left in Canada: The Institutional Framework of the RCMP Security and Intelligence Apparatus, 1918–1926," *Intelligence and National Security* 8, no. 3 (1993).

——— and Reg Whitaker, eds. *RCMP Security Bulletins: The Early Years, 1919–1929*. St. John's: Canadian Committee on Labour History, 1994.

Kealey, Linda. *Enlisting Women for the Cause: Women, Labour, and the Left in Canada, 1890–1920*. Toronto: University of Toronto Press, 1998.

John Thomas Keelor. "The Price of Lives and Limbs Lost at Work: The Development of No-Fault Workers' Compensation Legislation in British Columbia, 1910–1916." MA thesis, University of Victoria, 1996.

Kornbluh, Joyce, ed. *Rebel Voices: An IWW Anthology*. Ann Arbor: University of Michigan Press, 1972.

Lacomb, Michele. "Theosophy and the Canadian Idealist Tradition." *Journal of Canadian Studies* 17 (1983).

Leier, Mark. *Where the Fraser River Flows:The IWW In British Columbia*.Vancouver: New Star Books, 1990.

———. *Red Flags and Red Tape:The Making of a Labour Bureaucracy*.Toronto: University ofToronto Press, 1995.

———. "Workers and Intellectuals:TheTheory of the New Class and Early Canadian Socialism." *Journal of History and Politics*, 10 (1992).

———. "W[h]ither Labour History: Regionalism, Class, and theWriting of BC History." *BC Studies* 111 (Autumn 1996).

———. "Plots, Shots, and LiberalThoughts: ConspiracyTheory and the Shooting of Ginger Goodwin." *Labour/LeTravail* 39 (Spring 1997).

Lukas, J.Anthony. *BigTrouble:A Murder in a SmallWestern Town Sets Off a Struggle for the Soul of America*. NewYork: Simon and Schuster, 1997.

Mayse, Susan. *Ginger:The Life and Death of Albert Goodwin*. Madeira Park, BC: Harbour Publishing Co., 1990.

McCallum,Todd. "'A ModernWeapon for Modern Man': Marxist Masculinity and the Social Practices of the One Big Union, 1919–1924." MA thesis, SFU, 1995.

———. "The StrangeTale ofTom Cassidy and Catherine Rose, or, Free Love, Heterosexuality, and the One Big Union." *Journal of the Canadian HistoricalAssociation* (1998).

McCormack, A. Ross. *Reformers, Rebels, and Revolutionaries:TheWestern Canadian Radical Movement, 1899–1919*.Toronto: University ofToronto Press, 1977; *second edition*, 1991.

Naylor, James. *The New Democracy: Challenging the Social Order in Industrial Ontario, 1914–1925*.Toronto: University ofToronto Press, 1991.

Newsome, Eric. *The Case of the Beryl G*.Victoria: Orca Books, 1989.

Newton, Janice. *The Feminist Challenge to the Canadian Left, 1900–1918*.Montreal: McGill-Queen's University Press, 1995.

Noble, David. *Progress without People*. Chicago: Charles H. Kerr, 1993.

Norris, John. "TheVancouver Island Coal Miners, 1912–14:A Study of an Organizational Strike." *BC Studies* 45 (Spring 1980).

Palmer, Bryan D. "Listening to History Rather than Historians: Reflections onWorking Class History." *Studies in Political Economy* 20 (Summer 1986).

Phillips, Paul. *No Power Greater:A Century of Labour in BC*.Vancouver: BC Federation of Labour and Boag Foundation, 1967.

Robin, Martin. *Radical Politics and Canadian Labour*. Kingston: Industrial Relations Centre, Queen's University, 1968.

———. *The Rush for Spoils:The Company Province, 1871–1933*.Toronto: McClelland and Stewart, 1972.

———. *Pillars of Profit:The Company Province, 1934–1972*.Toronto: McClelland and Stewart, 1973.

Sale, Kirkpatrick. *Rebels against the Future: Lessons for the Computer Age*.Reading, MA: Addison/Wesley, 1995.

Schultz,Ted, ed. *The Fringes of Reason*. NewYork: Harmony Books, 1989.

Seager, Allen. "Socialists and Workers: The Western Canadian Coal Miners, 1900–21." *Labour/Le Travail* 16 (Fall 1985).

Shor, Francis. "Masculine Power and Virile Syndicalism: A Gendered Analysis of the IWW in Australia." *Labour History* 63 (June 1992).

Smith, Gibbs M. *Joe Hill*. Salt Lake City: Peregrine Smith Books, 1984.

Spielman, Jean E. *The Stool Pigeon and the Open Shop Movement*. Minneapolis: The American Publishing Company, 1923.

Sprouse, Martin, ed. *Sabotage in the American Workplace: Anecdotes of Dissatisfaction, Mischief, and Revenge*. San Francisco: Pressure Drop Press, 1992.

Stanton, John. *Never Say Die! The Life and Times of John Stanton, A Pioneer Labour Lawyer*. Ottawa: Steel Rail Publishing, 1987.

Stonebanks, Roger. Entry on Albert "Ginger" Goodwin in *Dictionary of Canadian Biography*, Volume XIV, 1911-1920. Toronto: University of Toronto Press, 1998.

Thomas, Philip J. *Songs of the Pacific Northwest*. Saanichton: Hancock House Publishers, 1979.

Thompson, E.P. *The Making of the English Working Class*. Harmondsworth: Penguin, 1975.

Tillotson, Shirley. "We may all soon be 'first-class Men': Gender and skill in Canada's early twentieth century urban telegraph industry." *Labour/Le Travail* 27 (Spring 1991).

Wargo, Alan J. "The Great Coal Strike: The Vancouver Island Coal Miners' Strike, 1912–1914." BA graduation essay, University of British Columbia, 1962.

Webb, James. *The Flight From Reason*. London: Macdonald, 1971.

Weber, Eugen. *My France: Politics, Culture, and Myth*. Cambridge: Harvard University Press, 1991.

Wejr, Patricia and Howie Smith, eds. *Fighting for Labour: Four Decades of Work in British Columbia, 1910–1950*. Sound Heritage, Volume Four. Victoria: Provincial Archives, 1978.

NEWSPAPERS

BC Federationist

BC Workers' News

Calgary Herald

Fernie District Ledger

Industrial Worker

Nanaimo Free Press

Prince Rupert Optimist

Vancouver Daily News-Advertiser

Vancouver Province

VTLC Independent

Victoria Daily Colonist

Victoria Daily Times

Western Clarion

INTERVIEWS

Gwen Arthur
Leon Gordon Arthur
Bill Bunyan
Captain John Bunyan
Richard Kennett
Owen Paulson
Alan Schwab

CORRESPONDENCE

David Frank, University of New Brunswick
Detective Sergeant Gary L. Hoving, San Luis Obispo County
    Sheriff-Coroner's Office
Ian Mackay, Queen's University
S.W. Horrall, former head, Historical Section, RCMP

ARCHIVAL MATERIAL

from BC Archives and Records Services, Glenbow Archives, National
Archives of Canada, Public Archives of Manitoba, UBC Special Collections, Vancouver City Archives.

INDEX

A Bibliography of
British Columbia
Labour History

INTRODUCTION

The history of British Columbia is a history of class struggle. From the time of the fur trade to the present, working people and their battles to make a better world have transformed the politics, economics, laws, and workplaces of the province. This bibliography will make this history more accessible to trade unionists, students, and the general public.

It is arranged in four sections: books, articles, theses, and newspapers. The entries in each section are listed alphabetically by the author's last name. Subsequent entries by the same author are indicated with an underline.

The bibliography was compiled by graduate students of Simon Fraser University's History Department: Dennis Pilon, Todd McCallum, Andy Parnaby, and David Sandquist.

BOOKS

Abella, Irving. *The Canadian Labour Movement, 1902–1960*. (Ottawa: Canadian Historical Association, 1975).

———. *Nationalism, Communism and Canadian Labour:The cio, the Communist Party and the Canadian Congress of Labour, 1935–1956*. (Toronto: University of Toronto Press, 1973).

Abella, Irving, and David Millar, eds. *The Canadian Worker in the Twentieth Century*. (Toronto: Oxford University Press, 1978).

Alexander, A. *Labour Turnover at Mackenzie*. (Vancouver: BC Research, 1974).

Allen, Robert C. *Trade Unions and the B.C. Economy*. (Vancouver: BC Economic Policy Institute, 1985).

Andrews, Ralph. *Glory Days of Logging*. (New York: Bonanza Books, 1956).

Angus, Ian. *Canadian Bolsheviks:The Early Years of the Communist Party of Canada*. (Montreal: Vanguard, 1981).

Anton, Frank. *The Role of the Government in the Settlement of Industrial Disputes in Canada*. (Toronto: CCH Canadian, 1962).

Arrowsmith, David. *Canada's Trade Unions: An Information Manual*. (Kingston: Industrial Relations Centre, Queen's University, 1992).

Audain, James. *From Coalmine to Castle:The Story of the Dunsmuirs of Vancouver Island*. (New York: Pageant Press, 1955).

Avakumovic, Ivan. *The Communist Party of Canada*. (Toronto: McClelland and Stewart, 1975).

Avery, Donald. *"Dangerous Foreigners": European Immigrant Workers and Labour Radicalism in Canada, 1896–1932*. (Toronto: McClelland and Stewart, 1979).

Babcock, Robert H. *Gompers in Canada: A Study in American Continentalism Before the First World War*. (Toronto: University of Toronto Press, 1974).

Bains, Hardial S. *British Columbia Labour Code Bill*. (Toronto: Norman Bethune Institute, 1974).

Baird, Irene. *Waste Heritage*. (Toronto: Macmillan, 1939).

Baker, Leslie. *Employee/Employer Rights: A Guide for the British Columbia Work Force*. (North Vancouver: Self Counsel Press, 1997).

The Bank Book Collective. *An Account to Settle: The Story of the United Bankworkers (SORWUC)*. (Vancouver: Press Gang Publishers, 1979).

Baptie, Susan. *First Growth*. (Vancouver: J.J. Douglas, 1976).

Barman, Jean. *The West Beyond the West: A History of British Columbia*. (Toronto: University of Toronto Press, 1991).

Bartley, George. *An Outline History of Typographical Union No. 226, Vancouver, BC, 1887–1938*. (Vancouver: Typographical Union No. 226, n.d.).

Baskerville, Peter A., and Eric W. Sager. *Unwilling Idlers:The Urban Unemployed and Their Families in Late Victorian Canada*. (Toronto: University of Toronto Press, 1998).

Bennett, Marilyn. *Indian Fishing and Its Cultural Importance in the Fraser River System*. (Vancouver: BC Department of the Environment and the Union of BC Indian Chiefs, 1973).

Bennett, William. *Builders of BC*. (Vancouver: Broadway Printers, 1937).

Bercuson, David J. *Fools and Wise Men:The Rise and Fall of the One Big Union*. (Toronto: McGraw-Hill Ryerson Limited, 1978).

Bergen, Myrtle. *Tough Timber:The Loggers of BC – Their Story*. (Vancouver: Elgin Publication, 1979).

Bernard, Elaine. *The Long Distance Feeling: A History of the Telecommunications Workers Union*. (Vancouver: New Star Books, 1982).

Bjarnason, Emil. *ILWU Canadian Area: 25th Anniversary, 1959–1984.* (Vancouver: International Longshoremen's and Warehousemen's Union, 1984).

———. *The Case of the Tearful Tycoon.* (Vancouver: Trade Union Research Bureau, 1961).

Bjarnason, Emil, and Bert Marcuse. *Wages and the Cost of Living.* (Vancouver: Trade Union Research Bureau, 1950).

———. *The Case of the Dwindling Dollar: What Is Happening to the Cost of Living, Wages, Prices and Profits?* (Vancouver: Trade Union Research Bureau, 1948).

Blount, Gail. *Collective Bargaining in Canadian Education: An Annotated Bibliography.* (Toronto: Ontario Institute for Studies in Education, 1975).

Bowen, Lynne. *Boss Whistle: The Coal Miners of Vancouver Island Remember.* (Lantzville: Oolichan Books, 1982).

Bowman, Phyllis. *We Skirted the War!* (Prince Rupert: Superior Printers, 1975).

Braid, Kate. *Women in Non-Traditional Occupations in British Columbia: Resume of Research.* (Victoria: BC Human Rights Commission, 1979).

Briskin, Linda, and Lynda Yanz, eds. *Union Sisters: Women in the Labour Movement.* (Toronto: Women's Press, 1983).

British Columbia, Department of Labour, Unemployment Relief Branch. *Narrative History of Unemployment Relief from 1931–1937.* (Victoria: King's Printer, 1937).

British Columbia, Industrial Relations Council. *Annual Report.* (Victoria: The Industrial Relations Council, serial 1989–).

———. *Industrial Relations Council Decision Index.* (Vancouver: Industrial Relations Products Limited, serial 1987–).

British Columbia, Ministry of Labour and Consumer Services. *Guide to the Industrial Relations Act.* (Victoria: Province of British Columbia, Ministry of Labour and Consumer Services, 1988).

———. *Labour Legislation Review: A Report of the Minister of Labour and Consumer Services to the Premier of British Columbia.* (Victoria: Ministry of Labour and Consumer Services, 1987).

British Columbia, Ministry of Labour. *BC Labour Directory, 1983.* (Victoria: Ministry of Labour, 1983).

British Columbia, Ministry of Skills, Training and Labour. *Guide to the Labour Relations Code.* (Victoria: Ministry of Skills, Training and Labour, 1993).

British Columbia Federation of Labour. *Why it isn't working: a labour review of the Industrial Relations Council.* (Vancouver: BCFL, 1988).

———. *25 Years: From Past to Present.* (Vancouver: BCFL, 1980).

———. *Unionism in British Columbia.* (Vancouver: BCFL, 1967).

———. *Unions Are People.* (Vancouver: BCFL, 1967).

———. *Automation: Threat or Promise?* (Vancouver: BCFL, 1966).

British Columbia Government Employees' Union. *Catch-up, Keep-up: Bargaining '82.* (Burnaby: BCGEU, 1982).

Brodie, Steve. *Bloody Sunday —Vancouver, 1938.* (Vancouver: Young Communist League, 1974).

Buchanan, D.R., and B.A. Campbell. *The Incomes of Salmon Fishermen in British Columbia.* (Ottawa: Department of Fisheries, 1957).

Buck, Tim. *Thirty Years: The Story of the Communist Movement in Canada, 1922–1952.* (Toronto: Progress Books, 1975 [1952]).

Burley, Edith I. *Servants of the Honourable Company: Work, Discipline, and Conflict in the Hudson's Bay Company, 1770–1870.* (Toronto: Oxford University Press, 1997).

Bye, Shirley. *Labour Code of British Columbia.* (Vancouver: Butterworths, 1979–1987).

Cameron, Colin. *The Economy We Live In.* (Vancouver: The Boag Foundation, 1954–55).

———. *Forestry, BC's Devastated Industry.* (Vancouver: CCF (BC), 1941).

Campbell, Marie. *Women and Trade Unions in BC, 1900–1920: The Social Organization of Sex Discrimination.* (Vancouver: Women's Research Centre, 1978).

Canada, Department of Manpower and Immigration, Economic Analysis and Forecasts Branch. *Introductory guide to unions in British Columbia.* (Ottawa: Economic Analysis and Forecasts Branch, 1974).

Carrothers, A.W.R. *The British Columbia Trade Union Act, 1959.* (Ottawa: Canadian Bar Association, 1960).

———. *The Labour Injunction in British Columbia.* (Toronto: CCH Canadian, 1956).

Carrothers, W.A. *The British Columbia Fisheries.* (Toronto: University of Toronto Press, 1941).

Chan, Anthony B. *Gold Mountain: The Chinese In the New World.* (Vancouver: New Star Books, 1983).

Chicanot, Eugene, ed. *Rhymes of the Miner: An Anthology of Canadian Mining Verse.* (Gardenvale: Federal Publications, 1937).

Christensen, Sandra. *Unions and the Public Interest: Collective Bargaining in the Government Sector.* (Vancouver: The Fraser Institute, 1980).

Christie, Robert. *Empire in Wood.* (Ithaca: New York State School of Industrial and Labor Relations, 1956).

Coates, Mary Lou. *Is There A Future For The Canadian Labour Movement?* (Kingston: Industrial Relations Centre, Queen's University, 1992).

Cochrane, William. *Labour Disputes and the Metropolitan Press: A Catalogue of Editorial Reactions.* (Victoria: BC Project, University of Victoria, 1983).

Con, Harry, et al. *From China to Canada: A History of the Chinese Communities in Canada.* ed. Edgar Wickberg (Toronto: McClelland and Stewart, 1982).

Cox, Thomas. *Mills and Markets: A History of the Pacific Coast Lumber Industry to 1900.* (Seattle: University of Washington Press, 1974).

Craig, Andy. *Trucking: BC's Trucking History.* (Saanichton: Hancock House, 1977).

Creese, Gillian. *Contracting Masculinity: Gender, Class, and Race in a White-Collar Union, 1944–1994.* (Toronto: Oxford University Press, 1999).

Crispo, John. *International Unionism: A Study in Canadian-American Relations.* (Toronto: McGraw-Hill, 1967).

Curtis, Lynn. *The War is Over! A Study of Labour-Management Relations at St. Joseph's Hospital, BC.* (Victoria: Social Science Research, 1970).

Daykin, Harold. *The Role of Co-operatives.* (Vancouver: The Boag Foundation, 1954–55).

———. *Money and Jobs.* (Vancouver: The Boag Foundation, 1954–55).

———. *Some Social Credit Fallacies.* (Vancouver: The Boag Foundation, 1954–55).

DeWolf, John. *Wage Movements and Wage Determinants in British Columbia: A Formula for the Mechanical Construction Industry.* (Vancouver: Broadway Printers, 1966).

Diamond, Sara. *Women's Labour History in British Columbia: A Bibliography, 1930–1948.* (Vancouver: Press Gang Publishers, 1980).

Dorman, George. *Up in the Morning, Out on the Job.* (Nanaimo: Brechin Publishing, 1994).

Drucker, Philip. *The Native Brotherhoods: Modern Intertribal Organizations on the Northwest Coast.* (Washington, DC: USGPO, 1958).

Drushka, Ken. *Working in the Woods: A History of Logging on the West Coast*. (Madeira Park: Harbour Publishing, 1992).

————. *Against Wind and Weather: A History of Towboating in British Columbia*. (Vancouver: Douglas and McIntyre, 1981).

Ehrlich, Howard L., Sandra Banister, and the Continuing Legal Education Society of British Columbia. *Labour Relations Code: Materials prepared for a Continuing Legal Education*. (Vancouver: Continuing Legal Education Society of British Columbia, 1993).

Finely, Joseph. *White Collar Union: The Study of the OPEIU and Its People*. (New York: Octagon Books, 1975).

Fisher, Robin. *Duff Patullo of British Columbia*. (Toronto: University of Toronto Press, 1991).

Forester, Joseph, and Anne Forester. *Fishing: British Columbia's Commercial Fishing History*. (Saanichton: Hancock House, 1975).

Forsey, Eugene. *The Canadian Labour Movement 1812–1902*. (Ottawa: Canadian Historical Association, 1974).

Foster, V.W. *Vancouver Through the Eyes of a Hobo*. (Vancouver: n.p., 1934).

Friesen, Jean, and Keith H. Ralston, eds. *Historical Essays on British Columbia*. (Toronto: McClelland and Stewart, 1976).

Gamey, Carol. *Collective Bargaining and the Excluded Employee in the British Columbia Public Service*. (Victoria: BC Project, University of Victoria, 1983).

————. *The Impact of Collective Bargaining on the BC Government Nurses: The RNABC Record*. (Victoria: BC Project, University of Victoria, 1983).

Garner, Joe. *Never Chop Your Rope: A Story of British Columbia Logging and the People Who Logged*. (Nanaimo: Cinnibar Press, 1988).

Gibson, Gordon, and Carol Robinson. *Bull of the Woods: The Gordon Gibson Story*. (Vancouver: Douglas and McIntyre, 1980).

Glavin, Terry. *Dead Reckoning: Confronting the Crisis in Pacific Fisheries*. (Vancouver: Douglas & McIntyre, a Greystone Book, 1996).

Glynn-Ward, Hilda. *The Writing On The Wall: The Chinese and Japanese Immigration to British Columbia, 1920*. (Toronto: University of Toronto Press, 1974).

Gould, Edwin. *Logging: British Columbia's Logging History*. (Saanichton: Hancock House, 1975).

Graham, Clara, Ed Picard, and Angus Davis. *Kootenay Yesterdays: Three First Hand Accounts of Mining, Prospecting, Ranching, Teaching and Trapping in the Kootenay District in Pre-World War I Times*. (Vancouver: Alexander Nicholls Press, 1976).

Graham, Donald. *Keepers of the Light: A History of British Columbia's Lighthouses and Their Keepers*. (Madeira Park, BC: Harbour Publishing, 1985).

————. *Lights of the Inside Passage: A History of British Columbia's Lighthouses and Their Keepers*. (Madeira Park, BC: Harbour Publishing, 1986.)

Greenall, Jack. *The I.W.A. Fiasco*. (Vancouver: Progressive Workers Movement, 1965).

Greening, W.E. *It Was Never Easy: A History of the Canadian Brotherhood of Railway, Transport and General Workers, 1908–1958*. (Ottawa: Mutual Press, 1961).

Griffin, Harold. *British Columbia: The People's Early Story*. (Vancouver: Tribune Publishing Company, 1958).

Griffin, H., and G. North. *A Ripple, A Wave: The Story of Union Organization in the BC Fishing Industry*. (Vancouver: Fishermen Publishing Society, 1974).

Griffin, Sean, ed. *Fighting Heritage: Highlights of the 1930s struggle for jobs and militant unionism in British Columbia*. (Vancouver: Tribune Publishing, 1985).

Gutkin, Harry, and Mildred Gutkin. *Profiles In Dissent:The Shaping of Radical Thought in the Canadian West.* (Edmonton: NeWest Press, 1997).

Hallock, Ricard M. *Pick Up Sticks:A History of the Intercoastal Lumber Trade.* (Vancouver: Cordillera Publishing Co., 1995).

Hann, Richard, Gregory Kealey, Linda Kealey, and Peter Warrian. *Primary Sources in Working-Class History, 1860–1930.* (Kitchener: Dumont Press, 1973).

Harney, Robert F. *From the Shores of Hardship: Italians in Canada.* (Welland: Soleil Publishing, 1993).

Harris, Cole. *The Resettlement of British Columbia: Essays on Colonialism and Geographical Change.* (Vancouver: UBC Press, 1997).

Henderson, George. *Federal Royal Commissions in Canada, 1867–1966:A Checklist.* (Toronto: University of Toronto Press, 1967).

Hendsbee, Joe. *Hands Off the Unions.* (Vancouver: Seamen Militants Against Government Intervention, 1963).

Heron, Craig. *The Canadian Labour Movement:A Short History.* (Toronto: James Lorimer, 1996).

Heron, Craig, and Robert Storey, eds. *On The Job: Confronting the Labour Process in Canada.* (Kingston and Montreal: McGill-Queen's University Press, 1986).

Hill, A.V. *Tides of Change:A Story of Fishermen's Cooperatives in British Columbia.* (Prince Rupert: Prince Rupert Fishermen's Cooperative Association, 1967).

Hoar, Victor. *The On-to-Ottawa Trek.* (Vancouver: Copp Clark, 1970).

Holmes, Marjorie. *Publications of the Goverment of British Columbia, 1871–1947.* (Victoria: King's Printer, 1950).

———. *Royal Commissions and Commissions of Inquiry in British Columbia, 1872–1942.* (Victoria: King's Printer, 1945).

Hospital Employees Union, Local 180. *Local 180,The Union of BC Hospital Workers.* (Vancouver: n.p., 1963)

Hotel, Restaurant and Culinary Employees and Bartenders Union, Local 40. *Industry Report:The British Columbia Hotel Industry.* (Vancouver:The Union, 1979).

Howard, Irene. *The Struggle for Social Justice in British Columbia: Helena Gutteridge,The Unknown Reformer.* (Vancouver: UBC Press, 1992).

Hume, Gavin H.G., Stan Lanyon, Ian Donald, Patricia Janzen. *Industrial Relations Reform Act: Materials prepared for a Continuing Legal Education seminar held in Vancouver, B.C.* (Vancouver: Continuing Legal Education Society of British Columbia, 1986).

Hume, Gavin H.G., Ian Donald, A.M. Hickling, Joseph Arvay. *Labour relations – current issues: Materials prepared for a Continuing Legal Education Seminar held in Vancouver, B.C.* (Vancouver: Continuing Legal Education Society of British Columbia, 1986).

Hutcheson, Sydney. *Depression Stories.* (Vancouver: New Star Books, 1977)

International Brotherhood of Boilermakers, Iron Shipbuilders, Blacksmiths, Forgers and Helpers. *70 Years of Participation in the Development of British Columbia, 1898–1968.* (Vancouver: n.p., 1968).

International Longshoremen's and Warehousemen's Union, ILWU Local 500. *"Man Along the Shore":The Story of the Vancouver Waterfront, As Told By the Longshoremen Themselves, 1860s–1975.* (Vancouver: ILWU Local 500, 1975).

International Typographical Union, Local 201,Victoria. *75th Anniversary, Diamond Jubilee, Victoria Typographical Union No. 201, 1884–1959.* (Victoria:The Union, 1959).

International Woodworkers of America, Western Council No. 1. *The IWA in British Columbia.* (Vancouver: Broadway Printers, 1971).

Isbester, F., et al. Industrial and Labour Relations in Canada: A Select Bibliography. (Kingston: Industrial Relations Centre, Queen's University, 1965).

Jamieson, Stuart. Industrial Relations Reform Act, 1987. (Vancouver: British Columbia Economic Policy Institute, 1987).

———. Industrial Relations in Canada. (Toronto: MacMillan of Canada, 1968).

———. Times of Trouble: Labour Unrest and Industrial Conflict in Canada, 1900–1966. (Ottawa: Information Canada, 1968).

———. Boom or Bust. (Vancouver: The Boag Foundation, 1954–55).

Jarvis, Robert. The Workingman's Revolt: The Vancouver Asiatic Exclusion Rally of 1907. (Toronto: Citizens for Foreign Aid Reform, 1991).

Johnstone, Bill. Coal Dust in My Blood: The Autobiography of a Coal Miner. (Victoria: Provincial Museum, 1980).

Jones, Beverly. High Heels 'n' Oil Rigs. (Prince George: Caitlin Press, 1995).

Kealey, Gregory S. Canada Investigates Industrialism. (Toronto: University of Toronto Press, 1973).

Kealey, Gregory S., and Reg Whitaker. RCMP Security Bulletins: The Depression Years, Part V, 1938–39. (St. John's: Canadian Committee on Labour History, 1997).

———. RCMP Security Bulletins: The Depression Years, Part IV, 1937. (St. John's: Canadian Committee on Labour History, 1997).

———. RCMP Security Bulletins: The Depression Years, Part III, 1936. (St. John's: Canadian Committee on Labour History, 1996).

———. RCMP Security Bulletins: The Depression Years, Part II, 1935. (St. John's: Canadian Committee on Labour History, 1995).

Kealey, Linda. Enlisting Women For The Cause: Women, Labour, and the Left in Canada, 1890–1920. (Toronto: University of Toronto Press, 1998).

Keller, Betty C., and Rosella M. Leslie. Sea-Silver: Inside British Columbia's Salmon-Farming Industry. (Victoria: Horsdal & Schubart, 1996).

Kent, Duncan. British Columbia: A Bibliography of Industry, Labour, Resources and Regions for the Social Sciences. (Vancouver: UBC Press, 1978).

Kesselman, Amy. Fleeting Opportunities: Women Shipyard Workers in Portland and Vancouver During World War II and Reconversion. (Albany: State University of New York Press, 1990).

Knight, Phyllis. A Very Ordinary Life, As Told To Rolf Knight. (Vancouver: New Star Books, 1974).

Knight, Rolf. Traces of Magma: An Annotated Bibliography of Left Literature. (Vancouver: Draegerman, 1983).

———. Along the No. 20 Line: Reminiscences of the Vancouver Waterfront. (Vancouver: New Star Books, 1980).

———. Indians at Work: An Informal History of Native Indian Labour in British Columbia, 1858–1930. (Vancouver: New Star Books, 1978; revised ed., 1996).

———. Work Camps and Company Towns in Canada and the US: An Annotated Bibliography. (Vancouver: New Star Books, 1975).

Knight, Rolf, and Homer Stevens. Homer Stevens: A Life in Fishing. (Madeira Park: Harbour Publishing, 1992).

Knight, Rolf, and Moya Koizumi. A Man of Our Times: The Life-History of a Japanese Canadian Fisherman. (Vancouver: New Star Books, 1976).

Knox, Paul, and Philip Resnick, eds. Essays in BC Political Economy. (Vancouver: New Star Books, 1974).

Kobayashi, Sadaji. *Thirty-Five Year History of the Suchi Bushide, Fishermen's Benevolent Society.* (Richmond, Vancouver, Tokyo: n.p., 1935).

Kumar, Pradeep. *From Uniformity to Divergence: Industrial Relations in Canada and the United States.* (Kingston: Industrial Relations Centre, Queen's University, 1993).

————. *Canadian Unions' Response to the Challenge of the 1980s: Perspectives of the Leaders.* (Kingston: Industrial Relations Centre, Queen's University, 1988).

Lambie, Catherine, and Peter Watson. *The Canadian Worker.* (Don Mills: Thomas Nelson, 1974).

Latham, Barbara K., and Cathy Kess, eds. *In Her Own Right: Selected Essays on Women's History in British Columbia.* (Victoria: Camosun College, 1980).

Latham, Barbara K., and Roberta J. Pazdro, eds. *Not Just Pin Money: Selected Essays on the History of Women's Work in British Columbia.* (Victoria: Camosun College Press, 1984).

Laxer, Robert. *Canada's Unions.* (Toronto: James Lorimer, 1976).

Lazarus, Morden. *Years of Hard Labour: An Account of the Canadian Workingman, His Organizations and Tribulations Over a Period of More Than a Hundred Years.* (Don Mills: Co-operative Press Association, 1974).

————. *The Trade Union Movement in Canada.* (Toronto: Co-operative Press Association, 1972).

Leier, Mark. *Red Flags and Red Tape: The Making of a Labour Bureaucracy.* (Toronto: University of Toronto Press, 1995).

————. *Where the Fraser River Flows: The Industrial Workers of the World in British Columbia.* (Vancouver: New Star Books, 1990).

Leier, Mark, and M.C. Warrior. *Light at the End of the Tunnel: The First Forty Years, A History of the Tunnel and Rock Workers Union of British Columbia, Local 168.* (Vancouver: Tunnel and Rock Workers Union Local 168, 1992).

Lembcke, Jerry, and William M. Tattam. *One Union in Wood: A Political History of the International Woodworkers of America.* (Madeira Park: Harbour Publishing, 1984).

Leonard, Frank. *A Thousand Blunders: The Grand Trunk Pacific Railway and Northern British Columbia.* (Vancouver: University of British Columbia Press, 1996).

A Life in the Woods: Oral Histories from the West Kootenay Forest. 3 vols. (Nelson BC: Kootenay Museum Association and Historical Society, 1994).

Lind, Carol. *Big Timber, Big Men: A History of Loggers in a New Land.* (Saanichton: Hancock House, 1978).

Linnaird, James. *First Report: Special Commission of Inquiry into British Columbia Construction, October 1975.* (Victoria: British Columbia Department of Labour, 1975).

Lipton, Charles. *The Trade Union Movement of Canada 1827–1959.* (Montreal: Canadian Social Publications, 1966).

Liversedge, Ronald. *Reflections of the On-to-Ottawa Trek.* ed. Victor Hoar. (Toronto: McClelland and Stewart, 1973).

Livesay, Dorothy. *Right Hand, Left Hand.* (Erin: Press Porcepic, 1977).

Logan, Harold A. *Trade Unions in Canada.* (Toronto: MacMillan, 1948).

————. *The History of Trade Union Organization in Canada.* (Chicago: University of Chicago Press, 1928).

Lowther, Bruce. *A Better Life: The First Century of the Victoria Labour Council.* (Victoria: Victoria Labour Council, 1989).

Lucas, Frank. *In Defense.* (Vancouver: Canadian Labour Defense League, 1935).

MacDowell, Laurel Sefton, and Ian Radforth, eds. *Canadian Working-Class History: Selected Readings.* (Toronto: Canadian Scholars' Press, 1992).

MacInnis, Angus. *Labor: Servant or Partner?* (Vancouver: CCF Economic Relations Committee, 1942).

MacInnis, Grace. *The Welfare State.* (Vancouver: The Boag Foundation, 1954–55).

MacIntosh, Robert. *Boilermakers in British Columbia.* (Vancouver: Local No. 359, International Brotherhood of Boilermakers, Iron Ship Builders, Blacksmiths, Forgers and Helpers, 1976).

MacKay, Donald. *Empire in Wood: The MacMillan Bloedel Story.* (Vancouver: Douglas and McIntyre, 1982).

———. *The Lumberjacks.* (Toronto: McGraw-Hill Ryerson, 1978).

Mackie, Richard Somerset. *Trading Beyond the Mountains: The British Fur Trade on the Pacific 1793–1843.* (Vancouver: UBC Press, 1996).

MacNeil, Grant. *The IWA in British Columbia.* (Vancouver: Western Canadian Regional Council No. 1, International Woodworkers of America, 1971).

Magnusson, Warren, et al., eds. *The New Reality: The Politics of Restraint in British Columbia.* (Vancouver: New Star Books, 1984).

Marchak, Patricia. *Green Gold: The forest industry in British Columbia.* (Vancouver: UBC Press, 1983).

———, ed. *The Working Sexes.* (Vancouver: Institute of Industrial Relations, University of British Columbia, 1977).

Marine Retirees Association, Marine Workers' and Boilermakers' Industrial Union, Local 1. *A History of Shipbuilding in British Columbia: As Told by the Shipyard Workers.* (Vancouver: Marine Retirees Association, 1977).

Marlatt, Daphne, ed. *Steveston Recollected: A Japanese-Canadian History.* (Victoria: Provincial Archives of British Columbia, 1975).

Martin, John. *Early Labor Organizations in Victoria.* (Victoria: Allied Printing Trades Council, 1948).

May, Louise-Anne, George Brandak, Elaine Bernard, and Mark Thompson. *A guide to labour records and resources in British Columbia.* (Vancouver: Special Collections Division, University of British Columbia Library, 1985).

Mayse, Susan. *Ginger: The Life and Death of Albert Goodwin.* (Madeira Park: Harbour Publishing, 1990).

McClelland, R.H. *In the Dispute Between Metro Transit Operating Company and the Independent Canadian Transit Union, Locals 1, 2, and 3.* (Victoria: Ministry of Labour, 1984).

McCormack, A. Ross. *Reformers, Rebels and Revolutionaries: The Western Canadian Radical Movement, 1899–1919.* (Toronto: University of Toronto Press, 1977).

McDonald, Robert A.J. *Making Vancouver: Class, Status and Social Boundaries 1863–1913.* (Vancouver: UBC Press, 1996).

McEwen, Tom. *He Wrote For Us: The story of Bill Bennett, Pioneer Socialist Journalist.* (Vancouver: Tribune Publishing, 1951).

McGeer, G.G. *The Police Situation in Vancouver.* (Vancouver: Allied Printing Trades Council, 1935).

McKean, Fergus. *British Columbia's Contribution to Victory.* (Vancouver: British Columbia Communist-Labor Total War Committee, 1942).

McKnight, George A. *Sawlogs on Steel Rails: A Story of the 45 years of Railway Operation in the Logging Camps of the Port Alberni Area.* (Port Alberni: Forest Industry Seniors History Committee, 1995).

McLean, Bruce. *'A Union Amongst Government Employees': A History of the BC Government Employees' Union, 1919–1979.* (Burnaby: BCGEU, 1979).

McPherson, Kathryn. *Bedside Matters:The Trans-formation of Canadian Nursing*, 1900–1990. (Toronto: Oxford University Press, 1996).

McVeigh, Elspeth. *Vancouver Bus Driving:A Study in Stress.* (Burnaby: British Columbia Public Interest Group, 1982).

Michaels, Jane. *A Study of Labour Relations in the Colleges and Institutions in British Columbia.* (Burnaby: British Columbia Institute of Technology, 1981).

Montague, J.T. and S.M. Jamieson. *Labour-Management Conference in Industrial Relations in British Columbia.* (Vancouver: Institute of Industrial Relations, University of British Columbia, 1963).

Montero, Gloria. *We Stood Together: First-Hand Accounts of Dramatic Events in Canada's Labour Past.* (Toronto: James Lorimer, 1979).

Morgan, Nigel. *British Columbia Needs a New Forest Policy.* (Vancouver: Labour Progressive Party, B.C. Provincial Committee, n.d.).

Morrison, William R., and Kenneth A. Coates. *Working in the North: Labor and the Northwest Defense Projects, 1942–1946.* (Juneau: University of Alaska Press, 1994).

Morton, James. *In the Sea of Sterile Mountains:The Chinese in British Columbia.* (Vancouver: J.J. Douglas, 1973).

Morton, Desmond. *Working People.* Third edition. (Toronto: Summerhill Press, 1990).

———. *Labour in Canada.* (Toronto: Grolier, 1982).

Mouat, Jeremy. *The Business of Power: Hydroelectricity in Southeastern BC, 1897–1997.* (Victoria: Sono Nis Press, 1997).

———. *Roaring Days: Rossland's Mines and the History of British Columbia.* (Vancouver: UBC Press, 1995).

Muise, Del, and Robert McIntosh. *Coal Mining in Canada:A Historical and Comparative Overview.* (Ottawa: National Museum of Science and Technology, 1996).

Munro, Jack and Jane O'Hara. *Union Jack: Labour Leader Jack Munro.* (Vancouver: Douglas and McIntyre, 1988).

Muszynski, Alicja. *Cheap Wage Labour: Race and Gender in the Fisheries of British Columbia.* (Kingston: McGill/Queen's University Press, 1996).

Newell, Dianne. *Tangled Webs of History: Indians and the Law in the Canadian West Coast Fisheries.* (Toronto: University of Toronto Press, 1993).

Newell, Dianne, and Logan Hovis. *British Columbia's Salmon Canning Industry:A Preliminary Annotated Guide to Bibliographical and Archival Sources.* (Vancouver: 1985).

Newton, Janice. *The Feminist Challenge to the Canadian Left, 1900–1918.* (Montreal and Kingston: McGill-Queen's University Press, 1995).

Norris, John, and Margaret Prang, eds. *Personality and History in British Columbia: Essays in Honour of Margaret Ormsby.* (Vancouver: BC Studies, 1977).

O'Donnell, John C. *"And Now the Fields Are Green":A Collection of Coal Mining Songs in Canada.* (Sydney NS: University College of Cape Breton Press, 1992).

Palmer, Bryan D. *Working-Class Experience: Rethinking the History of Canadian Labour, 1800–1991.* Second edition. (Toronto: McClelland & Stewart, 1992).

———. *Work and Unions in Canada.* (Ottawa: Department of the Secretary of State, 1988).

———. *Solidarity: The Rise and Fall Of An Opposition in British Columbia.* (Vancouver: New Star Books, 1987).

———, ed. *A Communist Life: Jack Scott and the Canadian Workers Movement, 1927–1985.* (St. John's: Committee on Canadian Labour History, 1988).

Panitch, Leo, and Donald Swartz. *The Assault on Trade Union Freedoms*. (Toronto: Garamond Press, 1988).

Parkinson, Laura Margaret, Patricia Albrecht, and the Victory Square Law Office. *Annotated British Columbia Labour Relations Code*. (Vancouver: Butterworths, 1993).

Patullo, T.D. *Let Us Reason Together: The Labour Problem*. (Victoria: n.p., 1946).

———. *The Strike Situation*. (Victoria: n.p., 1946).

Paynter, Joe. *British Columbia Edition: The Workingman's Guide to Canadian Facts*. (Vancouver: The Author, 1954).

Pearlman, E.E. *Comments on Labour Management Relations in BC*. (Victoria: The Daily Colonist, 1954).

Pearse, Peter. *Turning the Tide: Final Report of the Commission on Pacific Fisheries Policy*. (Ottawa: Ministry of Supplies and Services, 1982).

Pennier, Henry, and H.L. McDonald. *Chiefly Indian: The Warm and Witty Story of a BC Half-Breed Logger*. (West Vancouver: Grey-McDonald Publishers, 1972).

Perry, Adele. *100th Anniversary: Vancouver & District Labour Council, 1889–1989*. (Vancouver: VDLC, 1989).

Perry, Elizabeth. *Bibliography of Masters and Doctoral Theses on Canadian Industrial Relations From 1867 to 1978*. (Toronto: Centre for Industrial Relations, University of Toronto, 1981).

Phillips, Paul. *No Power Greater: A Century of Labour In British Columbia*. (Vancouver: British Columbia Federation of Labour, 1967).

Pinfield, Lawrence. *Labour Turnover at Mackenzie: A Case Study of Deviation-Amplifying Mutual Causal Relationships*. (Burnaby: Simon Fraser University, 1981).

Pinfield, Lawrence, and G.C. Hoyt. *Manpower Planning in Northern British Columbia*. (Burnaby: Simon Fraser University, Department of Economics and Commerce, 1974).

———. *A Systems Analysis of the Impact of Increases in Labour Turnover*. (Burnaby: Simon Fraser University, Department of Economics and Commerce, 1974).

Porter, Allan. *Directory of Canadian Labour Statistics*. (Montreal: National Industrial Conference Board, 1963).

Power, Jeffery. *Injunctions Have No Place in Labour Disputes*. (Vancouver: Marine Workers' and Boilermakers' Industrial Union, 1966).

Queen's University, School of Commerce and Administration, Industrial Relations Section. *Trade Union Agreements in Canadian History*. (Kingston: Queen's University, 1942).

Rankin, Harry. *Rankin's Law: Recollections of a Radical*. (Vancouver: November House, 1975).

Rajala, Richard A. *The Legacy and the Challenge: A Century of the Forest Industry at Cowichan Lake*. (Lake Cowichan: Lake Cowichan Heritage Advisory Committee, 1993).

Reid, David. *The Development of the Fraser River Salmon Canning Industry, 1885–1913*. (Vancouver: Department of the Environment, 1973).

Reimer, Derek, ed. *Fighting for Labour: Four Decades of Work in British Columbia, 1910–1950*. (Victoria: Provincial Archives, 1978).

Rhodes, Frank. *A Study of the Impact of Minimum Wage Revisions on Selected Business Establishments in British Columbia*. (Victoria: Department of Labour, 1973).

Riddell, W. Craig. *Unionization in Canada and the United States: A Tale of Two Countries*. (Kingston: Industrial Relations Centre, Queen's University, 1993).

Robideau, Henri. *Flapjacks and Photographs: A History of Mattie Gunterman, Camp Cook and Photographer.* (Vancouver: Polestar Press, 1995).

Robin, Martin. *Pillars of Profit: The Company Province, 1934–1972.* (Toronto: McClelland and Stewart, 1973).

———. *The Rush for Spoils: The Company Province, 1871–1933.* (Toronto: McClelland and Stewart, 1972).

———. *Radical Politics and Canadian Labour 1880–1930.* (Kingston: Queen's University Industrial Relations Centre, 1968).

Robinson, Garnet. *In Spite of the Stuffed Shirts I Am Not Going To Vote CCF.* (Vancouver: n.p., 1945).

Robson, Peter, and Michael Skog, eds. *Working the Tides: A Portrait of Canada's West Coast Fishery.* (Madeira Park, BC: Harbour Publishing, 1996).

Roddan, Andrew. *God in the Jungles: the story of the man without a home.* (Vancouver: n.p., 1931).

Rush, Maurice. *We Have a Glowing Dream: Recollection of Working-Class and Peoples Struggles in BC from 1935–1996.* (Vancouver: Centre for Socialist Education Society, 1996).

———. *V-Day in the Woods: The significance to labour of the woodworkers strike victory.* (Vancouver: Labour Progressive Party, n.d.).

Sangster, Joan. *Dreams of Equality: Women on the Canadian Left, 1920–1950.* (Toronto: McClelland & Stewart, 1989).

Schalwyk, Johanna. *Technology, Technological Change and Manpower: A Bibliography.* (Victoria: Minister of Labour, 1978).

Schwantes, Carlos A. *Radical Heritage: Labor, Socialism, and Reform in Washington and British Columbia, 1885–1917.* (Seattle: University of Washington Press, 1979).

Schroeder, Drew. *Labour Law.* (Vancouver: The Vancouver People's Law School, 1974).

Scott, Jack. *Canadian Workers, American Unions.* (Vancouver: New Star Books, 1978).

———. *Plunderbund and Proletariat: A History of the IWW in BC, 1911–1913.* (Vancouver: New Star Books, 1975).

———. *Sweat and Struggle: Working Class Struggles in Canada, 1789–1899.* (Vancouver: New Star Books, 1974).

———. *Martyrs and Militia.* (Vancouver: Mother Earth Books, 1973).

Scotton, Clifford A. *Brief History of Canadian Labour.* (Ottawa: Woodsworth House Publishers, 1956).

Shakespeare, Mary, and Rodney Pain. *West Coast Logging, 1840–1910.* (Ottawa: National Museum of Man, 1971).

Sivertz, Bent Gestur. *The Sivertz Family, Book 1: Christian Sivertz of Victoria and of Canada's Early Labor Movement.* (Parksville: Arrowmaker Graphics, 1984).

Smart, Tom, ed. *Material Relevant to British Columbia Labour History in Record Group 27, Canadian Department of Labour.* (Ottawa: Public Archives of Canada, 1975).

Smith, F. W. *The First Thirty Years: The Canadian Airline Pilots' Association.* (Vancouver: Mitchell Press, 1970).

Stacey, Duncan. *Sockeye and Tinplate: Technological Change in the Fraser River Canning Industry, 1871–1912.* (Victoria: British Columbia Provincial Museum, 1982).

Stainsby, Cliff, and John Malcolmson. *The Fraser Institute, the Government and a Corporate Free Lunch.* (Vancouver: Solidarity Coalition, 1983).

Stainsby, Jill, et al. *AUCE & TSSU: Memoirs of a Feminist Union, 1972–1993.* (Burnaby: Teaching Support Staff Union Publishing, 1994).

Stanbury, W.T., and Mark Thompson. *People, Productivity and Technological Change.* (Vancouver: Industrial Relations Management Association, 1973).

Stanton, John. *My Past is Now: Further Memoirs of a Labour Lawyer.* (St. John's: Canadian Committee on Labour History, 1994).

———. *Never Say Die! The Life and Time of John Stanton, A Pioneer Labour Lawyer.* (Ottawa: Steel Rail Publishing, 1987).

———. *Labour Arbitrations: Boom or Bust for Unions?* (Vancouver: Butterworths, 1983).

———. *The Life and Death of a Union: The Canadian Seamen's Union, 1936–1949.* (Toronto: Steel Rail Educational Publishing, 1978).

Stanton, Patrick. *Women in the Labour Market, 1983.* (Vancouver: Ministry of Labour, 1984).

Steeves, Dorothy. *Builders and Rebels: Short History of the ccf in British Columbia, 1932–1961.* (Vancouver: BC Committee for a New Democratic Party, 1961).

———. *The Compassionate Rebel: Ernest E. Winch and His Times.* (Vancouver: Boag Foundation, 1960).

Stonebanks, Roger. *The Guild at Forty: the struggle continues.* (Victoria: Victoria Newspaper Guild, 1986).

Strong-Boag, Veronica. *The New Day Recalled: Lives of Girls and Women in English Canada, 1919–1939.* (Toronto: Copp Clark Pitman, 1988).

Stuart Research Service Ltd. *The 1946 Strike in the Lumber Industry of British Columbia.* (Vancouver: Stuart Research Service Ltd., n.d.).

Swankey, Ben, ed. *Building British Columbia: The Story of the Carpenters' Union and the Trade Union Movement Since 1881.* (Vancouver: Carpenter Pensioners' Association of British Columbia, 1979).

Swankey, Ben, and Jean Evans Sheils. *"Work and Wages!": A Semi-Documentary Account of the Life and Times of Arthur H. (Slim) Evans.* (Vancouver: Trade Union Research Bureau, 1977).

Sykes, Ella. *A Home-Help in Canada.* (London: Smith, Elden and Co., 1912).

Taylor, Don, and Bradley Dow. *The Rise of Industrial Unionism in Canada: A History of the cio.* (Kingston: Industrial Relations Centre, Queen's University, 1988).

Taylor, Geoffrey. *Mining: BC's Mining History.* (Saanichton: Hancock House, 1977).

———. *Timber: A History of the Forest Industry in British Columbia.* (Vancouver: J.J. Douglas, 1975).

Templeton, R.J. *Rights and Duties of Labour.* (Vancouver: BC Federation of Trade and Industry, 1946).

———. *The Right To Strike.* (Vancouver: BC Federation of Trade and Industry, 1946).

———. *The Closed Shop.* (Vancouver: BC Federation of Trade and Industry, 1940s).

———. *Labour Managment Must Be Equally Responsible.* (Vancouver: BC Federation of Trade and Industry, 1940s).

———. *Do Unions Really Raise Wages?* (Vancouver: BC Federation of Trade and Industry, 1940s).

———. *The Labour Problem.* (Vancouver: BC Federation of Trade and Industry, 1946).

———. *Labour Won't Accept Socialism.* (Vancouver: BC Federation of Trade and Industry, 1945).

Thompson, John Herd, with Allen Seager. *Canada 1922–1939: Decades of Discord.* (Toronto: McClelland & Stewart, 1988).

Trade Union Research Bureau. *The Mackenzie Story: A Study in the History and Development of a Forest Industry and Town at Mackenzie, British Columbia.* (Mackenzie: Citizens Committe of Mackenzie, 1974).

Turner, Michael. *Company Town.* (Vancouver: Pulp Press, 1991).

United Brotherhood of Carpenters and Joiners of America, Local 452. *The First Hundred Years: United Brotherhood of Carpenters and Joiners of America, Local 452,Vancouver, B.C.* (Vancouver: United Brotherhood of Carpenters and Joiners of America, Local Union 452, Vancouver, B.C., 1990).

Vaisey, G. Douglas, comp. *The Labour Companion: A Bibliography of Canadian Labour History Based on Materials Printed from 1950–1975.* (Halifax: Committee on Canadian Labour History, 1980).

Veit, Suzanne. *Labour Turnover and Community Stability: Implications for Northeast Coal Development in British Columbia.* (Victoria: Ministry of Labour, 1978).

———. *Women in Mining: An Exploratory Study.* (Victoria: Ministry of Economic Development, 1976).

Verner, Coolie, and Gary Dickinson. *Union Education in Canada: A Report of the Educational Activities of Labour Organizations.* (Vancouver: Adult Education Research Centre, University of British Columbia, 1974).

Wachtel, Eleanor. *"What This Country Did to Us, It Did to Itself": A Report of the BC Human Rights Commission on the Farmworkers and Domestic Workers.* (Victoria: British Columbia Human Rights Commission, 1983).

Warburton, Rennie, and David Coburn, eds. *Workers, Capital and the State in British Columbia: Selected Essays.* (Vancouver: UBC Press, 1988).

Weaver, George. *Economics forWorkers.* (Vancouver: BC Educational Committee, CCF, 1942).

Webb, Patricia G. *The Heart of Healthcare: The Story of the Hospital Employees' Union: The First 50 Years.* (Vancouver: Hospital Employees' Union, 1994).

Webster, Daisy. *Growth of the ndp in BC, 1900–1970: 81 Political Biographies.* (Vancouver: New Democratic Party, 1970).

Weiler, Joseph M. and Peter A. Gall, eds. *The Labour Code of British Columbia in the 1980s.* (Calgary: Carswell, 1984).

Weiler, Paul. *Reconcilable Differences: New Directions in Canadian Labour Law.* (Agincourt: Carswell, 1980).

Weinrich, Peter. *Social Protest from the Left in Canada, 1870–1970.* (Toronto: University of Toronto Press, 1982).

Wells, Merle. *Miners' Unions in British Columbia and North Idaho.* (Boise: Idaho State Historical Society, 1984).

Western Surveys-Research Ltd. *The Public's Attitudes Towards Unions and Labour-Management Relations, GreaterVancouver and GreaterVictoria, April, 1958: An Introductory Report.* (Vancouver: Wester Surveys-Research Ltd., 1958).

White, Bill. *Shipyards atWar.* (Vancouver: Arsenal Pulp Press, 1983).

White, Howard. *A Hard Man to Beat: The Story of BillWhite, Labour Leader, Historian, Shipyard Worker, Raconteur.* (Vancouver: Arsenal Pulp Press, 1983).

White, Julie. *Sisters and Solidarity:Women and Unions in Canada.* (Toronto:Thompson Educational Publishing, 1993).

———. *Mail and Female:Women and the Canadian Union of PostalWorkers.* (Toronto:Thompson Educational Publishing, 1990).

Winch, Harold. *The Politics of a Derelict.* (Vancouver: BC Clarion, 1933).

Woodcock, George. *British Columbia: A History of the Province.* (Vancouver: Douglas & McIntyre, 1990).

Woods, Harry, ed. *Patterns of Industrial Dispute Settlement in Five Canadian Industries.* (Montreal: Industrial Relations Centre, McGill University, 1958).

Woodsworth, J.S. *On theWaterfront:With the Workers on the Docks ofVancouver.* (Ottawa: Mutual Press, 1928).

Working Lives Collective. *Working Lives:Vancouver, 1886–1986.* (Vancouver: New Star Books, 1985).

Youds, Mike. *Firing Iron:The History of the Operating Engineers, Local 115, 1909–1982.* (Vancouver: Mitchell Press, 1982).

Zirul, Graham J. *An Analysis of the Statutory Exclusion of "Managers" from Application of the BC Labour Code:The Right of Union Representation and Collective Bargaining.* 1993.

Zuehlke, Mark. *The Gallant Cause: Canadians in the Spanish Civil War, 1936–1939.* (Vancouver: Whitecap Books, 1996).

ARTICLES

Abella, Irving. "Communism and Anti-Communism in the British Columbia Labour Movement, 1940–1948." in *Western Perspectives.* ed. David J. Bercuson. (Toronto: Holt, Rinehart and Winston, 1974): 88–100.

———. "The CIO, the Communist Party and the Canadian Congress of Labour, 1936–1941." *Canadian Historical Association, Historical Papers.* (1969): 112–128.

Ainsworth, Jackie. "Getting Organized in the Feminist Unions." in *Still Ain't Satisfied: Canadian Feminism Today.* ed. Maureen Fitzgerald. (Toronto:The Women's Press, 1982): 132–140.

Aitchison, Catherine. "The Victoria Police Department, 1902." *British Columbia Genealogist.* 11. (December 1982): 86–91.

Akers, David. "Rebel or Revolutionary? Jack Kavanagh and the Early Years of the Communist Movement in Vancouver, 1920–1925." *Labour/Le Travail.* 30. (Fall 1992): 9–44.

Anderson, Robert John. "Domestic Service: The YWCA and Women's Employment Agencies in Vancouver, 1898–1915." *Histoire Sociale/Social History.* 50. (November 1992): 307–334.

Anderson, Robin. "Sharks and Red Herrings: Vancouver's Male Employment Agencies." *BC Studies.* 98. (Summer 1993): 43–84.

Andrews, C.D. "Cominco and the Manhattan Project." *BC Studies.* 11. (Fall 1971): 51–62.

Apostle, Richard, Don Clairmont, and Lars Osberg. "Segmentation and Labour Force Strategies." *Canadian Journal of Sociology.* 10:3. (Summer 1985): 253–277.

Artibise, Alan. "'A Worthy, If Unlikely Enterprise':The Labour Relations Board and the Evolution of Labour Policy and Practice in British Columbia, 1973–1980." *BC Studies.* 56. (Winter 1982–83): 3–43.

Armstrong, Lawrin, and Mark Leier. "Canadians in the Spanish Civil War, 1936–1938:The Mackenzie-Papineau Battalion in Spain." *The Beaver.* 77:5. (1997): 19–26.

Atherton, Jay. "The British Columbia Origins of the Federal Department of Labour." *BC Studies.* 32. (Winter 1976–77): 93–105.

Avery, Donald. "Continental European Immigrant Workers in Canada, 1896–1919: From 'Stalwart Peasants' to Radical Proletariat." *Canadian Review of Sociology and Anthropology.* 12:1. (1975): 53–64.

Avery, Donald, and Peter Neary. "Laurier, Borden and a White British Columbia." *Journal of Canadian Studies.* 12:4. (Summer 1977): 24–34.

Bacher, John C., and J. David Hulchanski. "Keeping Warm and Dry:The Policy Response to the Struggle for Shelter Among Canada's Homeless, 1900–1960." *Urban History Review.* 16:2. (October 1987): 147–163.

Bailey, Lloyd. "Captain Evans Represented the Miners." *British Columbia Historical News.* 26:2. (Spring 1993): 27–30.

Baker, Maureen, and Mary-Anne Robeson. "Trade Union Reactions to Women Workers and Their Concerns." *Canadian Journal of Sociology.* 6:1. (Winter 1981): 19–33.

Barman, Jean. "Reflections on the Role of the School in the Transition to Work in Resource Towns." in *Rethinking Vocationalism: Whose Work/Life Is It?*, eds. Rebecca Priegert Coulter and Ivor F. Goodson. (Toronto: Our Schools/Our Selves Education Foundation, 1993): 10–27.

———. "The West Beyond the West: The Demography of Settlement in British Columbia." *Journal of Canadian Studies.* 25:3. (Fall 1990): 5–18.

———. "'Knowledge is Essential for Universal Progress but Fatal to Class Privilege': Working People and Schools in Vancouver During the 1920s." *Labour/Le Travail.* 22. (Fall 1988): 9–66.

"Barristas of the World Unite! CAW Organizer Laurie Banong interviewed by L/LT." *Labour/Le Travail.* 42. (1998): 335–343.

Bartlett, Eleanor. "Real Wages and the Standard of Living in Vancouver, 1901–1929." *BC Studies.* 51. (Autumn 1981): 3–62.

Baskerville, Peter A. "'She has already hinted at board': Enterprising Urban Women in British Columbia, 1863–1989." *Histoire Sociale/Social History.* 26:52. (November 1993): 205–28.

Baskerville, Peter, and Eric Sager. "The First National Unemployment Survey: Unemployment and the Canadian Census of 1891." *Labour/Le Travail.* 23. (Spring 1989): 171–178.

Baureiss, Gunter. "Chinese Immigration, Chinese Stereotypes and Chinese Labour." *Canadian Ethnic Studies.* 19:3. (1987): 15–34.

Belshaw, John Douglas. "The British Collier in British Columbia: Another Archetype Reconsidered." *Labour/Le Travail.* 34. (Fall 1994): 11–36.

———. "The Standard of Living of British Miners on Vancouver Island, 1848–1900." *BC Studies.* 84. (Winter 1989–90): 37–64.

Benyon, J., K. Tooney, and N. Kishor. "Do Visible Minorities in British Columbia Want Teaching as a Career?" *Canadian Ethnic Studies.* 24:3. (1992).

Bercuson, David J. "Syndicalism Sidetracked: Canada's One Big Union." in *Revolutionary Syndicalism: An International Perspective.* eds. Marcel van der Linden and Wayne Thorpe. (Aldershot: Scholar Press, 1990): 221–236.

———. "Labour Radicalism and the Western Industrial Frontier." *Canadian Historical Review.* 58:2. (June 1977): 154–175.

———. "Western Labour Radicalism and the One Big Union: Myths and Realities." in *The Twenties in Western Canada.* ed. Susan Mann Trofimenkoff. (Ottawa: National Museums of Canada, 1972): 32–49.

Bernard, Richard, and Michael R. Smith. "Hiring, Promotion, and Pay in a Corporate Head Office: An Internal Labour Market in Action?" *Canadian Journal of Sociology.* 16:4. (Fall 1991): 353–375.

Bernsohn, Kenneth. "How Wobbly Are BC's Forest Unions?" *Forestalk.* 6. (Summer 1982): 26–31.

———. "Loggers, Highballers and the Green Chain Gang." *Forestalk.* 3. (Fall 1979): 11–19.

Binkley, Clark S. "A Crossroads in the Forest: The Path to a Sustainable Forest Sector in BC." *BC Studies.* 113. (Spring 1997): 39–68.

Bish, Robert. "The Case for 'Property Rights' in the Pacific Salmon Fishery." *Western Fisheries.* 110:3. (1984): 17–20.

Bishop, Mary F. "The Early Birth Controllers of BC." *BC Studies.* 61. (Spring 1984): 64–84.

Black, John. "Strike/Lockout at North Vancouver City Library." *BCLA Reporter*. 23. (January/February 1980): 1–3.

Blake, Donald. "The Electoral Significance of Public Sector Bashing." *BC Studies*. 62. (Summer 1984): 29–43.

Blomley, Nicholas K. "Federalism, Place and the Regulation of Worker Safety." *Economic Geography*. (January 1990): 22–47.

Bolotenko, George. "The National Archives and Left-Wing Sources from Russia: Records of the Mackenzie-Papineau Battalion, the Communist Party of Canada, and Left-Wing Internationals." *Labour/Le Travail*. 37. (1996): 179–203.

Bowles, Paul. "APEC: No Place For Labour." *Labour/Le Travail*. 41. (1998): 330–1.

Bradbury, J.H. "New Settlements Policy in British Columbia." *Urban History Review*. 8:2. (October 1979): 47–76.

———. "Class Structures and Class Conflicts in 'Instant' Resource Towns in British Columbia, 1965–1972." *BC Studies*. 37. (Spring 1978): 3–18.

Braid, Kate. "Women in Trades in British Columbia." in *Still Ain't Satisfied: Canadian Feminism Today*. ed. Maureen Fitzgerald. (Toronto: The Women's Press, 1982): 222–229.

Brandak, George. "Forest Industry Photographs." *BC Studies*. 113. (Spring 1997): 68.

———. "Labour Sources in the UBC Library's Special Collections Division." *Archivaria*. 4. (Summer 1977): 23–26.

———. "Acquisition of Records and Papers Relating to Labour History, University of British Columbia." *Newsletter of the Committee on Canadian Labour History*. 7. (Fall 1975): 14–15.

Bray, Bonita. "Against All Odds: The Progressive Arts Club's Production of Waiting For Lefty." *Journal of Canadian Studies*. 25:3. (Fall 1990): 106–123.

Brocks, Julian. "Joseph Hunter: Forgotten Builder of British Columbia." *British Columbia Historical News*. 28:2. (Spring 1995): 27–30.

Brown, Lorne. "Breaking Down Myths of Peace and Harmony in Canadian Labour History." *Canadian Dimension*. 9. (May 1973): 11–35.

Brown, Richard. "Picketing: Canadian Courts and the Labour Relations Board of British Columbia." *University of Toronto Law Journal*. 31. (Spring 1981): 153–199.

Brummelen, Harro Van. "Shifting Perspectives: Early British Columbia Textbooks From 1872–1925." *BC Studies*. 60. (Winter 1983–4): 3–27.

Brym, Robert J. "Incorporation versus Power: Models of Working-Class Radicalism With Special Reference to North America." *Canadian Journal of Sociology*. 11:3. (Fall 1986): 227–253.

Brown, Helen. "Gender and Space: Constructing the Public School Teaching Staff in Nanaimo, 1891–1914." *BC Studies*. 105/106. (Spring/Summer 1995): 59–79.

Burrows, James K. "'A Much Needed Class of Labour': The Economy and Income of the Southern Interior Plateau Indians, 1897–1910." *BC Studies*. 71. (Autumn 1986): 27–59.

Campbell, Marie. "Sexism in British Columbia Trade Unions, 1900–1920." in *In Her Own Right: Selected Essays on Women's History in BC*. eds. Barbara Latham and Cathy Kess. (Victoria: Camosun College, 1980): 167–186.

Campbell, Peter. "'Making Socialists': Bill Pritchard, the Socialist Party of Canada, and the Third International." Labour/Le Travail. 30. (Fall 1992): 45–63.

———." In Defence of the Labour Theory of Value: The Socialist Party of Canada and the Evolution of Marxist Thought." Journal of History and Politics. 10. (1992): 61–86.

Carroll, William K., and Rennie Warburton. "Feminism, Class Consciousness and Household-Work Linkages Among Registered Nurses in Victoria." Labour/Le Travail. 24. (Fall 1989): 131–145.

Carrothers, A.W.R. "The British Columbia Labour Relations Amendment Act, 1961." University of Toronto Law Journal. 14. (1962): 263–268.

———. "Legislative History of the BC Trade Unions Act: The Rossland Miners Case." UBC Legal Notes. 2. (March 1956): 339–346.

———. "The Right to Picket in BC: A Study in Statute Interpretation." University of Toronto Law Journal. 9. (1951–52): 250–287.

Carrothers, W.A. "Forest Industries in British Columbia." in The North American Assault on the Canadian Forest. ed. A.R.M. Lower. (Toronto: Ryerson Press, 1938): 227–344.

Cassin, A. Marguerite, and Alison I. Griffith. "Class and Ethnicity: Producing the Differences that Count." Canadian Ethnic Studies. 13:1. (1981): 109–129.

Caves, R.E., and R.H. Holton. "An Outline of the Economic History of British Columbia, 1818–1951." in Historical Essays on British Columbia. eds. G. Friesen and K. Ralston. (Toronto: McClelland and Stewart, 1976): 152–166.

Cayley, David. "The CAIMAW Story: Back to Basics for Labour." This Magazine. 14. (September/October 1980): 37–44.

Chan, Anthony B. "Bachelor Workers." in A Nation of Immigrants: Women, Workers, and Communities in Canadian History, 1840s–1960s. eds. Franca Iacovetta, Paula Draper, and Robert Ventrusca. (Toronto: University of Toronto Press, 1998): 231–251.

Clement, Wallace. "Canada's Coastal Fisheries: Formation of Unions, Co-operatives and Associations." Journal of Canadian Studies. 19:1. (1984): 5–33.

———. "The Subordination of Labour in Canadian Mining." Labour/Le Travail. 5. (Spring 1980): 133–148.

Cole, Douglas. "The Intellectual and Imaginative Development of British Columbia." Journal of Canadian Studies. 24:3. (Fall 1989): 70–79.

Collier, E. "Mining in the Cariboo: The Grouse Creek War." BC Perspectives. 4. (August 1973): 3–13.

Conley, James R. "Rethinking the Canadian Working Class." Journal of Canadian Studies. 30:3. (Fall 1995): 214–22.

———. "Open Shop Means Closed to Union Men: Carpenters and the 1911 Vancouver Building Trades General Strike." BC Studies. 91–92. (Autumn-Winter 1991–2): 127–151.

———. "Perculiarities of the British Columbians." Labour/Le Travail. 27. (1991): 190–192.

———. "Frontier Labourers, Crafts in Crisis, and the Western Labour Revolt: The Case of Vancouver, 1900–1919." Labour/Le Travail. 23. (Spring 1989): 9–37.

———. "More Theory Less Fact? Social Reproduction and Class Conflict in a Sociological Approach to Working-Class History." Canadian Journal of Sociology. 13:1–2. (Winter-Spring 1988): 75–103.

Corman, Jane. "Dissension Within the Ranks: The Struggle Over Employment Practices During a Recession." *Studies in Political Economy*. 32. (Summer 1990): 85–111.

Costigliola, Bozica. "BCFL's Unemployment Action Centres." *Canadian Labour*. 28. (February 1983): 10–12.

Craven, Paul and Tom Traves. "The Class Politics of the National Policy, 1872–1933." *Journal of Canadian Studies*. 14:3. (Fall 1979): 14–38.

Creese, Gillian. "Power and Pay: The Union and Equal Pay at B.C. Electric/Hydro." *Labour/Le Travail*. 32. (Fall 1993): 225–46.

———. "Exclusion or Solidarity? Vancouver Workers Confront the 'Oriental Problem.'" in *Canadian Working-Class History*. eds. Laurel Sefton MacDowell and Ian Radforth. (Toronto: Canadian Scholars' Press, 1992): 311–332.

———. "The British Columbian Working Class: New Perspectives on Ethnicity/Race and Gender." *Labour/Le Travail*. 27. (1991): 192–195.

———. "The Politics of Dependence: Women, Work, and Unemployment in the Vancouver Labour Movement Before World War II." *Canadian Journal of Sociology*. 13:1–2. (Winter-Spring 1988): 121–143.

———. "Organizing Against Racism in the Workplace: Chinese Workers in Vancouver Before the Second World War." *Canadian Ethnic Studies*. 19:3. (1987): 35–46.

Cruikshank, Douglas, and Gregory S. Kealey. "Canadian Strike Statistics, 1891–1950." *Labour/Le Travail*. 20. (Fall 1987): 85–145.

Crutchfield, J.A. "Collective Bargaining in the Pacific Coast Fisheries: The Economic Issues." *Industrial and Labor Relations Review*. 8. (July 1955): 541–556.

Darroch, Gordon A. and Michael D. Ornstein. "Ethnicity and Occupational Structure in Canada in 1871: The Vertical Mosaic in Historical Perspective." *Canadian Historical Review*. 61:3. (September 1980): 305–333.

Davis, Donald. "Competition's Moment: The Jitney-Bus and Corporate Capitalism in the Canadian City, 1914–1929." *Urban History Review*. 18:2. (October 1989): 103–121.

Davis, Donald F., and Barbara Lorenzkowski. "A Platform for Gender Tensions: Women Working and Riding on Canadian Urban Public Transit in the 1940s." *Canadian Historical Review*. 79:3. (1998): 431–65.

Davitt, Patricia. "When All The Secretaries Demand What They Are Worth." in *Still Ain't Satisfied: Canadian Feminism Today*. ed. Maureen Fitzgerald. (Toronto: The Women's Press, 1982): 195–209.

Diamond, Sara. "Women in the BC Labour Movement." *Canadian Oral History Association Journal*. 6. (1996): 7–10.

Dorsey, James. "Abandonment of Trade Union Bargaining Rights and the Labour Code of British Columbia." *UBC Law Review*. 11:1. (1977): 40–80.

Dossa, Parin. "Women's Space/Time: An Anthropological Perspective on Ismaili Immigrant Women in Calgary and Vancouver." *Canadian Ethnic Studies*. 20:1. (1988): 45–65.

Drache, Daniel. "The Formation and Fragmentation of the Canadian Working Class: 1820–1920." *Studies in Political Economy*. 15. (Fall 1984): 43–89.

Drent, Jan. "Labour and the Unions in a Wartime Essential Industry: Shipyard Workers in BC, 1939–1945." *The Northern Mariner/Le Marin du nord*. 6:4. (1996): 47–64.

Drystek, Henry F. "'The Simplest and Cheapest Mode of Dealing With Them': Deportation From Canada Before W.W.II." *Histoire Sociale/Social History*. 30. (November 1982): 407–442.

Dunn, Timothy. "Teaching the Meaning of Work: Vocational Education in British Columbia, 1900–1929." in *Shaping the Schools of the Canadian West*. ed. David Jones. (Calgary: Detselig Enterprises, 1979): 236–256.

Dwyer, Melva J. "Bibliography of British Columbia." *BC Studies*. 90. (Summer 1991).

Eastman, S. Mark. "Workers Education in Canada." *International Labour Review*. 40. (September 1939): 220–231.

Egan, Brian, and Suzanne Klausen. "Female in a Forest Town: The Marginalization of Women in Port Alberni's Economy." *BC Studies*. 118. (Summer 1998): 5–40.

Eleen, John. "Freight Trains and Memory Lanes: The On-to-Ottawa Trek." *Our Times*. 14:4. (1995): 24–31.

Elliot, Robbins. "The Canadian Labour Press from 1867: A Chronological Annotated Directory." *Canadian Journal of Economics and Political Science*. 14:2. (1948): 220–231.

Epstein, Rachel. "Domestic Workers: The Experience in BC." in *Union Sisters: Women in the Labour Movement*. eds. Linda Briskin and Lynda Yanz. (Toronto: The Women's Press, 1983): 222–237.

———. "I Thought There Was No More Slavery In Canada." *Canadian Dimension*. 14. (May 1980): 29–35.

Featherstone, Liza. "The Burger International." *Labour/Le Travail*. 43. (1999): 301–306.

Fillmore, Catherine J. "Gender Differences in Earnings: A Re-Analysis and Prognosis for Canadian Women." *Canadian Journal of Sociology*. 15:3. (Summer 1990): 275–301.

Fisher, Edward. "Strike Activity and Wildcat Strikes in British Columbia, 1945–1975." *Relations Industrielles/Industrial Relations*. 37:2. (1982): 284–312.

Fisher, Robin. "The Decline of Reform: British Columbia Politics in the 1930s." *Journal of Canadian Studies*. 25:3. (Fall 1990): 74–89.

Fitzgerald, Maureen. "Whither the Feminist Unions? SORWUC, AUCE and the CLC." *Sources For Feminist Research*. 10. (July 1981): 19–20.

Forsey, Eugene. "Distribution of Income in British Columbia." *Canadian Forum*. 22. (August 1942): 148–149.

Forward, Charles N. "The Development of Canada's Five Leading National Ports." *Urban History Review*. 10:3. (February 1982): 25–46.

Fowler, Kathryn. "Understanding the Opposition." *Equity*. 1:4. (1983): 32–35.

Fox, Bonnie, and John Fox. "Effects of Women's Employment on Wages." *Canadian Journal of Sociology*. 8:3. (Summer 1983): 319–329.

Fox, Paul. "Early Socialism in Canada." in *The Political Process in Canada: Essays in Honour of R. MacGregor Dawson*. ed. J.H. Atchinson. (Toronto: University of Toronto Press, 1963): 79–98.

Freund, Alexander, and Laura Quilici. "Exploring Myths in Women's Narratives: Italian and German Immigrant Women in Vancouver, 1947–1961." *BC Studies*. 105–106. (1995): 159–82.

Friesen, Gerald. "'Yours In Revolt': The Socialist Party of Canada and the Western Canadian Labour Movement." *Labour/Le Travailleur*. 1. (1976): 139–157.

Fryer, John. "Revolt of the People: Operation Solidarity." *Canadian Labour*. 28. (1983): 13–16.

Gervin, J., and J. Stevenson. "Labour's Growth in Vancouver." *American Federationist.* 58. (February 1951): 25–27.

Gladstone, Percy. "Native Indians and the Fishing Industry of BC." *Canadian Journal of Economics and Political Science.* 19. (February 1953): 20–34.

Gladstone, Percy, and Stuart Jamieson. "Unionism in the Fishing Industry of British Columbia." *Canadian Journal of Economics and Political Science.* 16. (1950): 1–11.

Glavin, Terry. "BCGEU: The Fight That Fizzled." *Canadian Dimension.* 16. (January 1983): 10–11.

———. "Breaking the Back of Back-Breaking Labour." *Canadian Dimension.* 14. (August 1980): 18–19.

Grove, Alan, and Ross Lambertson. "Pawns of the Powerful: The Politics of Litigation in the Union Colliery Case." *BC Studies.* 103. (Autumn 1994): 3–32.

Guppy, Neil. "Property Rights and Changing Class Formations in the BC Commercial Fishing Industry." *Studies in Political Economy.* 19. (Spring 1986): 59–83.

Gutstein, D. "How the Lawyers Came to Labour." *Vancouver Magazine.* 15. (March 1982): 36–44, 141–143.

Hak, Gordon. "'Line Up or Roll Up': The Lumber Workers Industrial Union in the Prince George District." *BC Studies.* 86. (Summer 1990): 57–774.

———. "The Socialist and Labourist Impulse in Small-Town British Columbia: Port Alberni and Prince George, 1911–1933." *Canadian Historical Review.* 70:4. (December 1989): 519–542.

———. "British Columbia Loggers and the Lumber Workers Industrial Union, 1919–1922." *Labour/Le Travail.* 23. (Spring 1989): 67–90.

———. "The Communists and the Unemployed in the Prince George District, 1930–1935." *BC Studies.* 68. (Winter 1985–86): 45–61.

Hall, David J. "The Construction Workers' Strike on the Canadian Pacific Railway, 1879." *Labour/Le Travail.* 36. (1995): 11–35.

Hallet, May E. "A Governor-General's Views on Oriental Immigration to British Columbia, 1904–1911." *BC Studies.* 14. (Summer 1972): 51–72.

Harding, James. "The New Left in British Columbia." *Our Generation.* 7. (June/July 1970): 21–44.

Hardwick, W.G. "The Forest Industry in Coastal British Columbia, 1870–1970." in *Readings in Canadian Geography.* ed. R.M. Irving. (Toronto: Holt, Rinehart and Winston, 1972): 318–323.

Harper, Bill and John Cleveland. "Railway Unions Under Siege." *Canadian Dimension.* 9. (July 1973): 10–12.

Harris, Cole. "The Lower Mainland, 1820–1881." in *Vancouver and Its Region.* eds. Graeme Wynn and Timothy Oke. (Vancouver: UBC Press, 1992): 36–68.

———. "Industry and the Good Life around Idaho Peak." *Canadian Historical Review.* 66:3. (September 1985): 315–343.

Harrison, Joan. "The Role of the Vancouver Temporary-Help Service Industry." *UBC Business Review.* 14. (1979): 85–93.

Harrison, Peter. "Life in a Logging Camp." *BC Studies.* 54. (Summer 1982): 88–104.

Hayter, Roger. "High Performance Organizations and Employment Flexibility: A Case Study of In Situ Change at the Powell River Paper Mill, 1980–1994." *Canadian Geographer/ Le geographe canadien.* 41:1. (1997): 26–40.

Hayter, Roger, and Trevor Barnes. "The Restructuring of British Columbia's Coastal Forest Sector: Flexibility Perspectives." BC Studies. 113. (Spring 1997): 7–34.

Hayward, Brian. "The Co-op Strategy." Journal of Canadian Studies. 19:1. (1984): 48–64.

Hazel, James P. "The Incidence of Crime in Vancouver During the Great Depression." BC Studies. 69–70. (Spring/Summer 1986): 211–248.

Heron, Craig. "National Contours: Solidarity and Fragmentation." in The Workers' Revolt in Canada, 1917–1925. ed. Craig Heron. (Toronto: University of Toronto Press, 1998): 268–304.

———. "Communists, Gangsters and Canadian Sailors." Labour/Le Travail. 24. (Fall 1989): 231–238.

———. "Labourism and the Canadian Working Class." Labour/Le Travail. 13. (Spring 1984): 45–76.

Heron, Craig, and Myer Siemiatycki. "The Great War, the State and the Working-Class Canada." in The Workers' Revolt in Canada, 1917–1925. ed. Craig Heron. (Toronto: University of Toronto Press, 1998): 11–42.

Heron, Craig, and Steve Penfold. "The Craftsmen's Spectacle: Labour Day Parades in Canada, The Early Years." Histoire sociale/Social History. 29:58. (1996): 357–89.

Hewlett, Edward. "The Chilcotin Uprising of 1864." BC Studies. 19. (Autumn 1973): 21–49.

High, Steven. "Native Wage Labour and Independent Production during the 'Era of Irrelevance'." Labour/Le Travail. 37. (1996): 243–64.

Hinde, John R. "'Stout Ladies and Amazons': Women in the British Columbia Coal–Mining Community of Ladysmith, 1912–14." BC Studies. 113. (Spring 1997): 38–58.

Holmes, John. "In Search of Competitive Efficiency: Labour Process Flexibility in the Canadian Newsprint Mills." Canadian Geographer/ Le geographe canadien. 41:1. (1997): 7–25.

Holmes, Richard, and Robert Rogow, "Time to Certification of Unions in British Columbia." Relations industrielles/ Industrial Relations. 49:1. (1994): 133–151.

Horn, Michiel. "The League for Social Reconstruction and the Development of a Canadian Socialism." Journal of Canadian Studies. 7:4. (November 1972): 3–17.

Horrall, S.W. "The Royal North-West Mounted Police and Labour Unrest in Western Canada." Canadian Historical Review. 61:2. (June 1980): 169–190.

Howard, Irene. "Vancouver Swedes and the Loggers." Swedish Pioneer Historical Quarterly. 21:3. (1970): 163–182.

Howard [Hoar], Victor. "The On-To-Ottawa Trek." Canada: An Historical Magazine. 3. (March 1976): 34–47 and (June 1976): 2–14.

———. "The Vancouver Relief Camp Strike of 1935: A Narrative of the Great Depression." Canada: An Historical Magazine. 1. (March 1973): 9–16, 26–33.

Howlett, Michael and Keith Brownsey. "The Old Reality and the New Reality: Party Politics and Public Policy in British Columbia, 1941–1987." Studies in Political Economy. 25. (Spring 1988): 141–177.

Ireland, Ralph. "Some Effects of Oriental Immigration on the Canadian Trade Union Ideology." American Journal of Economics and Sociology. 19. (January 1960): 217–221.

————. "Ideology Versus Expediency." *Indian Journal of Social Research*. 7:2. (1960): 120–127.

Irving, Allan. "The Development of a Provincial Welfare State: British Columbia, 1900–1939." in *The Benevolent State: The Growth of Welfare in Canada*. eds. Allan Moscovitch and Jim Albert. (Toronto: Garamond Press, 1987): 155–175.

James, Rick. "Staying Afloat: Saving BC's Lumber Industry by Shipbuilding." *British Columbia Historical News*. 29:4. (1996): 17–21.

————. "Finnish Immigrants and Their Political Ideology." *British Columbia Historical News*. 28:1. (Winter 1994–5): 20–4.

Jamieson, Stuart. "Regional Factors in Industrial Conflict: The Case of BC." *Canadian Journal of Economics and Political Science*. 28. (August 1962): 405–416.

————. "Native Indians and the Trade Union Movement in British Columbia." *Human Organization*. 20. (Winter 1961–62): 219–225.

————. "Labour Disputes Settlement in the Construction Industry of BC." in *Patterns of Industrial Disputes Settlements in Five Canadian Industries*. ed. H.D. Woods. (Montreal: Industrial Relations Centre, McGill University, 1958): 187–261.

Jewell, Gary. "The I.W.W. in Canada." *Our Generation*. 11. (Summer 1976): 35–45.

Johnson, Paul, and Jake Muller. "Pulp and Paperworkers Hold the Line." *Canadian Dimension*. 18:3. (1984): 33, 36.

Joseph, Philip. "Perfecting the Administrative Solution to Labour Disputes: The British Columbia Experiment." *Relations industrielles/Industrial Relations*. 38:2. (1983): 380–414.

Kealey, Gregory S. "1919: The Canadian Labour Revolt." *Labour/Le Travail*. 13. (Spring 1984): 11–44.

Kealey, Gregory S., and Andrew Parnaby. "World War I and State Repression of Labour and the Left in Canada, 1914–22." in *Topics in Canadian History*, Volume 2. ed. J.M. Bumsted. (Toronto: Oxford University Press, 1999).

Kealey, Linda. "'No Special Protection – No Sympathy': Women's Activism in the Canadian Labour Revolt of 1919." in *Class, Community and the Labour Movement: Wales and Canada, 1850–1930*. eds. Deian R. Hopkin and Gregory S. Kealey. (St. John's: Canadian Committee on Labour History, 1989): 134–159.

————. "Canadian Socialism and the Woman Question, 1900–1914." *Labour/Le Travail*. 13. (Spring 1984): 77–100.

Kilehmainen, J.I. "Harmony Island: A Finnish Utopian Venture in British Columbia." *British Columbia Historical Quarterly*. 5. (April 1941): 111–123.

Klausen, Susanne. "The Plywood Girls: Women and Gender Ideology at the Port Alberni Plywood Plant, 1942–1991." *Labour/Le Travail*. 41. (1998): 199–235.

Knott, Ernie. "BC Woodworkers and the Employers' Offensive." *Communist Viewpoint*. 13. (September/December 1981): 68–71.

Kobayashi, Audrey, and Peter Jackson. "Japanese Canadians and the Racialization of Labour in the British Columbian Sawmill Industry." *BC Studies*. 103. (Autumn 1994): 33–58.

Koenig, D.J., and T.B. Proverbs. "Class, Regional and Institutional Sources of Party Support Within British Columbia." *BC Studies*. 24. (Winter 1974–75): 19–28.

Kruger, Arthur. "The Direction of Unionism in Canada." in *Canadian Labour in Transition*. eds. R. Miller and F. Isbester. (Scarborough: Prentice Hall, 1971): 85–118.

Kube, Arthur. "Port Alberni Labour Council – A Decade of Progress." *Canadian Labour*. 19. (December 1974): 24–26.

Labonte, Ronald. "Racism and Labour: The Struggle of British Columbia's Farmworkers." *Canadian Forum*. 62. (June/July 1982): 9–11.

Lai, Chuen–Yan David. "Chinese Imprints in British Columbia." *BC Studies*. 39. (Autumn 1978): 20–29.

———. "Chinese Attempts to Discourage Emigration to Canada: Some Findings from the Chinese Archives in Victoria." *BC Studies*. 18. (Summer 1973): 33–49.

———. "The Chinese Consolidated Benevolent Association in Victoria: Its Origins and Functions." *BC Studies*. 15. (Fall 1972): 53–67.

Laidlaw, Blair, and Bruce Curtis. "Inside Postal Workers: The Labour Process, State Policy, and the Worker's Response." *Labour/Le Travail*. 18. (Fall 1986): 139–162.

Langan, Joy. "BCFL Women's Rights Committee." *Canadian Labour*. 20. (June 1975): 11–12.

Langdon, Steven. "The Emergence of the Canadian Working–Class Movement, 1845–1875." Part One. *Journal of Canadian Studies*. 8:2. (May 1973): 3–12.

———. "The Emergence of the Canadian Working–Class Movement, 1845–1875." Part Two. *Journal of Canadian Studies*. 8:3. (August 1973): 8–25.

Langford, Tom. "Workers' Subordinate Values: A Canadian Case Study." *Canadian Journal of Sociology*. 11:3. (Fall 1986): 269–293.

Layton, Steve and Robert Edwards. "The Right to Organize: Labour Law and Its Impact in British Columbia." in *Labour in a Global Economy: Perspectives from the US and Canada*. eds. Steve Hecker and Margaret Hallock. (Eugene: University of Oregon Books, 1991): 196–215.

Lebowitz, Michael. "Trade and Class: Labour Strategies in a World of Strong Capital." *Studies in Political Economy*. 27. (Autumn 1988): 137–149.

Lee, David. "Chinese Construction Workers on the Canadian Pacific." *Railroad History*. 148. (1983): 42–57.

Leier, Mark. "Portrait of a Labour Spy: The Case of Robert Raglan Gosden, 1882–1961." *Labour/Le Travail*. 42. (1998): 55–84.

———. "Plots, Shots, and Liberal Thoughts: Conspiracy Theory and the Death of Ginger Goodwin." *Labour/Le Travail*. 39. (1997): 215–24.

———. "W[h]ither Labour History: Regionalism, Class, and the Writing of BC History." *BC Studies*. 111. (Autumn 1996): 61–75.

———. "Response to Professors Palmer, Strong–Boag, and McDonald." *BC Studies*. 111. (Autumn 1996): 93–98.

———. "Ethnicity, Urbanism and the Labour Aristocracy: Rethinking Vancouver Trade Unionism, 1889–1909." *Canadian Historical Review*. 74:4. (December 1993): 510–534.

———. "Workers and Intellectuals: The Theory of the New Class and Early Canadian Socialism." *Journal of History and Politics*. 10. (1992): 87–108.

———. "Solidarity on Occasion: The Vancouver Free Speech Fights of 1909 and 1912." *Labour/Le Travail*. 23. (Spring 1989): 39–66.

Lembcke, Jerry. "The International Woodworkers of America in British Columbia, 1942–1951." *Labour/Le Travail*. 6. (Autumn 1980): 113–148.

Leslie, Susan. "Little Unions, Big Unions, and the Banks." *Urban Reader*. 7:4. (1979): 5–9.

Levine, Gilbert. "The Waffle and the Labour Movement." *Studies in Political Economy*. 33. (Autumn 1990): 185–193.

Lipsig-Mumme, Carla. "The 'Positive Strike': Union Strategy and State Control." *Studies in Political Economy*. 31. (Spring 1990): 181–185.

Lockhead, Richard. "Labour History, Oral History and the Ginger Goodwin Case." *Reynoldston Research and Studies Publication*. 2. (Fall 1973): 20–26.

Logan, Harold A. "Trends in Collective Bargaining: A Study in Causal Analysis." *Canadian Journal of Economics and Political Science*. 4. (August 1943): 331–347.

———. "The Rise of the One Big Union in Canada." *Journal of Political Economy*. 36:2. (1928): 240–279.

Loo, Tina. "'A Delicate Game': The Meaning of Law on Grouse Creek." *BC Studies*. 96. (Winter 1992–1993): 41–65.

Lorentzen, Edith, and Evelyn Woolner. "Fifty Years of Labour Legislation in Canada." *Labour Gazette*. 50. (September 1950): 1412–1459.

Lorimer, James. "Citizens and the Corporate Development of the Contemporary Canadian City." *Urban History Review*. 12:1. (June 1983): 3–10.

Lowe, Graham. "Women, Work and the Office: The Feminization of Clerical Occupations in Canada, 1901–1931." *Canadian Journal of Sociology*. 5:4. (Fall 1980): 361–381.

Lundstrum, Fred, and Myrtle Bergren. "1934 – The First Test." *Labour History*. 2. (Winter 1979–80): 14–17.

Lutz, John. "After the Fur Trade: The Aboriginal Labouring Class of British Columbia, 1849–1890." *Journal of the Canadian Historical Association*. 3. (1992): 69–94.

———. "Losing Steam: The Boiler and Engine Industry as an Index of British Columbia's Deindustrialization, 1880–1915." *Journal of the Canadian Historical Association*. (1988): 168–208.

Mackenzie, Suzanne, and Glen Norcliffe. "Restructuring the Canadian Newsprint Industry." *Canadian Geographer/ Le geographe canadien*. 41:1. (1997): 2–6.

MacKinnon, Mary. "New Evidence on Canadian Wage Rates, 1900–1930." *Canadian Journal of Economics/Revue canadienne d'économique*. 29:1. (1996): 114–31.

Mackinnon, T.J. "The Forest Industry of British Columbia." *Geography*. 61. (July 1971): 231–236.

MacLachlan, M. "The Blubber Bay Strike." *Labour History*. 2. (Winter 1979–80): 26–27.

———. "The Success of the Fraser Valley Milk Producers' Association." *BC Studies*. 24. (Winter 1974–75): 52–64.

Mahon, Rianne. "Canadian Labour in the Battle of the Eighties." *Studies in Political Economy*. 11. (Summer 1983): 149–177.

Manley, John. "'Starve, Be Damned!': Communists and Canada's Urban Unemployed, 1929–39." *Canadian Historical Review*. 79:3. (September 1998): 466–491.

Manley, John. "Does the International Labour Movement Need Salvaging? Communism, Labourism, and the Canadian Trade Unions, 1921–1928." *Labour/Le Travail*. 41. (1998): 147–80.

Marchak, Patricia. "British Columbia: 'New Right' Politics and a New Geography." in *Canadian Politics in the 1990s*. Third edition. eds. Michael S. Wittington and Glen Williams. (Scarborough: Nelson Canada, 1990): 45–59.

———. "Public Policy, Capital and Labour in the Forest Industry." in *Workers, Capital and the State in British Columbia*. eds. Rennie Warburton and David Coburn. (Vancouver: University of British Columbia Press, 1988).

———. "Women, Work and Unions." *International Journal of Sociology*. 5. (Winter 1975–76): 39–61.

———. "Class, Regional and Institutional Sources of Social Conflicts in BC." *BC Studies*. 27. (Autumn 1975): 30–49.

Martinello, Felice. "Correlates of Certification Application Success in British Columbia, Saskatchewan and Manitoba." *Relations industrielles/Industrial Relations*. 51–3. (1996): 544–562.

———. "Insurance in a Unionized Labour Market: An Empirical Test." *Canadian Journal of Economics*. 21. (May 1988): 394–409.

Matkin, James. "Government Intervention in Labour Disputes in British Columbia." in *Collective Bargaining in the Essential and Public Service Sector*. ed. M. Gunderson. (Toronto: University of Toronto Press, 1975): 79–118.

Matters, Diane. "Public Welfare Vancouver Style, 1910–1920." *Journal of Canadian Studies*. 14. (Spring 1979): 3–15.

May, Louise, and John Shields. "Labour Records at the University of British Columbia." *History Workshop*. 18. (Autumn 1984): 74–76.

McBride, Stephen. "The State and Labour Markets: Towards a Comparative Political Economy of Unemployment." *Studies in Political Economy*. 23. (Summer 1987): 141–155.

McCallum, Margaret. "Corporate Welfarism in Canada, 1919–1939." *Canadian Historical Review*. 71:1. (March 1990): 46–79.

———. "Keeping Women in their Place: The Minimum Wage in Canada, 1910–1925." *Labour/Le Travail*. 17. (Spring 1986): 29–56.

McCallum, Todd. "'Not a Sex Question': The One Big Union and the Politics of Radical Manhood." *Labour/Le Travail*. 42. (1998): 15–54.

McCandless, Richard. "Vancouver's Red Menace of 1935: The Waterfront Situation." *BC Studies*. 22. (Summer 1974): 56–71.

McClean, John. "BC and the Faculty Associations." *Canadian Personnel and Industrial Relations Review*. 25. (January 1978): 20–21.

McCormack, A. Ross. "The Industrial Workers of the World in Western Canada, 1905–1914." in *Canadian Working-Class History*. eds. Laurel Sefton MacDowell and Ian Radforth. (Toronto: Canadian Scholars' Press, 1992): 289–310.

———. "British Working-Class Immigrants and Canadian Radicalism: The Case of Arthur Puttee." *Canadian Ethnic Studies*. 10:2. (1978): 22–37.

———. "The Emergence of the Socialist Movement in British Columbia." *BC Studies*. 21. (Spring 1974): 3–27.

McDonald, Robert A.J. "The West is a Messy Place." *BC Studies*. 111. (Autumn 1996): 88–92.

———. "Lumber Society on the Industrial Frontier: Burrard Inlet, 1863–1886." *Labour/Le Travail*. 33. (Spring 1994): 69–96.

———. "Vancouver's 'Four Hundred': The Quest for Wealth and Status in Canada's Urban West, 1886–1914." *Journal of Canadian Studies*. 25:3. (Fall 1990): 55–73.

———. "Working Class Vancouver. 1886–1914: Urbanism and Class in British Columbia." *BC Studies*. 69–70. (Spring/Summer 1986): 33–69.

————. "'Holy Retreat' or 'Practical Breathing Spot'?: Class Perceptions of Vancouver's Stanley Park, 1910–1913." *Canadian Historical Review*. 65:2. (June 1984): 127–153.

McKee, William. "Vancouver City Archives: Some Additional Sources for Labour History." *Archivaria*. 4. (Summer 1977): 177–178.

McLaren, Angus. "Males, Migrants, and Murder in British Columbia, 1900–1923." in *On The Case: Explorations in Social History*. eds. Franca Iacovetta and Wendy Mitchinson. (Toronto: University of Toronto Press, 1998): 159–180.

————. "The Creation of a Haven for 'Human Thoroughbreds': The Sterilization of the Feeble-Minded and the Mentally Ill in British Columbia." *Canadian Historical Review*. 67:2. (June 1986): 127–150.

————. "The First Campaigns for Birth Control Clinics in British Columbia." *Journal of Canadian Studies*. 19:3. (Fall 1984): 50–64.

————. "'What Has This To Do With Working Class Women?' Birth Control and the Canadian Left, 1900–1939." *Histoire sociale/Social History*. 28. (November 1981): 435–454.

McLean, Bruce. "BC Government Employees' Union." *Canadian Labour*. 18. (March 1973): 10–15.

McMillan, Murray. "The Unionization of U.B.C.: The Academic Cloth Cap." *UBC Alumni Chronicle*. 29. (Spring 1975): 9–10, 12–13.

McMullan, John. "State, Capital and Debt in the British Columbia Fishing Fleet, 1970–1982." *Journal of Canadian Studies*. 19:1. (1984): 65–88.

McNaught, Kenneth. "E.P. Thompson vs. Harold Logan: Writing about Labour and the Left in the 1970s." *Canadian Historical Review*. 62:2. (June 1981): 141–168.

McNay, Diane. "The Teachers of British Columbia and Superannuation." *BC Studies*. 2. (Spring 1969): 30–44.

McPherson, Kathryn. "Science and Technique: Nurses' Work in a Canadian Hospital." in *Caring and Curing: Historical Perspectives on Women and Healing in Canada*. (Ottawa: University of Ottawa Press, 1994): 71–101.

McPhillips, David. "Employer Free Speech During Organization Drives and Decertification Attempts." *Osgoode Hall Law Journal*. 20. (March 1982): 138–154.

————. "Exclusion from the Bargaining Unit: An Alternative Approach." *Advocate*. 39. (November 1981): 473–480.

————. "Duty to Bargain in Good Faith in British Columbia." *Advocate*. 39. (January 1981): 217–233.

————. "Duty of Fair Representation: Recent Attitudes in British Columbia and Ontario." *Relations industrielles/Industrial Relations*. 36:4. (1981): 803–827.

McTiernan, Miriam. "Focus: The British Columbia Credit Union Archives." *Archivaria*. 5. (Winter 1977–78): 177–180.

Meltz, Noah M. "Interstate vs. Interprovincial Differences in Union Density." *Industrial Relations*. 28:2. (Spring 1989): 142–158.

Meredith, T.C. "Boosting in British Columbia: The Creation and Rise of Invermere." *Urban History Review*. 16:3. (February 1988): 271–279.

Morgan, Peter. "The Resurrection of TLRA." *BC Business Magazine*. 10. (November 1982): 21–22.

————. "A Man Constrained." *BC Business Magazine*. 10. (November 1982): 16–17, 19.

Morgan, Richard E. "Informal Participation Patterns in the Railroad Running Trades." *Labour/Le Travail*. 27. (Spring 1991).

Morley, Terry. "Politics as Theatre: Paradox and Continuity in British Columbia." *Journal of Canadian Studies*. 25:3. (Fall 1990): 19–37.

———. "Public Affairs: Labour in British Columbia Politics." *Queen's Quarterly*. 83. (Summer 1976): 291–298.

Mouat, Jeremy. "Vic Midgley Writes Home: A Letter From New Zealand, 1939." *Labour/Le Travail*. 30. (Fall 1992): 205–22.

———. "The Genesis of Western Exceptionalism: British Columbia's Hard-Rock Miners, 1895–1903." *Canadian Historical Review*. 71:3. (September 1990): 317–345.

———. "Creating a New Staple: Capital, Technology and Monopoly in British Columbia's Resource Sector, 1901–1925." *Journal of the Canadian Historical Association*. (1990): 215–238.

———. "The Politics of Coal: A Study of the Wellington Miners' Strike of 1890–91." *BC Studies*. 77. (Spring 1988): 3–29.

Mouat, Jeremy, and Hovis W. Logan. "The history of mining in British Columbia: a bibliography." Working draft. (Vancouver: University of British Columbia Special Collections, 1984).

Muller, Jack. "Dishing It Out in BC: Tune In, Turn On, Lay Off." *Canadian Dimension*. 17:2. (1983): 31–32.

Murphy, David G. "The Entrepreneurial Role of Organized Labour in the British Columbia Motion Picture Industry." *Relations industrielles/Industrial Relations*. 52:3. (1997): 531–552.

Muszynski, Alicja. "Race and Gender: Structural Determinants in the Formation of British Columbia's Salmon Cannery Labour Force." *Canadian Journal of Sociology*. 13:1–2. (Winter–Spring 1988): 103–121.

———. "Class Formation and Class Consciousness: The Making of Shoreworkers in the BC Fishing Industry." *Studies in Political Economy*. 20. (Summer 1986): 85–117.

———. "The Organization of Women and Ethnic Minorities in a Resource Industry: A Case Study of the Unionization of Shoreworkers in the BC Fishing Industry, 1937–1949." *Journal of Canadian Studies*. 19:1. (Spring 1984): 89–107.

Nearing, S. "Crow's Nest Pass." *Labour Monthly*. 9. (February 1927): 120–123.

———. "The Labour Situation in Western Canada." *Labour Monthly*. 7. (May 1925): 228–293.

Nelles, H. V. "Horses of a Shared Colour: Interpreting Class and Identity in Turn-of-the-Century Vancouver." *Labour/Le Travail*. 40. (1997): 269–75.

Newton, Janice. "From Wage Slave to White Slave: The Prostitution Controversy and the Early Canadian Left." in *Beyond the Vote: Canadian Women and Politics*. eds. Linda Kealey and Joan Sangster. (Toronto: University of Toronto Press, 1989): 217–236.

Nicol, Janet Mary. "'Unions Aren't Native': The Muckamuck Restaurant Labour Dispute, Vancouver, BC (1978–1983)." *Labour/Le Travail*. 40. (Fall 1997): 235–251.

Noel, Alain, and Keith Gardner. "The Gainers Strike: Capitalist Offensive, Militancy, and the Politics of Industrial Relations in Canada." *Studies in Political Economy*. 31. (Spring 1990): 31–73.

Norris, John. "The Vancouver Island Coal Miners, 1912–1914: A Study of An Organizational Strike." *BC Studies*. 45. (Spring 1980): 56–72.

North, George. "Public Sector Under the Gun in BC." *Canadian Dimension*. 16:4. (1982): 30–32.

O'Bannon, Patrick. "Technological Change in the Pacific Coast Canned Salmon Industry, 1900–1925: A Case Study." *Agricultural History*. 56. (January 1982): 151–166.

Ofori-Amoah, B., and Roger Hayter. "Labour Turnover Characteristics at the Eurocan Pulp and Paper Mill, Kitimat: A Log Linear Analysis." *Environment and Planning.* A. 21. (November 1989): 1491–1510.

Ormsby, Margaret. "The United Farmers of British Columbia – An Abortive Third Party Movement." *British Columbia Historical Quarterly.* 17:1/2. (1953): 53–74.

Owen, Thelma Dillon. "Legendary Kelowna Teamster. (George Dillon)." *Okanagan History 60th Annual Report.* 163–164.

Palmer, Bryan D. "Class and the Writing of History: Beyond BC." *BC Studies.* 111. (Autumn 1996): 76–84.

———. "Labour Protest and Organization in 19th-Century Canada, 1820–1890." *Labour/Le Travail.* 20. (Fall 1987): 61–84.

———. "Listening to History Rather than Historians: Reflections on Working Class History." *Studies in Political Economy.* 20. (Summer 1986): 47–84.

———. "Fighting On Two Fronts." *Canadian Dimension.* 17:6. (1983): 13–15.

Panitch, Leo. "Capitalist Restructuring and Labour Strategies." *Studies in Political Economy.* 24. (Autumn 1987): 131–151.

Panitch, Leo and Donald Swartz. "Toward Permanent Exceptionalism: Coercion and Consent in Canadian Industrial Relations." *Labour/Le Travail.* 13. (Spring 1984): 133–157.

Papenbrook, Wiho. "Fighting for a Healthy Workplace in Kitimat." *Canadian Dimension.* 16. (July/August 1982): 14–15.

Parker, Keith. "Ginger Goodwin: Union Organizer." *British Columbia Historical News.* 30:2. (1997): 24–8.

———. "Arthur Evans: Western Radical." *Alberta History.* 26. (Spring 1978): 21–29.

Parkin, Al. "Saga of the Loggers Navy." *Labour History.* 2. (Winter 1979–80): 8–10.

Payne, Raymond. "Corporate Power, Interest Groups and the Development of Mining Policy in British Columbia, 1972–1977." *BC Studies.* 54. (Summer 1982): 3–37.

Peck, Gunther. "Divided Loyalties: Immigrant Padrones and the Evolution of Industrial Paternalism in North America." *International Labor and Working-Class History.* 53. (1998): 49–68.

Pentland, H.C. "The Western Canadian Labour Movement, 1897–1919." *Canadian Journal of Political and Social Theory.* 3. (Spring 1979): 53–78.

Pentland-Smith, Janice. "Provisions for Women in BC Union Contracts." in *Women and Work: A Resource Kit.* (Ottawa: Secretary of State, Women's Programme, 1978).

Perry, Adele. "'Fair Ones of a Purer Caste': White Women and Colonialism in Nineteenth-Century British Columbia." *Feminist Studies.* 23:3. (1997): 501–24.

Peterson, Larry. "The One Big Union in International Perspective: Revolutionary Industrial Unionism, 1900–1925." *Labour/Le Travail.* 7. (Spring 1981): 41–66.

Petryslyn, J. "R.B. Bennett and the Communists, 1930–1935." *Journal of Canadian Studies.* 9:4. (1974): 43–55.

Phillips, Paul. "The National Policy and the Development of the Western Canadian Labour Movement." in *Prairie Perspectives.* eds. A.W. Rasporich and H.C. Klassen. (Toronto: Holt, Rinehart and Winston, 1973).

Pierson, Ruth. "Women's Emancipation and the Recruitment of Women into the Canadian Labour Force in World War II." *Journal of the Canadian Historical Association.* (1976): 141–173.

Piva, Michael J. "Urban Working-Class Incomes and Real Incomes in 1921: A Comparative Analysis." *Histoire sociale/Social History.* 31. (May 1983): 145–167.

Poisson, Myrna. "Right-to-work Laws." *UBC Business Review*. 14. (1979): 73–83.

Ponak, Allen, and Mark Thompson. "Faculty Views of Collective Bargaining: The Voice of Experience." *Relations industrielles/Industrial Relations*. 39:3. (1984): 449–465.

———. "Faculty Attitudes and the Scope of Bargaining." *Industrial Relations*. 18. (Winter 1979): 97–102.

Purdy, Sean. "Industrial Efficiency, Social Order, and Moral Purity: Housing Reform Thought in English Canada." *Urban History Review/Revue d'histoire urbaine*. 25:2. (1997): 30–40.

Rae, W. "Narrative and Appreciation of Events on Vancouver Island, August 14th–31st, 1913." *BC Studies*. 43. (Autumn 1979): 83–93.

Rajala, Richard A. "Clearcutting the British Columbia Coast: Work, Environment and the State 1880–1930." In *Making Western Canada: Essays on European Colonization and Settlement*. eds. Catherine Cavanaugh and Jeremy Mouat. (Toronto: Garamond Press, 1996): 104–132.

———. "The Forest as Factory: Technological Change and Worker Control in the West Coast Logging Industry, 1880–1930." *Labour/Le Travail*. 32. (Fall 1993): 73–104.

Ralston, Keith. "Patterns of Trade and Investment on the Pacific Coast, 1867–1892: The Case of the British Columbia Salmon Canning Industry." *BC Studies*. 1. (Winter 1968–69): 37–45.

Rands, Jean. "Towards an Organization of Working Women." in *Women Unite: An Anthology of the Canadian Women's Movement*. (Toronto: Canadian Women's Educational Press, 1972): 141–148.

Rees, Kevin, and Roger Hayter. "Flexible Specialization, Uncertainty, and the Firm: Enterprise Strategies in the Wood Remanufacturing Industry of the Vancouver Metropolitan Area, British Columbia." *Canadian Geographer/Le geographe canadien*. 40:3. (1996): 203–219.

Reid, David. "Company Mergers in the Fraser River Salmon Canning Industry, 1885–1902." *Canadian Historical Review*. 56:3. (September 1975): 282–302.

Resnick, Phillip. "Social Democracy in Power: The Case of British Columbia." *BC Studies*. 34. (Spring 1977): 3–20.

Ripmeester, Michael. "Mines, Homes, and Halls: Place and Identity as a Gold Miner in Rossland, British Columbia, 1898–1901." *Canadian Geographer/Le geographe canadien*. 38:2. (Summer 1994): 98–109.

Roberge, Roger. "Resource Towns: The Pulp and Paper Communities." *Canadian Geographical Journal*. 94. (February/March 1977): 28–35.

Robin, Martin. "British Columbia: The Politics of Class Conflict." in *Canadian Provincial Politics*. ed. Martin Robin. (Scarborough: Prentice-Hall, 1972): 27–68.

Rodney, William. "Russian Revolutionaries in the Port of Vancouver, 1917." *BC Studies*. 16. (Winter 1972–73): 25–31.

Rosenthal, Star. "Union Maids: Organized Women Workers in Vancouver, 1900–1915." *BC Studies*. 41. (Spring 1979): 36–55.

Roy, Patricia. "Vancouver: The Mecca of Unemployed, 1907–1929." in *Town and City: Aspects of Western Canadian Urban Development*. ed. Alan Artibise. (Regina: Canadian Plains Research Center, University of Regina, 1981): 393–413.

———. "British Columbia's Fear of Asians, 1900–1950." *Histoire sociale/Social History*. 25. (May 1980): 161–172.

————. "The British Columbia Electric Railway and Its Street Railway Employees: Paternalism in Labour Relations." BC Studies. 16. (Winter 1972–73): 3–24.

————. "The Fine Art of Lobbying and Persuading: The Case of BC Electric Railway." in Canadian Business History: Selected Studies, 1947–1971. ed. D.S. Macmillan. (Toronto: McClelland and Stewart, 1972): 239–254.

Roy, Reginald H. "The Seaforths and the Strikers: Nanaimo, August 1913." BC Studies. 43. (Autumn 1979): 81–93.

Russell, Bob. "A Fair or a Minimum Wage? Women Workers, the State, and the Origins of Wage Regulation in Western Canada." Labour/Le Travail. 28. (Fall 1991): 59–88.

Sager, Eric W., and Peter Baskerville. "Locating the Unemployed in Urban British Columbia: Evidence From the 1891 Census." Journal of Canadian Studies. 25:3. (Fall 1990): 38–54.

Sangster, Joan. "The Communist Party and the Woman Question, 1922–1929." Labour/Le Travail. 15. (Spring 1985): 25–56.

Satzewich, Victor, and Peter S. Li. "Immigrant Labour in Canada: The Loss and Benefit of Ethnic Origin in the Job Market." Canadian Journal of Sociology. 12:3. (Fall 1987): 229–242.

Sautter, Udo. "The Origins of the Employment Service of Canada, 1900–1920." Labour/Le Travail. 6. (Autumn 1980): 89–112.

Saywell, John. "Labour and Socialism in British Columbia: A Survey of Historical Development Before 1903." British Columbia Historical Quarterly. 15. (July/October 1951): 129–150.

Scardellato, Gabrielle P. "Italian Immigrant Workers in Powell River, BC: A Case Study of Settlement Before World War Two." Labour/Le Travail. 16. (Fall 1985): 145–163.

Schwindt, R. "The Pearse Commission and the Industrial Organization of the British Columbia Forest Industry." BC Studies. 41. (Spring 1974): 3–35.

Seager, Allen. "Right, Left, and Centre – News and Views of the Canadian West." Labour/Le Travail. 18. (Fall 1986): 209–215.

————. "Socialists and Workers: The Western Canadian Coal Miners, 1900–21." Labour/Le Travail. 16. (Fall 1985): 23–59.

————. "The Pass Strike of 1932." Alberta History. 25. (Winter 1977): 1–11.

Seager, Allen, and Adele Perry. "Mining the Connections: Class, Ethnicity, and Gender in Nanaimo, British Columbia, 1891." Histoire sociale/Social History. 30:59. (1997): 55–76.

Seager, Allen, and David Roth. "British Columbia and the Mining West: A Ghost of a Chance." in The Workers' Revolt in Canada, 1917–1925. ed. Craig Heron. (Toronto: University of Toronto Press, 1998): 231–67.

Seixas, Peter. "Teaching Working Class History in BC." Labour/Le Travail. 27. (1991): 195–199.

Selman, Gordon. "Mechanics' Institutes in British Columbia." Continuous Learning. 10. (May/June 1971): 126–130.

Septer, Dirk. "James Cronin: Mining Pioneer," British Columbia Historical News. 29:1. (Winter 1995–96): 27–8.

Silverman, Peter. "Military Aid to the Civil Power in British Columbia: The Labour Strikes in Wellington and Steveston, 1890 and 1900." Pacific Northwest Quarterly. 61:3. (1970): 156–164.

Simpson, Wayne, and Frank Peters. "The Economics of Mileage Restrictions for Railway Workers in Western Canada." Relations industrielles/Industrial Relations. 38:1. (1983): 95–103.

Sinnot, Emmett, and Paul Tennant. "The Origins of Taxicab Limitation in Vancouver City. (Or Good Try Anyway, Stanley Anderson)." *BC Studies*. 49. (Spring 1981): 40–53.

Smith, Allan. "The Myth of the Self-Made Man in English Canada, 1850–1914." *Canadian Historical Review*. 59:2. (June 1978): 189–218.

Smith, Michael R. "The Effects of Strikes on Workers: A Critical Analysis." *Canadian Journal of Sociology*. 3:4. (Fall 1978): 457–473.

Smucker, Joseph, and Axel Vanden Berg. "Some Evidence of the Effects of Labour Market Policies on Workers' Attitudes Toward Change in Canada and Sweden." *Canadian Journal of Sociology*. 16:1. (Winter 1991): 51–75.

"Sources for Labour History at the Public Archives of Canada." *Newsletter of the Committee on Canadian Labour History*. 2. (1973): 18–23.

Stainsby, Jill. "'It's the Smell of Money': Women Shoreworkers of British Columbia." *BC Studies*. 103. (Autumn 1994): 59–81.

Stanbury, W.T., D.B. Fields, and D. Stevenson. "BC Indians in An Urban Environment: Income, Poverty, Education and Vocational Training." *Manpower Review Pacific Region*. 5. (July/September 1972): 11–33.

———. "Unemployment and Labour Force Participation Rates of BC Indians Living Off Reserves." *Manpower Review Pacific Region*. 5. (April/June 1972): 21–45.

Stewart, Bruce. "The Housing of Our Immigrant Workers." *Canadian Political Science Association Papers and Proceedings*. 1. (1913): 98–111.

Stewart, George. "Tales of Pioneer Miners." *BC Outdoors*. 28. (November/December 1972): 48–53.

Stewart, John. "The Canadian Northern Strike of 1912." *Labour History*. 3:1. (1981): 8–10.

Stewart, Ian. "A Retrospective Look at Labour Legislation in British Columbia and Manitoba: Much Ado About Little?" *British Journal of Canadian Studies*. 9:2. (1994): 348–359.

Stocks, Alex. "Union Raiding: Rivalry in BC Mines, Smelters and Metal Industries." *Labour Files*. 4:2. (1985): 2–23.

Storey, Robert. "Studying Work in Canada." *Canadian Journal of Sociology*. 16:3. (Summer 1991): 241–265.

Stortz, Paul J., and J. Donald Wilson, "Education on the Frontier: Schools, Teachers and the Community Influence in North Central British Columbia." *Histoire sociale/Social History*. 26:52. (November 1993): 265–90.

Strong-Boag, Veronica. "'Moving Beyond Tired Truths': Or, Let's Not Fight Old Battles." *BC Studies*. 111. (Autumn 1996): 84–87.

Struthers, James. "Prelude to Depression: The Federal Government and Unemployment, 1918–1929." *Canadian Historical Review*. 58:3. (September 1977): 277–293.

Stuart-Stubbs, Basil. "The Employment Situation for Recent Graduates of the UBC School of Librarianship." *BCLA Reporter*. 26. (March 1983): 16–19.

Stunden, Nancy. "Canadian Labour Archives: Some Recent Acquisitions." *Labour/Le Travail*. 5. (Spring 1980): 148–159.

Sutherland, Neil. "'I Can't Recall When I Didn't Help': The Working Lives of Pioneering Children in Twentieth Century British Columbia." *Histoire sociale/Social History*. 48. (November 1991).

———. "'We Always Had Things To Do':
The Paid and Unpaid Work of Anglo-
phone Children Between the 1920s and
the 1960s." *Labour/Le Travail*. 25. (Spring
1990): 105–141.

Sutherland, Ruby. "Vancouver's Labour Arts
Guild." *Food For Thought*. 6. (May–June
1946): 10–13.

———. "The Labour Arts Guild." *Canadian
Art*. 3. (November 1945): 6–9, 40.

Swartz, Donald. "New Forms of Worker Par-
ticipation: A Critique of the Quality of
Working Life." *Studies in Political Economy*. 5.
(Spring 1981): 55–79.

Sweeney, Robert C.H. "Understanding Work
Historically: A Reflection Prompted by
Two Recent Studies of the Fur Trade."
Labour/Le Travail. 41. (1998): 243–52.

Szychter, Gwen. "The War Work of Women
in Rural British Columbia 1914–1919."
British Columbia Historical News. 27:4. (Fall
1994): 5–9.

Tan, Jim. "Chinese Labour and the Reconsti-
tuted Social Order of British Columbia."
Canadian Ethnic Studies. 19:3. (1987): 68–88.

Tanner, Julian. "Skill Levels of Manual Workers and Beliefs about Work, Management,
and Industry: A Comparison of Craft and
Non-Craft Workers in Edmonton." *Canadian Journal of Sociology*. 9:3. (Summer
1984): 303–319.

Taylor, John H. "Mayors a la Mancha: An
Aspect of Depression Leadership in Canadian Cities." *Urban History Review*. 9:3. (February 1981): 3–14.

———. "'Relief from Relief': The Cities'
Answer to Depression Dependency." *Journal of Canadian Studies*. 14:1. (Spring 1970):
16–23.

Taylor, Ronald and Mark Thompson. "Work
Value Systems of Young Workers." *Academy
of Management Journal*. 19. (December 1976):
522–536.

Thomas, Phil. "'Where the Fraser River
Flows' by Joe Hill." *Labour History*. 3:1.
(1981): 11–12.

Thompson, Mark. "Restraint and Labour
Relations: The Case of British Columbia."
Canadian Public Policy. 11. (June 1985):
171–179.

———. "Anatomy of a Crisis in Labour
Relations: Restraint Legislation and the
Public Sector in British Columbia." in
Managing Industrial Relations in an Era of Change.
(Montreal: McGill University, 1984):
141–157.

Thompson, Mark, and Allen Ponak. "Faculty
Perceptions of Decision Making Influence
and Support for Collective Bargaining." in
*Proceedings of the Thirty-Sixth Annual Winter Meet-
ing of the Industrial Relations Research Association*.
ed. Barbara Dennis. (Madison: IRRA,
1984): 337–344.

———. "Arbitration and Alcohol Abuse." in
Current Problems in Labour Arbitration. ed. J.M.
Weiler. (Toronto: Carswell, 1981).

Thompson, Mark, and Albert A. Blum.
"International Unionism in Canada: The
Move to Local Control." *Industrial Relations*.
22:1. (Winter 1983): 71–86.

Thompson, Mark, and J. Cairne. "Reply."
Industrial and Labour Relations Review. 28. (April
1975): 435–438.

———. "Compulsory Arbitration: The Case
of British Columbia Teachers." *Industrial and
Labour Relations Review*. 27. (October 1973):
3–17.

Tieleman, Bill. "The BC Spirit." *Canadian
Dimension*. 17:5. (1983): 10–11.

Tillotson, Shirley. "Class and Community in
Canadian Welfare Work, 1933–1960." *Journal of Canadian Studies/ Revues d'études
canadiennes*. 32:1. (1997): 63–92.

———. "'When Our Membership awakens': Welfare Work and Canadian Union Activism, 1950–1965." *Labour/Le Travail*. 40. (1997): 137–69.

Trower, Peter. "An Old Logger Remembers." *Vancouver*. 13. (October 1980): 122–126, 128–130.

Tuck, J. Hugh. "The United Brotherhood of Railway Employees in Western Canada, 1898–1905." *Labour/Le Travail*. 11. (Spring 1983): 63–88.

Turiff, Gordon. "British Columbia's Proposed Labour Ombudsman." *University of British Columbia Law Review*. 10:1. (1975): 64–85.

Vaselenak, J.R. "British Columbia Logging and Lumber Industry, 1946–1953." in *Patterns of Industrial Dispute Settlement in Five Canadian Industries*. ed. H.D. Woods. (Montreal: Industrial Relations Centre, McGill University, 1958): 325–375.

Wade, Jill. "Home or Homelessness? Marginal Housing in Vancouver, 1886–1950." *Urban History Review/Revue d'histoire urbaine*. 25:2. (1997): 19–29.

———. "The 'Sting' of Vancouver's Better Housing 'Spree'." *Urban History Review*. 21:2. (March 1993): 92–103.

———. "Wartime Housing Limited, 1941–1947: Canadian Housing Policy at the Crossroads." *Urban History Review*. 15:1. (June 1986): 41–60.

———. "The 'Gigantic Scheme': Crofter Immigration and Deepsea Fisheries Development for British Columbia, 1817–1893." *BC Studies*. 53. (Spring 1982): 28–44.

Wade, Susan. "Helena Gutteridge: Votes for Women and Trade Unions." in *In Her Own Right: Selected Essays on Women's History in BC*. eds. Barbara Latham and Cathy Kess. (Victoria: Camosun College, 1980): 187–203.

Warburton, Rennie. "Race and Class in British Columbia: A Comment." *BC Studies*. 45. (Spring 1980): 17–35.

Warburton, Rennie, and David Coburn. "The Rise of Non-Manual Work in British Columbia." *BC Studies*. 59. (Autumn 1983): 5–27.

Ward, Doug. "Stop the Presses." *Canadian Dimension*. 14. (July/August 1979): 11–13.

Ward, W. Peter. "Class and Race in the Social Structure of British Columbia, 1870–1939." *BC Studies*. 45. (Spring 1980): 17–35.

———. "British Columbia and the Japanese Evacuation." *Canadian Historical Review*. 57:3. (September 1976): 289–308.

Warskett, George. "Capital's Strength and Labour's Weakness Under Free Trade." *Studies in Political Economy*. 33. (Autumn 1990): 113–135.

Warskett, Rosemary. "Wage Solidarity and Equal Value: Or Gender and Class in the Structuring of Work Place Hierarchies." *Studies in Political Economy*. 32. (Summer 1990): 55–85.

———. "Bank Worker Unionization and the Law." *Studies in Political Economy*. 25. (Spring 1988): 41–75.

Watkins, Lyndon. "Will We Revive Our Merchant Marine?" *Canadian Geographic*. 10:10. (February/March 1981): 10–20.

Webb, Roland H. "Burrard Drydock Co. Ltd.: The Rise and Demise of Vancouver's Biggest Shipyard." *The Northern Mariner/Le marin du nord*. 6:3. (1996): 1–10.

Webber, Jeremy. "Compelling Compromise: Canada Chooses Conciliation Over Arbitration, 1900–1907." *Labour/Le Travail*. 28. (Fall 1991): 15–57.

———. "The Malaise of Compulsory Conciliation: Strike Prevention in Canada During W.W.II." *Labour/Le Travail*. 15. (Spring 1985): 57–88.

Weber, Ralph. "Riot in Victoria, 1860." *Journal of Negro History*. 56. (April 1971): 141–148.

Weinrich, Peter. "The Censor and the BC Federationist, 1916–1919." *Bulletin of the Committee on Canadian Labour History*. 7. (Spring 1979): 6–9.

White, Julie. "Service, Office and Retail Workers' Union of Canada." in *Women and Work: A Resource Kit*. (Ottawa: Secretary of State, Women's Programme, 1978).

Widenor, Marcus R. "Diverging Patterns: Labour in the Pacific Northwest Wood Products Industry." *Industrial Relations*. 34:3. (July 1995): 441–463.

Wilkey, Craig D. "British Columbia's Error Regarding the Chinese Immigrants." *British Columbia Historical News*. 31:2. (1998): 14–7.

Wilson, J. Donald. "Workshops on Canadian Working-Class History, Victoria, May 1990." *Labour/Le Travail*. 27. (Spring 1991): 185–213.

———. "'I Am Here To Help If You Need Me': British Columbia's Rural Teachers' Welfare Officer, 1928–1934." *Journal of Canadian Studies*. 25:2. (Summer 1990): 94–118.

Wilson, J. Donald, Matti Kurikka, and A.B. Makela. "Socialist Thought Among Finns in Canada, 1900–1932." *Canadian Ethnic Studies*. 10:2. (1978): 9–21.

Wong, Daryl. "The Pacific Coast Logging Industry in the 1930s." *British Columbia Historical News*. 29:3. (1996): 26–30.

Wotherspoon, Terry. "Occupational Divisions and Struggles for Unity Among British Columbia Public School Teachers." *BC Studies*. 107. (Autumn 1995): 30–59.

———. "The Incorporation of Public School Teachers into the Industrial Order: British Columbia in the First Half of the Twentieth Century." *Studies in Political Economy*. 46. (Spring 1995): 119–151.

———. "From Subordinate Partners to Dependent Employees: State Regulation of Public School Teachers in 19th-Century British Columbia." *Labour/Le Travail*. 31. (Spring 1993): 75–110.

Wright, Robert. "The Plight of Rural Women Teachers in the 1920s." *British Columbia Historical News*. 28:1. (Winter 1994–5): 26–29.

Wynne, Robert. "American Labor Leaders and the Vancouver Anti-Oriental Riot." *Pacific Northwest Quarterly*. 57:4. (1966): 172–179.

Yarmie, Andrew. "The Right To Manage: Vancouver Employer's Associations, 1900–1923." *BC Studies*. 90. (Summer 1991): 40–74.

Young, Walter. "Ideology, Personality and the Origin of the CCF in British Columbia." *BC Studies*. 32. (Winter 1976–77): 139–162.

———. "The New Democratic Party: British Columbia's Labour Party." in *Papers on the 1962 Election*. ed. John Meisel. (Toronto: University of Toronto Press, 1964): 181–200.

Yu, Miriam. "Human Rights, Discrimination, and Coping Behaviour of the Chinese in Canada." *Canadian Ethnic Studies*. 19:3. (1987): 114–124.

THESES AND UNPUBLISHED PAPERS

Allum, James R. "Smoke Across the Border: An Environmental History of the Trail Smelter Investigation, 1900–45." (Ph.D. Thesis, Queen's University, 1995).

Anderson, Clifford. "Collective Bargaining Under a Compulsory Conciliation System in the British Columbia Coast Forest Industry." (M.A. Thesis, University of British Columbia, 1971).

Anderson, Donald E. "The Growth of Organized Labour in the Lumbering Industry of British Columbia." (B.A. Essay, University of British Columbia, 1944).

Anderson, Robin J. "The Vancouver Employment Business, 1900–1915: Sharks and White Slavers." (M.A. Thesis, Simon Fraser University, 1991).

Angel, Elizabeth Sharon. "In Search of Parity: The Hospital Employees' Union in the British Columbia Long Term Care Industry." (M.Sc.Bus.Admin. Thesis, University of British Columbia, 1985).

———. "Journalism and the Newspaper Guild." (M.B.A. Essay, University of British Columbia, 1981).

Armstrong, Myrtle. "The Development of Trade Union Political Activity in the CCF." (M.A. Thesis, University of Toronto, 1959).

Atherton, Pat. "CAIMAW – Portrait of a Canadian Union." (M.Sc. Thesis, University of British Columbia, 1979).

———. "The Professional Association of Residents and Interns." (M.B.A. Essay, University of British Columbia, 1979).

Bartlett, Eleanor Anne. "Real Wages and the Standard of Living in Vancouver, 1901–1929." (M.A. Thesis, University of British Columbia, 1980).

Bartlett, Jon. "The 1877 Wellington Miners' Strike." (B.A. Essay, University of British Columbia, 1975).

Baum, Rainer. "The Social and Political Philosophy of Trade Unions." (M.A. Thesis, University of British Columbia, 1962).

Belshaw, John. "The Administration of Relief to Vancouver's Unemployed, 1929–1939." (M.A. Thesis, Simon Fraser University, 1982).

Bernard, Elaine. "Long Distance Feeling: A History of the Telecommunications Workers Union." (Ph.D. Thesis, Simon Fraser University, 1989).

———. "The Rod Young Affair in the British Columbia Co–operative Commonwealth Federation." (M.A. Thesis, University of British Columbia, 1979).

Bjarnason, Emil Grover. "Mechanization and Collective Bargaining in the British Columbia Longshore Industry." (Ph.D. Thesis, Simon Fraser University, 1976).

———. "Collective Bargaining in the Coal Mining Industry in Canada." (M.A. Thesis, Queen's University, 1965).

Bjonback, R.D. "The Factors of Growth in Manufacturing Employment in Metropolitan Vancouver, 1949–1958." (M.A. Thesis, Simon Fraser University, 1971).

Bordeleau, Gisele. "The Professional Institute of the Public Service of Canada: The Difficult Situation of a Multi-Group Union." (M.B.A. Essay, University of British Columbia, 1979).

Boucher, Gerald R. "The 1901 Rossland Miners' Strike: The Western Federation of Miners responds to Industrial Capitalism." (B.A. Essay, University of Victoria, 1986).

Bowen, Lynn Elizabeth. "Friendly Societies in Nanaimo: The British Tradition of Self-Help in a Canadian Coal Mining Community." (M.A. Thesis, University of Victoria, 1980).

Bradbury, Bettina. "The Road To Receivership: Unemployment and Relief in Burnaby, North Vancouver City and District, and West Vancouver, 1929–1933." (M.A. Thesis, Simon Fraser University, 1975).

Braid, Kate. "Invisible Women: Women in Non-Traditional Occupations in British Columbia." (M.A. Thesis, Simon Fraser University, 1980).

Bray, Bonita D. "The Weapon of Culture: Working–Class Resistance and Progressive Theatre in Vancouver, 1930–1938." (M.A. Thesis, University of Victoria, 1990).

Brinley, John. "The Western Federation of Miners." (Ph.D. Thesis, University of Utah, 1972).

Brown, Maria J. "Adult Education among Members of a North Vancouver Labour Union." (M.A. Thesis, University of British Columbia, 1972).

Brown, Patrick. "Workers' Participation: A Survey of Employees' Attitudes." (M.Sc. Thesis, University of British Columbia, 1982).

Bruce, Peter G. "Political Parties and the Evolution of Labor Law in Canada and the United States." (Ph.D. Thesis, Massachusetts Institute of Technology, 1988).

Burnell, Thomas. "Labour Unrest and Justice: The Case of Blubber Bay." (B.A. Essay, University of British Columbia, 1980).

Burns, Janet Mary Christine. "Trade Union Membership, Working-Class Self-Identification, and Support for the New Democratic Party." (M.A. Thesis, University of Victoria, 1981).

Burrill, William J. "Class Conflict and Colonialism: The Coal Miners of Vancouver Island During the Hudson's Bay Company Era, 1848–1862." (M.A. Thesis, University of Victoria, 1987).

Busche, Kelly. "Real Wages and the Supply of Labour in Canada, 1926–1977." (M.A. Project, Simon Fraser University, 1980).

Cameron, Ian Julian. "School Board–Public Conflict in British Columbia." (Ed.D. Thesis, University of British Columbia, 1981).

Campbell, Annie. "Historical Sketch of the Economic and Social Conditions and the Legislation Affecting Oriental Immigration in California and British Columbia." (B.A. Essay, University of British Columbia, 1922).

Campbell, J. Peter. "'Stalwarts of the Struggle': Canadian Marxists of the Third Way, 1879–1939." (Ph.D. Thesis, Queens University, 1991).

Carle, Judith Jane. "Analysis of Membership Education: A Study of the CCF Party in BC, 1933–1961." (M.A. Thesis, University of British Columbia, 1982).

Casaday, Lawren Wilde. "Labor Unrest and the Labor Movement in the Salmon Industry of the Pacific Coast." (Ph.D. Thesis, University of California, Berkley, 1937).

Chafetz, Israel. "Decertification: The British Columbia Experience." (M.Sc.Bus.Admin. Thesis, University of British Columbia, 1977).

Chaklader, Anjan. "The Impact of Royal Commissions on Public Policy: Workers' Compensation in British Columbia, 1941–1968." (M.A. Thesis, University of British Columbia, 1992).

Chin, Siu-Miu Luda. "Job Transferability of Chinese Immigrant Women in Vancouver: Their Voices." (Ph.D. Thesis, University of British Columbia, 1994).

Church, J.S. "Mining Companies in the West Kootenay and Boundary Regions of British Columbia, 1890–1900: Capital Formation and Financial Operations." (M.A. Thesis, University of British Columbia, 1961).

Cleveland, Deborah Jean. "First Agreement Arbitration in British Columbia: 1974–1979." (M.Sc.Bus.Admin. Thesis, University of British Columbia, 1982).

Colli, Terry. "Wage Structure and the Wage Determining Process for Six British Columbia Industries." (M.A. Thesis, University of British Columbia, 1970).

Coneybeer, Ian Tom. "The Origins of Workman's Compensation in British Columbia: State Theory and Law." (M.A. Thesis, Simon Fraser University, 1990).

Conley, James Robert. "Employers' Strategies and Workers' response to Five Vancouver Industries." (Paper presented at the Fifth B.C. Studies Conference, 1988).

———. "Class conflict and collective action in the working class of Vancouver, British Columbia, 1900–1919." (Ph.D. Thesis, Carleton University, 1986).

Cooper, Lesley. "More Than Mere Survival: Placer Gold and Unemployment in 1930s British Columbia." (M.A. Thesis, University of Victoria, 1995).

Creese, Gillian Laura. "Working class politics, racism and sexism: the making of a politically divided working class in Vancouver, 1900–1939." (Ph.D. Thesis, Carleton University, 1986).

Crockford, Cairn. "Making a Living: Nuu-Chah-Nulth Men and Women in the Pelagic Sealing Industry." (M.A. Thesis, University of Victoria, 1996).

Curran, John. "The Causes of Canadian Unemployment: A New Approach." (M.A. Thesis, Simon Fraser University, 1980).

Currie, Ian Douglas. "British Columbia Industrial Conciliators: A Study in Role Perception, Performance and Conflict." (M.A. Thesis, University of British Columbia, 1961).

Daniels, Peter L. "The Geography of Unemployment in Vancouver." (M.A. Thesis, University of British Columbia, 1985).

Derhak, William. "The Economic Determinants of Strike Activity in BC." (M.A. Essay, Simon Fraser University, 1979).

———. "The Short-run Behaviour of Wage Differentials by Skill in BC." (M.A. Essay, Simon Fraser University, 1979).

Dunn, Timothy Allan. "Work, Class and Education: Vocationalism in British Columbia's Public Schools, 1900–1929." (M.A. Thesis, University of British Columbia, 1978).

Edelson, Miriam. "Unions and the Fiscal Crisis in the Local State: A History of British Columbia Governments' Strategies to Organize Local Employers, 1973–1982." (M.A. Thesis, Carleton University, 1985).

Eeckhout, Tomi Richard. "An Analysis of Discharge Arbitrations in British Columbia, 1974–1977." (M.Sc. Bus. Admin. Thesis, University of British Columbia, 1981).

Egri, Carolyn. "Women Bank Managers in British Columbia." (M.Sc. Thesis, University of British Columbia, 1983).

Elliott, Oliver Kent. "Determinants of labour bargaining structure in the British Columbia forest industry." (M.B.A. Project, Simon Fraser University, 1984).

Felske, Larry William. "Studies in the Crow's Nest Pass Coal Industry from its Origins to the End of World War I." (Ph.D. Thesis, University of Toronto, 1991).

Fisher, Edward George. "The Effects of Changes in Labour Legislation On Strike Activity in British Columbia: 1945–1975." (Ph.D. Thesis, University of British Columbia, 1979).

Foley, Sheryl Catherine. "Non-Profit Monopolies and De-unionization: Some Outcomes of the Privatization of Youth Corrections in British Columbia." (M.A. Thesis, Simon Fraser University, 1993).

Foster, John. "Education and Work in a Changing Society: British Columbia, 1870–1930." (M.A. Thesis, University of British Columbia, 1970).

Frecker, John Peter. "Militant and Radical Unionism in the British Columbia Fishing Industry." (M.A. Thesis, University of British Columbia, 1973).

Friesen, Gerald Arnold. "Studies in the Development of Western Canadian Regional Consciousness, 1870–1925." (Ph.D. Thesis, University of Toronto, 1974).

Frogner, Raymond. "'Within Sound of the Drum': Currents of Anti-Militarism in the British Columbia Working Class in the 1930s." (M.A. Thesis, University of Victoria, 1991).

Fynn, Sonia. "A Discussion of the Factors Affecting the Decision of Married Women to Participate in the Labour Force." (M.A. Essay, Simon Fraser University, 1973).

Gallacher, Daniel. "Men, Money, Machines: Studies Comparing Colliery Operations and Factors of Production in the British Columbia Coal Industry to 1891." (Ph.D. Thesis, University of British Columbia, 1979).

———. "City in Depression: The Impact of the Years 1929–1930 on Greater Victoria, British Columbia." (M.A. Thesis, University of Victoria, 1970).

Geddes, Graham. "Agreement and agitation: the movement for comprehensive workmen's compensation legislation in British Columbia, 1891–1917." (B.A. Essay, University of British Columbia, 1986).

Gladstone, Percy Henry. "Industrial Disputes in the Commercial Fisheries of British Columbia." (M.A. Thesis, University of British Columbia, 1959).

Goldstone, Irene Lynn. "The Origins and Development of Collective Bargaining By Nurses in British Columbia, 1912–1976." (M.Sc. Thesis, University of British Columbia, 1981).

Gorter, Rob. "Wage Differentials and CPR Construction: An Analysis of Chinese Immigrant Labour in British Columbia, 1880–1885." (M.A. Thesis, Simon Fraser University, 1995).

Grantham, Ronald. "Some Aspects of the Socialist Movement in British Columbia." (M.A. Thesis, University of British Columbia, 1942).

Grass, Eric. "Employment and Production: The Mature Stage in the Life Cycle of a Sawmill: Youbou, British Columbia, 1929–1989." (Ph.D. Thesis, Simon Fraser University, 1991).

Gray, Stephen. "Woodworkers and Legitimacy: The IWA in Canada, 1937–1957." (Ph.D. Thesis, Simon Fraser University, 1989).

Griffin, Robert. "The Shawinigan Lake Lumber Company, 1889–1943." (M.A. Thesis, University of Victoria, 1979).

Hak, Gordon Hugh. "On the Fringes: Capital, Labour and Class Formation in the Forest Economies of the Port Alberni and Prince George Districts, British Columbia, 1910–1939." (Ph.D. Thesis, Simon Fraser University, 1986).

Hampton, Warren. "Highway for Hire: Trucking and its Economic Regulation in BC: A History." (M.B.A. Project, Simon Fraser University, 1979).

Hansen, James Lyle. "Farmers Outstanding In Their Field: The Ginger Group in Politics, 1921–1935." (M.A. Thesis, University of Victoria, 1993).

Hayward, Brian Gordon. "The Development of Relations of Production in the British Columbia Salmon Fishery." (M.A. Thesis, University of British Columbia, 1981).

Hill, Patrick. "A Failure of Unity: Communist Party-CCF Relations in British Columbia, 1935–1939." (M.A. Thesis, University of Victoria, 1977).

Hobbs, Basil, and Brian Walisser. "The Rise and Fall of the International Union of Mine, Mill and Smelter Workers." (B.A. Essay, University of British Columbia, 1973).

Hobbs, Edmond W. "Courses and programs in labour studies at Canadian universities and colleges: an analysis." (M.A. Thesis, Simon Fraser University, 1984).

Hobbs, Margaret. "Gendering Work and Welfare: Women's Relationship to Wage-Work and Social Policy in Canada during the Great Depression." (Ph.D. Thesis, University of Toronto, 1995).

Hommen, Leif. "Setting Patterns: Technological Change, Labour Adjustment and Training in British Columbia's Lumber Manufacturing Industry." (Ph.D. Thesis, University of British Columbia, 1994).

Hovis, Logan. "Technological Change and Mining Labour: Copper Mining and Milling Operations at the Britannia Mines, British Columbia, 1898–1937." (M.A. Thesis, University of British Columbia, 1986).

Hudson, Douglas. "Traplines and Timber: Social and Economic Change Among the Carrier." (Ph.D. Thesis, University of Alberta, 1983).

Hudson, Stephanie Lee. "Freedom of Association in Canada: The Dilemma for Trade Unions in a Liberal Society." (M.A. Thesis, University of British Columbia, 1989).

Humphreys, Elizabeth. "Role Bargaining: A Means of Adaptation to Strain Within Dual Work Families." (M.A. Thesis, University of British Columbia, 1974).

Jackson, Karen. "The Ideology of the NDP in BC: Manifest Socialism, 1966, 1969 and 1972 Elections Campaigns." (Working Paper, University of Victoria, 1983).

Jamal, Muhammad. "Task Specialization and Organizational Attachment: An Empirical Study of Industrial Blue-collar Workers in Vancouver." (M.A. Thesis, University of British Columbia, 1972).

Jansen, Jan W. "Management-labour relations in the forest industry in British Columbia." (B.S.F. Thesis, Faculty of Forestry, University of British Columbia, 1973).

Jelking, Robert. "The Public Interest in Collective Bargaining: An Analysis of the Changing Role of the Government." (M.B.A. Thesis, University of British Columbia, 1969).

Jenkins, Ernst Ault. "British Columbia's Labour Legislation Compared With That Existing in Other Canadian Provinces." (B.A. Essay, University of British Columbia, 1930).

Jhappan, Carol. "Resistance to Exploitation: East Indians and the Rise of the Canadian Farmworkers Union in British Columbia." (M.A. Thesis, University of British Columbia, 1983).

Johnson, Ross Alfred. "No Compromise – No Political Trading: The Marxian Socialist Tradition in British Columbia." (Ph.D. Thesis, University of British Columbia, 1975).

Jordan, Donald James. "Unit Determination Under the Labour Code." (LL.M. Thesis, University of British Columbia, 1979).

Joseph, Norman. "A Study of Job Satisfaction Attitudes Among Female White Collar Union Workers in a University Setting." (M.B.A. Project, Simon Fraser University, 1977).

Joseph, Philip Austin. "The Policies Underlying Interest Dispute Settlement in British Columbia and New Zealand." (LL.M. Thesis, University of British Columbia, 1984).

Kaliski, S.F. "The Growth and Development of the Manufacturing Industry in British Columbia." (B.A. Essay, University of British Columbia, 1952).

Kantrowiz, Peter. "Investigating the effects of discrimination by gender in the labour market: a study using cross-sectional B.C. data." (M.A. Project, Simon Fraser University, 1985).

Karas, Frank Paul. "Labour and coal in the Crowsnest Pass, 1925–1936." (M.A. Thesis, University of Calgary, 1972).

Keelor, John Thomas. "The Price of Lives and Limbs Lost at Work: The Development of No-Fault Workers' Compensation Legislation in British Columbia, 1910–1916." (M.A. Thesis, University of Victoria, 1996).

Kennedy, Hugh. "A Study of White Collar Workers' Attitudes Towards Unions." (M.B.A. Project, Simon Fraser University, 1977).

Kerin, Theresa. "The Power of Indigenous Capital in a Company: An Analysis of the Ruling Class of British Columbia." (M.A. Thesis, University of Victoria, 1978).

Kilbank, Alfred. "The Economic Basis of Collective Bargaining in the Lumbering Industry of British Columbia." (B.A. Essay, University of British Columbia, 1947).

Kittredge, Anne. "The Feminist Movement: Its Effects on Married Women's Labour Market Participation." (M.A. Essay, Simon Fraser University, 1979).

———. "The Male-Female Wage Gap – A Canadian Study." (M.A. Essay, Simon Fraser University, 1979).

Knox, Paul Graham. "The Passage of Bill 39: Reform and Repression in British Columbia's Labour Policy." (M.A. Thesis, University of British Columbia, 1974).

Kummer, Burkhard C. "Does centralization of the bargaining structure contribute to the stabilization of industrial relations? A conceptual analysis." (M.A. Thesis, University of British Columbia, 1985).

Lacroix, Roland Andre. "Problems of Plant Closures and Worker Relocation: A Case Study of James Island, B.C." (M.A. Thesis, University of Victoria, 1981).

Lambert, Paul Gerald. "The Determinants of Collective Bargaining Strategy in the British Columbia Hospital Industry." (M.Sc.Bus.Admin. Thesis, University of British Columbia, 1980).

Lane, Marion. "Unemployment During the Depression: The Problem of the Single Unemployed Transient in British Columbia, 1930–1938." (B.A. Essay, University of British Columbia, 1966).

Lapper, Robert. "From compulsion to voluntarism: B.C. labour policy 1968–1978." (B.C. Project, University of Victoria, 1983).

Lawrence, Joseph. "Markets and Capital: A History of the Lumber Industry of British Columbia." (M.A. Thesis, University of British Columbia, 1957).

———. "A Historical Account of the Early Salmon Canning Industry in British Columbia, 1870–1900." (B.A. Essay, University of British Columbia, 1951).

Leier, J. Mark, "Bureaucracy, Class, and Ideology: The Vancouver Trades and Labour Council, 1889–1909." (Ph.D. Thesis, Memorial University of Newfoundland, 1991);

———. "Through the Lens of Syndicalism: Fragmentation on the Vancouver and British Columbia Left Before the Great War." (M.A. Thesis, Simon Fraser University, 1987).

Lembcke, Jerry Lee. "The International Woodworkers of America: An Internal Comparative Study of Two Regions." (Ph.D. Thesis, University of Oregon, 1978).

Leonard, Anne. "Employment Trends for Women in British Columbia." (M.A. Thesis, University of British Columbia, 1966).

Leonard, Frank Edward. "Class conflict in the Canadian coal mining industry to 1925." (B.A. Essay, University of Victoria, 1982).

Lewis, Richard Francis Victor. "A Comparison Between British Columbia and New Zealand Labour Movements." (M.B.A. Thesis, University of Alberta, 1970).

Littlefield, Loraine. "Gender, Class and Community: The History of Sne-nay-muxw Women's Employment." (Ph.D. Thesis, University of British Columbia, 1995).

Lofthouse, Mark James. "The theory of regulation and the structure of provincial minimum wages." (M.A. Project, Simon Fraser University, 1983).

Logan, Roderick MacKenzie. "The Geography of Salmon Fishing Conflicts: The Case of Noyes Island." (M.A. Thesis, University of British Columbia, 1967).

Loosmore, Thomas Robert. "The British Columbia Labour Movement and Political Action, 1879–1906." (M.A. Thesis, University of British Columbia, 1954).

Lotzkar, Joseph. "Seasonal Variations in British Columbia Coastal Lumber Industry With Particular Regard to Labour Matters." (B.A. Essay, University of British Columbia, 1950).

Lucas, Robert. "Origins of Social Exchange." (M.Sc. Thesis, University of British Columbia, 1977).

Luckhurst, Leland. "Job Evaluation in the Forest Industry in British Columbia." (M.B.A. Thesis, University of British Columbia, 1973).

Lutz, John S. "Work, Wages and Welfare in Aboriginal-non-aboriginal Relations, British Columbia, 1849–1970." (Ph.D. Thesis, University of Ottawa, 1995).

MacKay, Dean. "A Survey of Labour Relations in the Metal Mining Industry of British Columbia." (M.A. Thesis, University of British Columbia, 1949).

MacKenzie, Bruce. "Party and Press Portrayals of the British Columbia CCF-NDP, 1937–1979." (M.A. Thesis, University of British Columbia, 1981).

Mackie, Richard. "Hudson's Bay Company on the Pacific, 1821–1843." (Ph.D. Thesis, University of British Columbia, 1993).

——. "Colonial Land, Indian Labour, and Company Capital: The Economy of Vancouver Island, 1849–1858." (M.A. Thesis, University of Victoria, 1985).

MacKinnon, David. "The Forest Industry, Community, and Place: Currents of Ecological Re-development in Three Forest Sector Impacted BC Communities." (M.A. Thesis, Trent University, 1995).

Maclean, Diane. "Strikes and the Economy: A Study of the Choice of an Appropriate Dependent Variable." (M.A. Essay, Simon Fraser University, 1980).

——. "Strikes and Their Relationship to Economic Variables: A Critical Survey." (M.A. Essay, Simon Fraser University, 1980).

Mainguy, J.W. "Workers in the Logging Industry of British Columbia." (B.A. Essay, University of British Columbia, 1941).

Malcolmson, J.D. "Resource Development and the State in Early British Columbia." (M.A. Thesis, Simon Fraser University, 1980).

Marchak, Maureen Patricia. "Bargaining Strategies of White-Collar Workers in British Columbia." (Ph.D. Thesis, University of British Columbia, 1970).

Martinello, Felice F. "Wage and employment determination in a unionized industry: the I.W.A. in the B.C. wood products industry." (Ph.D. Thesis, University of British Columbia, 1984).

Mathes, Raymond Walter. "The mediative role of the Labour Relations Board of British Columbia in disputes involving illegal work stoppages." (M.Sc. Thesis, University of British Columbia, 1982).

———. "B.C. industrial relations, issues, roles and responsibilities: a workshop/conference held in Vancouver, British Columbia, 25/26 October 1979, summary of proceedings." (Vancouver: Industrial Relations Management Association of B.C., 1979).

McCallum, Todd. "'A Modern Weapon for Modern Man': Marxist Masculinity and the Social Practices of the One Big Union, 1919–1924." (M.A. Thesis, Simon Fraser University, 1995).

McCormack, Andrew Ross. "The origins and extent of western labour radicalism, 1896–1919." (Ph.D. Thesis, University of Western, Ontario, 1973).

McCririck, Donna. "Opportunity and the Workingman: A Study of Land Opportunity and the Growth of Blue Collar Suburbs in Early Vancouver." (M.A. Thesis, University of British Columbia, 1981).

McDonald, Ian. "Class Conflict and Political Factionalism: A History of the International Brotherhood of Electrical Workers, 1901–1961." (M.A. Thesis, Simon Fraser University, 1986).

McGeough, Maureen. "The Effectiveness of the RNABC as a Collective Bargaining Representative: An Analysis." (M.B.A. Essay, University of British Columbia, 1981).

McIntosh, Jean Elizabeth. "Mark Mosher's reconstruction of the development of the woodworkers union in the Alberni Valley: a participant's history." (M.A. Thesis, University of British Columbia, 1987).

McLeod, Heather. "'Not Another God-Damn Housewife': Ruth Bullock, The 'Woman Question' and Canadian Trotskyism." (M.A. Thesis, Simon Fraser University, 1993).

McLoughlin, Peter Martin. "The Japanese and the Labour Movement of British Columbia." (B.A. Essay, University of British Columbia, 1951).

McMillan, Charles J. "Trade unionism in District 18, 1900–1925: a case study." (M.B.A. Thesis, University of Alberta, 1969).

McNally, Gregory William. "Induction Practices Offered to Beginning Teachers by School Districts in British Columbia." (M.A. Thesis, Simon Fraser University, 1992).

McPherson, Kathryn Mae. "Skilled Service and Women's Work: Canadian Nursing, 1920–1939." (Ph.D. Thesis, Simon Fraser University, 1990).

McPhillips, David. "Employer Free Speech During Organization Drives and Decertification Campaigns." (LL.M. Thesis, University of British Columbia, 1979).

Meekison, James. "Forces of the Demand for British Columbia's Mining Labour: An Analysis of the Trends of Wage Rates and Employment of British Columbia's Mining Industry." (M.A. Thesis, University of British Columbia, 1962).

Midgley, Ian Harold. "The Share System and Its Effects on Innovation, Employment and Income in the British Columbia Salmon Fishing Industry." (M.A. Thesis, University of British Columbia, 1963).

Mikita, Jeanne. "State Policy and the Migration of Foreign Domestic Workers to Canada: The Migration of Filipina Nannies to Vancouver, BC." (M.A. Thesis, Simon Fraser University, 1994).

Moffat, Ben. "A Community of Working Men: The Residential Environment of Early Nanaimo, British Columbia, 1875–1891." (M.A. Thesis, University of British Columbia, 1982).

Mosher, Sheila. "The Social Gospel in British Columbia, 1900–1920." (M.A. Thesis, University of Victoria, 1974).

Mouat, Jeremy. "Mining in the Settler Dominions: A Comparative Study of the Industry in Three Communities from the 1880s to the First World War." (Ph.D. Thesis, University of British Columbia, 1988).

Muldoon, Don. "Capitalism Unchallenged: A Sketch of Canadian Communism, 1939–1949." (M.A. Thesis, Simon Fraser University, 1977).

Nadeau, Mary-Jo. "'Forgotten and Suddenly Remembered': A Feminist Critique of Socialist/Marxist Feminist Analyses of Women's Labour in Canada." (M.A. Thesis, York University, 1994).

Naismith, Earl George. "Profile and Problems of Part Time Faculty in Selected B.C. Community Colleges." (M.A. Thesis, University of British Columbia, 1978).

Nastich, Marion. "The Use of British Columbia Unemployment Statistics, 1952–1956." (B.A. Essay, University of British Columbia, 1958).

Nelson, Patricia Ann. "The solidarity coalition: the struggle for common cause." (M.A. Thesis, University of British Columbia, 1985).

Ng, Ignace. "Transaction costs, labour market institutions, and strikes." (Ph.D. Thesis, Simon Fraser University, 1985).

Nicholls, Paul James. "Peace River labour – a study." (B.Comm. Essay, University of British Columbia, 1968).

Nicol, Janet Mary. "Social Class Difference Between East and West Side Vancouver Public Schools, 1945–60." (M.A. Thesis, University of British Columbia, 1996).

Nijhar, Karnail Singh. "Teachers' Attitudes Towards the Application of Merit Pay Programs in British Columbia." (M.B.A. Thesis, University of British Columbia, 1965).

Nikaido, Roy. "The Air Line Pilots: A Model for Other Professions?." (M.B.A. Essay, University of British Columbia, 1979).

North, Roy Archibald. "The British Columbia Teachers' Federation and the Arbitration Process." (M.A. Thesis, University of British Columbia, 1964).

Oberg, Kalevero. "Sointula, a Communistic Settlement in British Columbia." (B.A. Essay, University of British Columbia, 1928).

Olligschlaeger, Andreas Matthias. "Neoclassical Economics and Labour Migration Theory: A Canadian Perspective." (M.A. Thesis, University of British Columbia, 1986).

Orr, Allen. "The Western Federation of Miners and the Royal Commission on Industrial Disputes in 1903 with Special Reference to the Vancouver Coal Miners' Strike." (M.A. Thesis, University of British Columbia, 1968).

Ottens, Johannes. "The Use of Regional Techniques to Analyse Forest Policy Impacts: The Case of the Impact of Close Utilization Policy on the Level of Employment Within the Kamloops Region." (M.F. Thesis, University of British Columbia, 1974).

Paarsch, Harry J. "Labour Stoppages and the Theory of the Offset Factor: Evidence from the British Columbia Logging and Lumber Sectors." (Ph.D. Thesis, Stanford University, 1987).

Parker, Helen R. "A Study of Employment and Wages in British Columbia Industries." (B.Comm. Essay, University of British Columbia, 1937).

Parkin, Frank. "Conflict in the Lumber Industry." (M.A. Thesis, University of British Columbia, 1962).

Parnaby, Andrew. "'We'll Hang All the Policemen from a Sour Apple Tree': Class, Law, and the Politics of State Power in the Blubber Bay Strike of 1938–39." (M.A. Thesis, Simon Fraser University, 1995).

Pavin, Eros. "Labour/management relations at Alberni Plywood Division." (B.S.F. Thesis, Faculty of Forestry, University of British Columbia, 1980).

Paulson, Marilee. "Ideological Practice in Labour News Reporting." (M.A. Thesis, University of British Columbia, 1975).

Peck, Gunther William. "Reinventing Free Labor: Immigrant Padrones and Contract Laborers in North America, 1880–1920." (Ph.D. Thesis, Yale University, 1994).

Pedlar, David John. "A Study of Domestic Service in Canada." (M.A. Thesis, University of British Columbia, 1982).

Pennington, Edward, and Ian Walker. "The Role of Trade Unions in Social Welfare: An Exploratory Study of the Attitude of Trade Union Members Towards Health and Welfare Services." (M.S.W. Thesis, University of British Columbia, 1962).

Pentland-Smith, Janice. "Women in the Canadian Labour Force: The Union Response." (M.A. Thesis, Simon Fraser University, 1977).

Phillips, Paul Arthur. "The British Columbia Labour Movement in the Inter-War Period: A Study of Its Social and Political Aspects." (Ph.D. Thesis, London School of Economics and Political Science, 1967).

Philpott, Stuart Bowman. "Trade Unionism and Acculturation: A Comparative Study of Urban Indians and Immigrant Italians." (M.A. Thesis, University of British Columbia, 1963).

Pilon, Dennis. "The Drive for Proportional Representation in British Columbia, 1917–1923." (M.A. Thesis, Simon Fraser University, 1996).

Poole, Peter. "Organized Labour versus the State in British Columbia: The Political Limitations of Trade Unions." (M.A. Thesis, Simon Fraser University, 1987)

Porsild, Charlene L. "Culture, Class, and Community: New Perspectives on the Klondike Gold Rush, 1896–1905." (Ph.D. Thesis, Carleton University, 1994).

Powell, Mary. "Response to the Depression: Three Representative Women's Groups in British Columbia." (M.A. Thesis, University of British Columbia, 1967).

Prittie, Robert W. "Some Aspects of the History of the Winnipeg General Sympathetic Strike and the General Strike Movement in Western Canada in 1919." (B.A. Essay, University of British Columbia, 1947).

Quilici, Laura. "We Were Strong Ladies: Italian Women's Work in Vancouver, 1947–1961." (M.A. Thesis, Simon Fraser University, 1995).

Rajala, Richard A. "The Rude Science: A Social History of West Coast Logging, 1890–1930." (M.A. Thesis, University of Victoria, 1987).

Ralston, Keith. "The 1900 Strike of Fraser River Sockeye Salmon Fishermen." (M.A. Thesis, University of British Columbia, 1965).

Ramirez, Carmen. "Collective Bargaining in British Columbia Colleges." (M.B.A. Essay, University of British Columbia, 1979).

Rankin, Bruce Howard. "The State and Labor Organization: Explaining Divergent Patterns of Unionization in Canada and the United States." (Ph.D. Thesis, University of Maryland, 1993).

Reimer, Chad. "The Origin and Development of BC History." (Ph.D. Thesis, York University, 1995).

Riddell, Susan Elizabeth. "Curing Society's Ills: Public Health Nurses and Public Health Nursing in Rural British Columbia, 1919–1946." (M.A. Thesis, Simon Fraser University, 1991).

Roald, Jerry Bruce. "Pursuit of Status: Professionalism, Unionism, and Militancy in the Evolution of Canadian Teachers' Organizations, 1915–1955." (Ed.D. Thesis, University of British Columbia, 1970).

Roberts, Dorothy. "Doctrine and Disunity in the BC Section of the CCF, 1932–1956." (M.A. Thesis, University of Victoria, 1973).

Roberts, Frank. "Re-examination of the Failure of Leadership in the Socialists Democratic Federation and the Socialists League, 1884–1890." (M.A. Thesis, Simon Fraser University, 1983).

Robertson, Irene. "The Business Community and the Development of Victoria, 1858–1900." (M.A. Thesis, University of Victoria, 1982).

Robertson, Struan Turner. "Minimum Wage Legislation in British Columbia." (B.A. Essay, University of British Columbia, 1939).

Robinson, Bruce Arnold. "Financial Incentives for Middle Management in British Columbia." (M.B.A. Thesis, University of British Columbia, 1963).

Robinson, Peter. "Integration of the Forest Industry of British Columbia." (M.B.A. Thesis, University of British Columbia, 1972).

Rose, Ramona Marie. "'Keepers of Moral': The Vancouver Council of Women 1939–1945." (M.A. Thesis, University of British Columbia, 1990).

Roth, David Michael. "A Union on the Hill: the International Union of Mine, Mill and Smelter Workers and the Organization of Trail Smelter and Chemical Workers." (M.A. Thesis, Simon Fraser University, 1991).

Roy, Patricia. "The British Columbia Electric Railway Company, 1897–1928." (Ph.D. Thesis, University of British Columbia, 1970).

Schofield, Andrew Mark. "Ideology, Space, and the Dialectics of Union Organization: A Case Study of the United Fishermen and Allied Worker's Union." (M.A. Thesis, Simon Fraser University, 1991).

Schwantes, Carlos Arnaldo. "Left-wing unionism in the Pacific Northwest: a comparative history of organized labour and socialist politics in Washington and British Columbia, 1885–1917." (Ph.D. Thesis, University of Michigan, 1976).

Schwartzenhauer, Walter George. "Public service grievance activity in British Columbia." (M.B.A. Project, Simon Fraser University, 1983).

Scott, Stephen O. "Primitive Accumulations: The BC Salmon Industry and Indian Labour." (M.A. Thesis, Carleton University, 1987).

Segger, Timothy. "Work, Nonwork, and the Relationship Between Job Satisfaction and Life Satisfaction: A Comparison Between the Police and the Public." (M.A. Thesis, University of Victoria, 1975).

Shalla, Vivian. "Working the Line: The Labour Process of Passenger Agents at Air Canada, 1937 to 1993." (Ph.D. Thesis, Carleton University, 1993).

Shaw, Ronald J. "Organized Labour and the Co-operative Commonwealth Federation in British Columbia, 1932–1937." (B.A. Essay, University of British Columbia, 1973).

Skolrood, Arthur. "The British Columbia Teachers' Federation: A Study of Its Historical Development, Interests and Activities from 1916–1963." (Ph.D. Thesis, University of Oregon, 1967).

Sloan, William. "The Crow's Nest Pass During the Depression: A Socio-Economic History of Southeastern British Columbia, 1918–1939." (M.A. Thesis, University of Victoria, 1968).

Smith, Matthew Eliot. "The Development of a Socialist Opposition: The Case of British Columbia, 1880–1945." (Ph.D. Thesis, University of North Carolina, 1978).

Smithers, Douglas. "A Study of the American Federation of Musicians." (M.A. Thesis, University of British Columbia, 1952).

Smythe, Limen. "The Lumber and Sawmill Workers' Union in British Columbia." (M.A. Thesis, University of Washington, 1937).

Sparrow, Leona. "Work History of a Coast Salish Couple." (M.A. Thesis, University of British Columbia, 1976).

Spence, Georgia. "The Enactment of a Role by New Members in Established Work Groups: The Community Psychiatric Nurses in British Columbia." (M.A. Thesis, University of Victoria, 1980).

Stainsby, Jill. "'It's the Smell of Money': Women Shoreworkers of British Columbia." (M.A. Thesis, Simon Fraser University, 1991).

Stewart, Eileen Barbara. "Job security issues in faculty collective bargaining experience in British Columbia colleges and institutions." (M.B.A. Project, Simon Fraser University, 1983).

Stewart, Ian Hampton. "Labour parties, labour unions, and labour laws: a comparative analysis of British Columbia and Manitoba." (M.A. Thesis, Queen's University, 1982).

Stobart, Anne Patricia. "The Situational Suitability of Job Evaluation Plans in Unionized Environments." (M.Sc. Bus. Admin. Thesis, University of British Columbia, 1986).

Storey, Gordon. "The Influence of Interorganizational Conflict Upon the Behaviour of a Collective Bargaining Team." (M.Sc. Thesis, University of British Columbia, 1978).

Strong, Gordon. "The Salmon Canning Industry in British Columbia." (B.A. Essay, University of British Columbia, 1934).

Stuart, Richard. "The Early Political Career of Angus MacInnis." (M.A. Thesis, University of British Columbia, 1970).

Sumida, Rigenda. "The Japanese in British Columbia." (M.A. Thesis, University of British Columbia, 1935).

Szychter, Gwen. "Farm Women and Their Work in Delta, British Columbia, 1900–1939." (M.A. Thesis, Simon Fraser University, 1992).

Tattam, William. "Sawmill Workers and Radicalism: Portland Oregon, 1929–1941." (M.A. Thesis, University of Oregon, 1970).

Taft, George. "Socialism in North America: The Case of BC and Washington State, 1900–1960." (Ph.D. Thesis, Simon Fraser University, 1983).

Thompson, Robert Bruce Douglas. "The impact of computer-mediated office technology on the labour requirements of office organizations." (M.A. Thesis, University of British Columbia, 1984).

Tilley, Wanda Florence Lilian. "Creating a Clause-finder: An Analysis of Articles in British Columbia College and Institute Faculty Collective Agreements." (M.A. Project, Simon Fraser University, 1982).

Timms, Diana. "Links Between Person-Thing Orientation, Organizational Images, and Allocation of Organizational Activities." (M.Sc. Thesis, University of British Columbia, 1979).

Tracy, Wilmot. "Vocational Training for Rehabilitation in British Columbia for W.W. Two Veterans to March 31, 1945." (M.A. Thesis, University of British Columbia, 1945).

Turner, Thomas Sydney. "An Analysis of Base Wage Rates for Select Bargaining Units in British Columbia." (M.B.A. Thesis, University of British Columbia, 1969).

Tweedy, Mark. "1880 and 1881 Strikes by the Miners of the Vancouver Coal Company." (B.A. Essay, University of British Columbia, 1978).

Underhill, Harold Fabian. "Labor Legislation in British Columbia." (Ph.D. Thesis, University of California, Berkeley, 1936).

Underwood, Morley. "Governor Douglas and the Miners, 1858 to 1859." (B.A. Essay, University of British Columbia, 1974).

Vakil, Thea. "The Political Model of Power in Organizations." (M.Sc. Thesis, University of British Columbia, 1983).

Venables, Kenneth A. "The Making of Protective Labour Legislation in British Columbia: The 1912 Royal Commission of Labour and Its Aftermath." (M.A. Thesis, Simon Fraser University, 1996)

Voigt, Barbara Carole. "A Comparison of Alberta, British Columbia, and Ontario Industrial Relations Systems in the Health Care Industry." (M.B.A. Thesis, University of Alberta, 1976).

Walsh, Susan. "Equality, Emancipation and a More Just World: Leading Women in the BC CCF." (M.A. Thesis, Simon Fraser University, 1983).

Wargo, Alan. "The Great Coal Strike: The Vancouver Island Coal Miner Strike, 1912–1914." (M.A. Thesis, University of British Columbia, 1962).

Warrian, Peter J. "The Challenge of the One Big Union Movement in Canada, 1919–1921." (M.A. Thesis, University of Waterloo, 1971).

Whittaker, Jo Ann M. "A Chronicle of Failure: Gender, Professionalization and the Graduate Nurses Association of British Columbia, 1912–1935." (M.A. Thesis, University of Victoria, 1990).

Williams, Charles Brian. "Canadian-American Trade Union Relations: A Study of the Development of Binational Unionism." (Ph.D. Thesis, Cornell University, 1964).

Williams, Margaret J. "Ethnicity and Class Conflict at Maillardville/Fraser Mills: The Strike of 1931." (M.A. Thesis, University of British Columbia, 1983).

Worswick, Christopher. "The Labour Market Adjustment of Immigrant Families." (Ph.D. Thesis, University of British Columbia, 1995).

Wright, A. James. "The Winter Years in Cowichan: A Study of the Depression in a Vancouver Island Community." (M.A. Thesis, University of British Columbia, 1967).

Wynne, Robert. "Reactions to the Chinese in the Pacific Northwest and British Columbia, 1880–1910." (Ph.D. Thesis, University of Washington, 1964).

Yerburgh, R.E.M. "An Economic History of Forestry in British Columbia." (M.A. Thesis, University of British Columbia, 1931).

Yorke, David. "The Workers' Unity League in BC." (Unpublished Essay, Simon Fraser University, 1973).

Young, David. "The Vancouver City Police Force, 1886–1914." (Unpublished Essay, University of British Columbia, 1976).

Yri, Marlene Ingrid. "The British Columbia Teachers' Federation and its Conversion to Partisanship, 1966–1972." (M.A. Thesis, University of British Columbia, 1979).

Zafer, Muhammad Masoud Uz. "Strikes in Essential Services in British Columbia." (LL.M. Thesis, University of British Columbia, 1984).

NEWSPAPERS

Across Campus. Local 1 – Association of University and College Employees, 1977–

The Advocate: for peace, progress and democracy. 1 September 1939–14 June 1940

The Amalgamator. January 1943–August 1947

BC Clarion. 1931–1936

BC District Union News. International Union of Mine, Mill and Smelter Workers. 10 June 1944–July 1955

BC Labor News. 29 July 1921–26 May 1922

The BC Labour Truth. National Labor Council of Vancouver. May 1934–February 1935

The BC Lumber Worker. International Woodworkers of America: BC District Council #1. September 1931–February 1960

BC Maritime Worker. April 1936–27 November 1936

BC Teamster. International Brotherhood of Teamsters. 23 January 1962–December 1974

BC Trades Unionist and Union Label Bulletin. Vancouver Trades and Labour Council. January 1908–January 1909

BC Workers' News: for unity in the struggle. 18 January 1935–26 March 1937

BC Workers' Review. January 1940–March 1943

BC Workman. 20 May 1899–12 Aug 1899

The Barker. Local 1-217 – International Woodworkers of America. April 1960–

The Bridge River Miner. Pioneer Local 308 – IUMMSW. 22 September 1939–14 February 1940

The British Columbia Federationist. Vancouver Trades and Labour Council. 4 November 1911–5 June 1925

The British Columbia Labour Truth. May 1934–November 1939

British Columbia Musician. Musicians' Union Local 145 – A.F. of M. 8 May 1923–September 1928

British Columbia Yukon Teamster. International Brotherhood of Teamsters. February 1975–

Broke Beater. Local 1123–Canadian Paper Workers' Union. July 1975–September 1976

The Camp Worker. B.C. Loggers' and Camp Workers' Union. 26 April 1919–28 June 1919

The Canadian Farmer: Labour Advocate. 12 June 1925–17 July 1925

The Canadian Labour Advocate. 24 July 1925–29 April 1926

The Canadian Labour Congress News. April 1956–April 1958

The Canadian Labour Herald. Vancouver Council of the Canadian Federation of Labour. October 1937–April 1942

The Canadian Labour Press. 15 February 1919–February 1963

The Canadian Trade Unionist. 22 November 1925–30 December 1933

The Canadian Seamen. Deepsea and Inlandboatmen's Union (BC Division). 18 August 1944–24 February 1945

The Canadian Tribune/Daily Tribune. 20 January 1940–20 January 1971

The Canadian Woodworker. 3 November 1948–15 December 1948

Chinese Lumber Worker. September 1948–1 June 1953

The Chipper. International Woodworkers of America. (New Westminster). May 1970–.

The Commentator. 2 November 1938–27 November 1944. January 1956–December 1966. January 1967–March 1969

The Communicator. Bralorne Community Club. 1938?–1971

Congress News. 5 September 1942–12 August 1944

Congress News/Canadian Labour. October 1949–June 1952

The Conveyor. Local 651 – United Steelworkers of America. 26 August 1974.

The Cooperator. 7 March 1939–21 March 1939

The District Ledger. Local 18 – United Mine Workers of America. 18 January 1908–1 August 1919

East Indian Lumber Worker. July 1950–April 1953

Forward look. Local 592 – Canadian Paperworkers Union. July 1976–May 1977

The Fisherman. Local 6 – Salmon Purse Seiners' Union and Pacific Coast Fishermen's Union. (B.C. Section). 26 February 1937–

Groundswell Rank and File News. February 1975–March 1975

The Heavy Lift. 8 May 1933–8 July 1935

The Independent. 31 March 1900–22 August 1904

The Indicator. Socialist Party of Canada. 18 October 1919–3 January 1920

The Industrial News. 26 December 1885–11 December 1886

Industrial World. Local 6 – Western Federation of Miners. 16 September 1899–27 April 1901

Island. Local 5115–United Steelworkers of America. January 11, February 8, August 30, October 11, 1971.

Job Steward. Local 1-85 – International Woodworkers. December 1975–October 1977.

Labour Herald. Prince Rupert Trades and Labour Council. December 1931–28 July 1933

Labor Star. 16 January 1919–20 March 1919

The Labor Statesman. Vancouver, New Westminster and District TLC. 25 April 1924–March 1969

Labour Review. 1 April 1932–1 September 1932

Labour Truth. National Labour Council of British Columbia. March 1935–November 1939

The Live Wire. 1950–June 1959

The Main Deck. Local 1 – Boilermakers' and Iron Shipbuilders' Union. 9 June 1943–1 December 1943

Men and Paper. 17 May 1946–3 June 1950

Nanaimo Clarion. 1900–1903

Northwest Worker. October 1977–April 1978

The Outsider. Pacific Press Newspaper Unions and the Vancouver–New Westminster Newspaper Guild. 20 February 1970–11 May 1970

Pacific Advocate. 4 November 1944–8 February 1946

Pacific Coast News: The B.C. Fisherman's Weekly. 1 August 1935–30 July 1936. 6 August 1936–1 February 1940.

Pacific Tribune. 15 February 1946–

Paystreak. 19 June 1897–11 October 1902

The People: Labor's Voice for Victory. 13 October 1942–28 October 1944

The People's Advocate. 2 April 1937—25 August 1939

The Plain Speaker and Public Opinion. 23 August 1918—15 October 1918

Post Office "Sitdowner's" Gazette. May 1938—June 1938

The Red Flag. Socialist Party of Canada. 28 December 1918—11 October 1919

Ship and Dock. Longshoremen and Water Transport Workers of Canada. December 1934—27 November 1935

Ship and Shop. Local 1 — Marine Workers and Boilermakers Industrial Union. 9 March 1951—November 1967

Ship's News. Seafarer's Industrial Unions. 9 September 1936—27 October 1939

Solidarity Times. Solidarity Coalition. 15 October 1983—20 December 1983

Strike Bulletin. Central Strike Committee, 1919. 4 June 1919—26 June 1919

Thunderbird News. Local 312—Canadian Paperworkers' Union. October 1975, January 1977

The Trades Unionist. Vancouver Trades and Labor Council. September 1905—December 1907

The Tradesman. Yukon Building and Construction Trades Council. March 1972—

The Typo Times. Local 226 —Typographical Union. 25 June 1946—20 January 1950

Unemployed Worker. Workers' Unity League. 31 May 1927—18 April 1934

The Union Woodworker. 29 December 1948—23 August 1950

The United Worker. December 1947—March 1956

Vancouver All-Canadian Labour Annual. Vancouver Labour Council. 1928

Vancouver Postal Club News. Vancouver Branch 12 Courier. May—August 1964

The Vancouver Typographer. Union Printers of Vancouver. 11 August 1892

Victoria Solidarity. Victoria Solidarity Coalition. October 1983—November 1983

The Voice of the Fisherman. Fishermen and Cannery Workers Industrial Union. March 1934—25 February 1935

Voice of the Unemployed. Provincial Worker's Council. 2 November 1934

Waterfront Organizer. Joint Policy Committee of the BC Maritime Workers. 1 May 1937—23 October 1937

Waterfront Strike Bulletin. Strike Committee of the v&DWWA. June 1935—August 1935

We Too. 16 February 1935—2 November 1935

The Western Canadian Lumber Worker. Int'l Woodworkers of America — BC District Council #1. March 1960—April 1985

The Western Clarion. 7 May 1903—21 December 1918

The Western Clarion. Socialist Party of Canada. 10 January 1920—16 February 1924

Western Lumberman. October 1919—December 1921

Western Pulp and Paper Worker. Western Canada Council of Pulp and Paper Mill Unions. April 1956—June 1969

Western Socialist. 1898—1 May 1903

The Western Steelworker. United Steelworkers of America District 6. April 1970—June 1975

The Western Wage-Earner. Vancouver Trades and Labour Council. 9 February 1909—January 1911

The Worker. The Lumber Workers' Industrial Union. 19 September 1919—30 October 1919

Workers' Voice. National Unemployed Workers' Association. 16 April 1932—14 May 1932

Your Union. Local 480—United Steelworkers of America. January 1973—1977